THE ART OF BIBLICAL PERFORMANCE

BIBLICAL PERFORMANCE CRITICISM AND THE DRAMA OF OLD TESTAMENT NARRATIVES

THE ART OF BIBLICAL PERFORMANCE

BIBLICAL PERFORMANCE CRITICISM AND THE DRAMA OF OLD TESTAMENT NARRATIVES

Travis West

GLOSSAHOUSE DISSERTATION SERIES 14

G_H

GLOSSAHOUSE
WILMORE, KY
www.glossahouse.com

The Art of Biblical Performance: Biblical Performance and the Drama of Old Testament Narratives

GlossaHouse, LLC
110 Callis Circle
Wilmore, KY 40309
www.GlossaHouse.com

West, Travis M.
the art of biblical performance: biblical performance criticism and the drama of old testament narratives / Travis West — Wilmore, KY: GlossaHouse © 2023

xiii, 284 p. cm. —
(GlossaHouse Dissertation Series 14; Ref.)
A revision of the author's Ph.D. dissertation, Vrije Universiteit Amsterdam, 2018

ISBN-13: 978-1-63663-071-7

Cover design by T. Michael W. Halcomb

Text layout and book design by Andrew J. Coutras and Fredrick J. Long

Volume Editing by Andrew J. Coutras and Fredrick J. Long

The fonts used to create this work are available from
www.linguistsoftware.com/lgku.htm

To the anonymous Hebrew dramatists and performers,
whose legacy continues to shape, inspire,
and baffle generation after generation.

GLOSSAHOUSE DISSERTATION SERIES

SERIES EDITORS

FREDRICK J. LONG   ◆   T. MICHAEL W. HALCOMB
CARL S. SWEATMAN   ◆   ANDREW J. COUTRAS

VOLUME EDITORS

ANDREW J. COUTRAS   ◆   FREDRICK J. LONG

GLOSSAHOUSE DISSERTATION SERIES

The purpose of GlossaHouse Dissertation Series is to publish innovative, affordable, and cutting-edge scholarly research in the field of Biblical Studies that treat ancient and modern texts and languages.

ACKNOWLEDGEMENTS

Many writers consider the words in their books—and the books themselves—to be like children. Writers nurture a book from the inception of an idea, through the gestation period and the initial struggle to birth it, then on through the long period of rearing it through the various stages of toddlerhood, awkward adolescence, and eventually—with great excitement and great anxiety—they release it into the world to become what it was destined to be. Every author—just like every parent—knows you cannot rear a child alone. Just as it takes a village to raise a child, it takes a village to write a book. I am so grateful for my village. I hereby offer an incomplete acknowledgement of the village that helped raise the book you hold.

In the first place, I am grateful for my very own personal Gandalf, Dr. Tom Boogaart—professor, friend, mentor, colleague, and sage. As my professor, you first captivated my heart and imagination for all things Hebrew and Old Testament. Then you invited me into the sacred circle as a co-teacher and colleague. You mentored me in the ways of biblical performance criticism all the way up to sitting on my dissertation committee and flying to Amsterdam for my defense on your own dime. For all that, and the week-long writing retreat at your cabin, and so much more, I am beyond grateful.

My PhD supervisor, Dr. Willem van Peursen, believed in my project and in me. Your steady hand guided my research through its awkward "middle school years" and convinced me not to drop out of school when the going got tough. Your generosity and understanding as I endured great personal challenges enabled me to finish what I had started.

Dr. Leanne Van Dyk, my dean throughout my PhD work, was a tireless cheerleader and encourager as I struggled to believe I could complete a degree while teaching full-time. Your emotional, financial, and personal support was essential to my success. Thank you (and the Board of Western Theological Seminary) for giving me a sabbatical to complete the last few critical chapters in a timely manner.

I'm grateful to my former president, Dr. Tim Brown, who gave me a faculty position when I was just a kid. You saw in me what I didn't see in myself. I am indebted also to Dr. Eric Williams for first suggesting I look into the Vrije Universiteit Amsterdam. Your invitation to guest lecture on performance criticism while I was still a student gave me confidence that I had something to contribute. You were an early waterer of the seed that grew into this book. And to Bruce Johnson who let me use his family's cabin for a week-long writing retreat—the progress I made there helped me stick with it when the light at the end of the tunnel was dim.

So many students over the years have engaged the material in this book in various stages of its development. From the early lectures I wrote for the OT Narratives class, to the Advanced Hebrew students who read my chapter on 2 Kings 5, to my class on Elijah and Elisha, to my Hebrew TAs who were conversation partners, your engagement and critical feedback sharpened my thinking and improved the book.

I am grateful to the editorial team at GlossaHouse—especially Dr. Michael Halcomb and Dr. Fred Long—for being willing to publish my dissertation, and for your creative and collaborative spirits. Also, Andrew Coutras for all your support from tracking down the right fonts to getting my footnote formatting approved—I am grateful for the dozens of hours of reformatting you saved me from having to do.

My research assistant, Larry "Modeh Ani" Figueroa almost single-handedly got this manuscript in the shape it needed to be in for publication. Your attention to detail, thoughtful questions, abundant competence, and joy in the work was instrumental and I am so grateful for your help and your friendship.

Finally, without the support, encouragement, grace, patience, generosity, and partnership of my wife Mariah, I would have quit long ago. Thank you for believing in me and supporting me, even when it scared you or meant we'd spend significant time apart. Your sacrifice and love mean the world to me

TABLE OF CONTENTS

A TEXTUAL BIAS IN OLD TESTAMENT SCHOLARSHIP

Over the last 150 years or so, scholars of the Old Testament (particularly those in the West) have almost uniformly agreed on one fundamental assumption about the nature of the Bible, namely, that it is a *book*, a *written* document, a *textual* corpus. The assumption is so fundamental that it almost does not even bear mentioning for fear of stating the obvious. Further, what *kind* of texts they are and how they ought to be interpreted *as texts* has been the subject of significant debate; that debate is more or less the history of the last 150 years of Western scholarship on the Bible. This is true with respect to the entirety of the Hebrew Bible, but it is perhaps most prevalent with the narrative portion consisting of roughly Genesis—2 Kings, excluding the legal and descriptive portions, while also including the other narrative portions of the Bible, such as the prophetic book of Jonah.

Examples of what could be called the textual/literary bias are literally ubiquitous in biblical scholarship. It has informed countless methodologies, from the documentary hypothesis and historical criticism in the late nineteenth century to form criticism, narrative criticism, rhetorical criticism, reader-response criticism and ideological criticism in the twentieth and twenty-first centuries, just to name a few. It has guided hypotheses about the process whereby biblical passages—and even entire books or collections of books—were edited, redacted, and eventually finalized. You can pick up almost any book or article written about the Old Testament over the last century and a half and will encounter statements that confirm this most basic assumption.

A sampling of random quotations from various scholars should suffice to demonstrate this pervasive reality. First, examples concerning the written nature of the stories. From Gerhard von Rad: "In other words, the Hexateuch itself may, and indeed must, be understood as representative of a type of literature of which we may expect to be able to recognise the early stages, the circumstances of composition, and the subsequent development until it reached the greatly extended form in which it now lies before us."[1] From Robert Alter: "Nevertheless, these stories are not, strictly speaking, historiography, but rather the imaginative reenactment of history by a gifted writer who organizes his materials along certain thematic biases and according to his own remarkable intuition of the psychology of the characters."[2] From John Barton: "To make coherent sense of the methods of Old Testament study, they must be set against the background of literary criticism in general, in the world of English literature and of the study of modern languages and literature."[3]

Secondly, the textualization of the stories lead to the development of sometimes mind-bendingly complex and imaginative reconstructions of the textual layers of the received text, or anachronistic ways of conceiving the ancient editing and transmission process as purely textual, as if texts (and the materials and spaces required to create them) were as ubiquitous and painless to work with then as they are now. From Donald Redford:

> The Genesis Editor was a compiler, loath to reject anything short of gross theological error. Consequently the Judah-expansion was made the point of departure; parts were re-arranged (e.g. the blessing of Ephraim and Manasseh), and new material was added (e.g. chapter 38, and 46; 8–27). The Genesis Editor himself added what he felt to be indispensable, e.g. 46:1–7, Jacob's audience with Pharaoh (47:7–10), Jacob's last words to Joseph (48:1–7, 21–22), Jacob's burial (50:7–14), and Joseph's death (50:22–26). He even reworked and otherwise embellished episodes which had been integral parts of the story, e.g. chapter 41.[4]

[1] Von Rad, *Problem of the Hexateuch*, 3.
[2] Alter, *Art of Biblical Narrative*, 35.
[3] Barton, *Reading the Old Testament*, 3.
[4] Redford, *Study of the Biblical Story of Joseph*, 180.

Finally, the written nature of the text demands that it be *read* in specific ways. A mundane example, from William Beardslee, is illustrative of countless similar statements: "Poststructuralist criticism includes several ways of reading a text."[5] The titles of various books on the narratives prioritize the act of reading, such as *Reading Biblical Narrative: An Introductory Guide*, by J. P. Fokkelman;[6] *Reading Biblical Narratives: Literary Criticism and the Hebrew Bible*, by Yairah Amit;[7] *Sex, Wives, and Warriors: Reading Biblical Narrative With Its Ancient Audience*, by Philip Esler;[8] and *Sexual Politics in the Biblical Narrative: Reading the Hebrew Bible as a Woman*, by Esther Fuchs.[9] The subtitle of Meir Sternberg's monumental study of biblical narrative frames the act of interpretation as precisely an act of reading: *The Poetics of Biblical Narrative: Ideological Literature and the Drama of Reading*.[10] A search of the ATLA Religion database with keywords "reading," and "Hebrew Bible or Old Testament" resulted in over 2,200 hits.

The Bible is assumed to be a book, and the narratives texts, for good reason. The reason, of course, is because it *is* a book, and they *are* texts. But this study will endeavor to demonstrate that the narratives, in particular, are *not* texts in the way modern scholarship has largely assumed they are. Susan Niditch names the situation well: "Too often Old Testament scholars imagine the process of composition and transmission to involve individuals in scriptoria, redactors, editors, and compilers rather that [*sic*] composers practicing their art in accordance with a set of cultural expectations for those who share in that culture."[11] Even though many scholars have begun to accept that the origins of the Bible are oral, their acceptance seems to be primarily intellectual as opposed to practical, for after making this acknowledgement they immediately revert back to treating the received text *as a text*. In other

---

[5] Beardslee, "Poststructuralist Criticism," 253.
[6] Fokkelman, *Reading Biblical Narrative*.
[7] Amit, *Reading Biblical Narratives*.
[8] Esler, *Sex, Wives, and Warriors*.
[9] Fuchs, *Sexual Politics*.
[10] Sternberg, *Poetics of Biblical Narrative*.
[11] Niditch, *Underdogs and Tricksters*, 12.

words, orality and its implications have not yet been sufficiently incorporated at the methodological level.

In this study I will argue that the cultural realities of ancient Israel suggest that the art practiced by the biblical composers was not of an essentially literary character, but rather of a dramatic character, which prioritized performance. I will argue that the narrative texts contained in the Hebrew Bible are more akin to dramatic scripts than a purely literary form of writing. In other words, the *textual* character of the biblical texts (particularly the narratives) is secondary, their literary quality penultimate. They are not intended to be read silently in one's head but enacted through one's body and voice in space and time before a gathered audience. They are most at home not on the page but on the stage.

Perhaps one way to describe what I intend to do in the following pages is to compare my efforts to the description the editors of the *Berit Olam* commentary series offer on the back cover to describe the approach taken by the authors in the series, which is an explicitly literary approach to interpreting the narrative and poetic portions of the Hebrew Bible. "This multi-volume commentary reflects a relatively new development in biblical studies. The readings of the books of the Hebrew Bible offered here all focus on the final form of the texts, approaching them as literary works, recognizing that the craft of poetry and storytelling that the ancient Hebrew world provided can be found in them and that their truth can be better appreciated with a fuller understanding of that art."[12] My purpose here is to do something similar, based on a similar assumption, but moving in a very different direction. Namely, I intend to show that the ancient crafts of *drama* and *performance* are evident in the texts we receive, and that a fuller understanding of Israel's performance tradition will lead to a greater appreciation of Israel's dramatic and theological achievement.

My interest in this topic of research is personal and professional, but it was personal before it was professional. Ten years ago (2007), when I was an M.Div. student at the seminary where I now teach, I took a class that incorporated a version of the performance approach that I

[12.]Cohn, *2 Kings*, back cover.

describe here, introduced to me and the rest of the class for the first time by our professor, Dr. Tom Boogaart. It was a trial run of sorts for him, an attempt to use the classroom as a lab to test a methodology he had been working on developing on his own for decades. In that class we spent the semester memorizing Jonah 1 in the original Hebrew, and at the end of the semester performed it in a worship service and also in various churches and ministries throughout West Michigan where we are located. It was a transformational experience for me, for my classmates, and for Tom as well. We began to ask questions of the biblical passage that we had never thought to ask before. Questions like: Where is God located in this passage? What posture do the sailors take when they cry out to the Lord? How do you use your body to depict the sailors' growing fear (vv. 5, 10), which ultimately is transformed into worship (v. 16)? With what tone of voice does Jonah confess God's sovereignty and his "fear" of YHVH to the sailors in verse 9 that captures the irony created between his words and his actions? How do you demonstrate the distinction between what the sailors do in verse 14 when they "cry out" to YHVH, as opposed to when they cried out to "their gods" earlier (v. 5)? And so on. The discoveries we made in pursuing answers to these and other questions led to a number of new insights into the story and the art by which it is told. It also pointed to this approach's potential to help revitalize the American church's relationship with the Old Testament, and also to shift the way scholars in the academy relate to the biblical passages they interpret. My personal investment in this new-to-me way of interpreting narratives continued the following year when, upon my graduation from seminary, Tom gave that class to me to teach as an adjunct.

Thus began my professional interest in biblical performance criticism (a moniker I was unaware of at the time). At the same time I began teaching that class, I also returned to Western Theological Seminary to begin a Th.M. degree, for which I wrote a thesis titled *Performance Criticism and the Narratives of the Hebrew Bible*, which I completed in the summer of 2009. That project helped establish a foundation upon which this dissertation has been built. Since that first performance in 2007 I have been involved in dozens of performances of

Old Testament dramas—in Hebrew as well as in English—as both a professor/participant and as an audience member. These performances have taken place during worship at the seminary where I teach, another seminary in a nearby town, various churches in West Michigan, a conference on pedagogy hosted by Vanderbilt Divinity School,[13] and in multiple sessions at an annual meeting of the Society of Biblical Literature.[14]

My interest in biblical performance criticism today remains both personal and professional. I find great satisfaction in the process of entering a story this deeply with a group of students and discovering along with them the great riches therein. I do not have formal theatrical training,[15] nor is that necessary to effectively practice biblical performance criticism. What seems to be required is: an awareness of one's body; an imagination about space and its use in telling a story; a capacity to interpret nonverbal communication; a willingness to be vulnerable; an openness towards being surprised by one's self, one's interpretive partners, as well as the story; a trust in the biblical story to speak through the bodies and voices of the participants. And this is to say nothing of the scholarly skills that are also employed in the process of biblical interpretation, ranging from knowledge of the original language to proficiency in critical methodologies to the self-awareness required in order to live into the practice Abraham Heschel famously

---

[13.]Travis West and Pam Bush, "Embodied Education: Learning Biblical Hebrew as Spiritual and Pastoral Formation," (presentation at the Pedagogical Possibilities: New Paradigms in Teaching for Ministry conference, Nashville, TN, June 3–5, 2016).

[14.]Travis West and Tom Boogaart, "Using Performance to Teach the Bible," (workshop presentation at the Annual Meeting of the Society of Biblical Literature, San Diego, CA, November 21, 2014; Travis West and Tom Boogaart, "Language Learning as Spiritual Formation: Teaching Hebrew in a Seminary Context," (presentation at the Annual Meeting of the Society of Biblical Literature, San Diego, CA, November 22–25, 2014).

[15.]I was in one musical in high school, and participated in the Theatre Company during my freshman year at Calvin College, a 1-credit class in which I studied a few theater principles, ironed all of the costumes for every performance of one of the main stage plays, and performed in two different productions—a musical based on the Song of Songs, and a play based on two works of Edgar Allen Poe.

described: "Our sight is suffused with knowing, instead of feeling painfully the lack of knowing what we see. The principle to be kept in mind is to know what we see rather than to see what we know."[16]

The dissertation is divided into two parts. Part 1 (Chapters 1–3) lays the theoretical foundation upon which biblical performance criticism of the narratives is built. These chapters combine orality studies, cultural anthropology, and performance studies with biblical studies in order to revisit the genre of the narratives and articulate an emerging methodology that enables the scholar to interpret them in such a way that has deeper resonance to their generic character. This methodology is called biblical performance criticism.

In Chapter 1, titled "A Genealogy of Orality: Tracing the Development of Orality in Old Testament Studies from Gunkel to Today," I identify the major scholarly voices over the past eleven decades or so who have written about the oral character of the Old Testament in some fashion. The publication of Hermann Gunkel's *The Legends of Genesis* in 1901 placed the oral tradition that stands behind the present form of the Old Testament at the center of biblical studies for the first time. In the ensuing decades, as we learned more about the character of orally composed works, the romanticized vision of the oral transmission process Gunkel introduced became much more sophisticated and complex, leading to Susan Niditch's conclusion that there is a dynamic "interplay" between the written and the oral, both in the historical process that resulted in the received texts, and in the received texts themselves. Niditch hypothesized that public performance played an important role in the process of oral transmission throughout the biblical period leading up to the exile. In Chapters 2 and 3 I further develop this idea by giving greater attention to the context of performance in the development of biblical narratives.

Chapter 2, "Drama and Performance: The Genre of the Biblical Narratives Revisited," develops the context of performance in three related yet distinct ways: reconsidering the genre of the narratives, defining and

---

[16.]Heschel, *The Prophets*, 1:xi.

describing what is meant by "performance," and fleshing out the methodological implications of the genre and performance sections. In the first section I will conclude that the best genre designation for the Old Testament narratives is drama; the stories are scripts of ancient plays. This reconsideration is tantamount to a paradigm shift in biblical studies. In the second section I engage the complex and multi-faceted term "performance," which Marvin Carlson calls an "essentially contested concept."[17] I offer a definition of performance drawn from its etymology in order to establish a boundary of meaning for performance within the context of this study. From there I draw on the work of performance theorists to help articulate what actually *happens* in a performance and how that might change the way we approach and understand the scripts contained in the narrative corpus of the Hebrew Bible, including what implications there may be on the function of scholarship itself. The primary oversight of text-oriented biblical scholarship (which is to say, the vast majority of Western biblical scholarship) has largely been its disregard for the historical and cultural context of Israel's orality, and its methodological implications. In this final section of the chapter I will tease out the methodological implications of these dramatic texts that incorporates performance and manifests the paradigm shift called for by the first two sections. The name of this methodology is biblical performance criticism.

The title of the dissertation is borrowed from Chapter 3: "The Art of Biblical Performance: Five Essential Elements of Israel's Dramatic Tradition." The title of this chapter, as well as its content, is a purposeful play on the title and content of Robert Alter's remarkable book *The Art of Biblical Narrative*, in which he identifies what he calls "literary conventions"[18] that demonstrate the artistry of Israel's *literary* achievement. Alter's logic is that sensitivity to these literary conventions enables the careful reader of the Bible to make more penetrating analyses of the biblical texts, while also giving the reader the tools to discern narrative

---

[17.]Carlson, *Performance*, 1.

[18.]Alter, *Art of Biblical Narrative*, 49. He also refers to these, on the same page, as "narrative conventions."

gaps in the story and the clues to unlock the possible meaning(s) of those gaps. This chapter takes a similar approach to Alter but with an altered trajectory: identifying five components of Hebrew performance that each contribute something significant to the artistry and profundity of Israel's *dramatic* tradition. The five elements are: dramatic structure, the role of the narrator (audience participation), dialogue, point of view, movement and gesture. I will argue, as Alter did, that sensitivity to these elements—and the manifold ways they intersect and overlap—can lead to deeper readings of the scripts, and to identify *and fill in* gaps in the stories that have remained inaccessible to other approaches.

In Part 2 (Chapters 4–6) I offer the fruit of biblical performance criticism by applying it to three specific dramas taken from the Elisha cycle in 2 Kgs Chapter 4 engages the story of the Widow's Oil found in 2 Kgs 4:1–7. Chapter 5 is on the entirety of 2 Kgs 5: the Healing of Naaman and the Downfall of Gehazi. Finally, Chapter 6 covers the Bands of Aram in 2 Kgs 6:8–23. I chose these particular stories for various reasons. First, I had previous experience performing each of these dramas multiple times with different classes of students over the past several years. Each performance was different and drew out different layers of insight into the drama, which afforded me a wide array of experiences from which to draw on the way to offering a performance critical interpretation of each passage. Second, the stories are wonderfully dramatic, and lent themselves to performance with relative ease and great profundity. Third, these stories demonstrate well the power of biblical performance criticism to identify and address gaps, draw out new insights from stories that have already received much attention by scholars over the years, and also provide a taste of the many ways performance can deal with unique challenges of representation in the stories, such as the movement of large armies, the occurrence of miracles, the passage of time, and the expression of human emotion. Fourth, the length of the dramas, as well as the number of characters in each made for a good fit between these dramas and the performance class that I taught for many years at the seminary where I am employed with respect to the number of students in the class and what is possible for beginner Hebrew students to memorize over the course of a semester. Fifth, and somewhat personally, I simply love all three of these dramas; they are powerful, profound, theologically rich, and spectacular stories of God's faithfulness in dire situations of personal, national, and international conflict. Finally, I debated whether to take all three dramas from the same book or from various parts of the Hebrew Bible for Part 2. There are merits and drawbacks to each decision, but in the end I felt like three dramas from the Elisha cycle was the clearer, more consistent, and simpler option. I felt this was the case especially in light of how I draw on enactments of a number of other dramas taken from several other books in Chapters 1–3.

I do not imagine a reader must read this book by taking a predetermined path. Many routes could lead to a happy ending. One could, of course, read it straight through, from cover to cover. But Part 2 could easily be read without reading Part 1 first. And the chapters in Part 2 could be read in any order, akin to how one would read a commentary. I hope this flexibility adds to the book's usability.

Throughout all six chapters, but particularly Chapters 4–6, I have included the original Hebrew text whenever it was both possible and profitable to do so. In each instance I have included also a transliteration of the Hebrew in italics, and a gloss of the word or phrase in quotation marks. I generally included the Hebrew in the body of the sentence and the transliteration and translation in parentheses. In certain circumstances, however, the syntax of the sentence obliged me to give priority to, say, the translation, in which case I placed the Hebrew and its transliteration in parentheses, and so on. This inconsistency is the result of my decision to prioritize the readability of the sentence over imposing a strict system to determine which of the three components appears in the text proper and which are placed in parentheses. Unless otherwise noted, all translations are my own.

I have included both translation and transliteration because I imagine my audience for this work to be not only scholars of the Bible—who are likely able to read the Hebrew without transliteration or translation—but also theater and performance scholars, as well as orality scholars and cultural anthropologists interested in the application of their disciplines to the Old Testament, and I did not imagine many of these readers would have a working knowledge of Hebrew. I also envision part of my readership to include pastors who desire to find more accessible and dynamic ways of opening the biblical texts to their congregations who may or may not have taken Hebrew during their theological education, and likely have forgotten much of it if they did! I personally believe biblical performance criticism holds great promise to help reinvigorate the Church's relationship to the scriptures by demonstrating one particularly powerful way that the Old Testament is living and active, that God still speaks to us through the Bible, and that these ancient stories are not irrelevant but rather speak clearly and powerfully today. To perform the story is to discover that the story is alive and present in the "now" of the performance, and that those bringing it to life are not removed from it but are essential parts of the story; it is in a very real sense now also *their* story. Another decision I needed to make was my citation method. I have chosen to include only shortened footnotes in the body of the paper, which give the reference to the author's last name, an abbreviated version of the title (with enough of the title given to be both memorable and to get a feel for the work), and page reference. A bibliography of every work referenced is given at the end, for any reader who desires more information about a source. In a couple of places I also included the date of publication. I did this only when the footnote included a long list of works arranged chronologically by date of publication, when explicit reference to the dates would aid the reader in getting a feel for the timeline for the scope of works referenced.

PART 1

THE FOUNDATION OF BIBLICAL PERFORMANCE CRITICISM

CHAPTER 1
A GENEALOGY OF ORALITY: TRACING THE DEVELOPMENT OF ORALITY IN OLD TESTAMENT STUDIES FROM GUNKEL TO TODAY

Introduction

In this introductory chapter I will summarize both the contributions and the complications of the research of a number of influential scholars who have considered the intersection of orality, textuality, and the Hebrew Bible. I will treat each successive scholar or group of scholars chronologically. This is not to suggest a straight line of development among the scholars I have included along this chronology, nor is it to suggest that each scholar simply took the insights of their temporal predecessors and either added nuance to them. Rather, it is an acknowledgement that each "generation" of scholars does read and engage in conversation with the work of their predecessors, even while making their own unique contributions to the ongoing discussion. Each "generation" interacts with the work of their "ancestors" in different ways. Some adopt and develop their forebears' work; others critique it and seek a new path, yet others reject it altogether. By the end I hope it is clear that not only has each generation developed the conversation by furthering their ancestors' lines of inquiry and discovering new insights, but also that the ancestors themselves had penetrating insights that set the trajectory for their "descendants," and have stood the test of time.

Hermann Gunkel

The field of Hebrew Bible/Old Testament has benefited considerably from research conducted over the last hundred years or so into the oral character of Ancient Near Eastern societies in general, and Israel in particular. Beginning with the publication of *The Legends of Genesis* in

1901,[1] Hermann Gunkel placed the oral tradition that stood behind the narrative portion of the Bible—particularly Genesis—at the center of the historical research of the Hebrew Bible. Form criticism, which he is credited with establishing,[2] was an attempt to deepen the researcher's understanding of the development of the biblical text "by isolating pre-literary stages in its growth," and "also as a tool in reconstructing the social life and institutions . . . of ancient Israel."[3] This was accomplished by discerning formal features of the text, as well as identifying the genre (German *Gattung*) of the particular passage under scrutiny through a process of identifying patterned content and generalizing those patterns to various classes or genres of literature (written or oral).[4] Gunkel and those who followed him "discovered that there were *Gattungen* embedded within the written form of the text that must originally have had a *Sitz im Leben*[5] in which they would have been *spoken*."[6]

Gunkel's work elevated the role of oral tradition in biblical studies, giving it a more prominent position in the historical research of the Bible. Although no one's work is wholly original, and Gunkel clearly had influences,[7] he nevertheless established the fact of Israel's orality and initiated the academic conversation about a period of oral transmission pre-dating the written documents. Gunkel's work was an

---

[1] *The Legends of Genesis* was an independent printing of the introduction to Hermann Gunkel's monumental commentary on Genesis, published in the same year.

[2] *Anchor Bible Dictionary*, s.v. "Form Criticism," 838.

[3] Barton, *Reading the Old Testament*, 31.

[4] "Form Criticism," 840.

[5] *Sitz im Leben* is German for "setting-in-life," and refers to the attempt to discern the particular life situation in which the text would have been used. This is distinguished from an attempt to discern what time period the text was written in. In other words, *Sitz im Leben* is concerned with identifying the particular setting or life context, such as the Passover festival or corporate worship in the Temple, as opposed to an historical period. Cf. "Form Criticism," 840.

[6] Barton, *Reading the Old Testament*, 33.

[7] For example, Gunkel credited Hugo Gressmann with introducing him to the significance of folktale, and *The Folktale in the Old Testament* is dedicated to him for this reason. Gunkel, *Folktale*, 13. Indeed, even Wellhausen identified the existence of an oral tradition that stood behind the documents he named J and E. Cf. Nielsen, *Oral Tradition*, 12; and Zink, "Scandinavian Oral Tradition," 249.

essential first step. In the last one hundred years many more steps have been taken down the road, but Gunkel's initial footprint set the trajectory for all that would follow. Not all of Gunkel's assumptions have withstood the test of time, however.

In particular, Gunkel's assumptions concerning the relationship between oral and literate societies have received nuance and complexification in important ways. Writing at the turn of the twentieth century, Gunkel articulated an evolutionary model in which "oral means early, primitive, and unsophisticated,"[8] and, by contrast, literate means late, refined, and complex. Gunkel describes his view of the early, oral Israelites throughout *The Legends of Genesis* variously as "uncivilised,"[9] "primitive,"[10] "simple artists"[11] who lack "intellectual power"[12] and a "creative grasp,"[13] and are therefore "not capable of constructing artistic works of any considerable extent."[14]

The result of this presumed simplistic naïveté is a romanticized imagination of the oral transmission process. According to Gunkel:

> In the leisure of a winter evening the family sits about the hearth; the grown people, but more especially the children, listen intently to the beautiful old stories of the dawn of the world which they have heard so often yet never tire of hearing repeated.[15]

Not only did Gunkel tend to romanticize and condescend toward this "primitive" phase in Israel's tradition history, he was adamant that no formal relationship remained between the unsophisticated folkloric "legends" in their (early) oral stage and the refined, sophisticated (late)

[8.] Niditch, *Oral World*, 2.

[9.] Gunkel, *Legends*, 1. I have kept the original spelling instead of changing to the American spelling of "uncivilized."

[10.] Gunkel, *Legends*, 47.

[11.] Gunkel, *Legends*, 62.

[12.] Gunkel, *Legends*, 40.

[13.] Gunkel, *Legends*, 55.

[14.] Gunkel, *Legends*, 47.

[15.] Gunkel, *Legends*, 41.

historical-religious documents of Israel's canon. In *The Folktale in the Old Testament*, published sixteen years after *The Legends of Genesis*, Gunkel articulated this unequivocally: "The elevated and rigorous spirit of biblical religion tolerated the folktale as such at almost no point and this near total eradication from the holy tradition is one of the great acts of biblical religion."[16] Implicit in this view is an assumption about the relationship between orality and literacy within a society. Gunkel drew a hard line between oral and literate cultures, assuming a society could be either one or the other, but not both simultaneously. Therefore, for Gunkel, orality and literacy are mutually exclusive cultural and historical realities.

Milman Parry and Albert Lord

This strict dichotomy between orality and literacy was reinforced by the pioneering work of Milman Parry and his disciple and successor Albert Bates Lord. They conducted wide ranging comparative analyses based on extensive field work of living oral traditions in Serbo-Croatia. They applied their findings to the Greek epics *Iliad* and *Odyssey* to demonstrate their oral compositional character. Although Lord's publication of *The Singer of Tales* in 1960 remains a watershed event with respect to the development of our understanding of oral tradition and transmission, and even inspired several attempts to discern the oral compositional nature of various biblical texts,[17] the oral-formulaic theory which it made famous has been widely criticized on precisely this point: Lord assumed "the absolute incompatibility of oral and written modes of composition,"[18] and, by implication, the absolute

---

[16] Quoted in Niditch, *Oral World*, 2.

[17] See Niditch, *Oral World*, 8–10. See also Person, "Orality Studies," 56. Person refers to Robert Culley, Robert Coote, and David Gunn as scholars inspired by Lord's analysis, though they were "somewhat more cautious" than others with respect to the "great divide thesis," which assumed a "tremendous gulf between orality and literacy" (Person, "Orality Studies," 56.).

[18] Carr, *Writing on the Tablet*, 6. Late in his career Lord allowed for the possibility of "transitional texts," produced by a culture on its way from orality to literacy. Although he maintained that the transition was swift and decisive, he did suggest that

incompatibility of oral and literate societies. Indeed, as David Carr has shown, Lord argued that the oral "mode of composition virtually required illiteracy on the part of the composer."[19] In *The Singer of Tales*, Lord presented this position in the clearest of terms:

> The written technique, on the other hand, is not compatible with the oral technique, and the two could not possibly combine, to form another, a third, a "transitional" technique. It is conceivable that a man might be an oral poet in his younger years and a written poet later in life, but it is not possible that he be *both* an oral and a written poet at any given time in his career. The two by their very nature are mutually exclusive.[20]

This suggests that if the composer gained a capacity to read and write, his or her ability—or desire—to generate oral performances of the tradition, and the community's capacity to receive and hold the tradition in its collective memory, would diminish considerably, and eventually disappear altogether. According to Carr, he believed "there was a decisive shift when a society moved from orality to literacy," indicated by "decisively different dynamics" between written texts and their oral counterparts.[21] The result would perhaps be the same one Gunkel envisioned: a literate society, broken from its oral past, which prefers verifiable historical documents over so-called legends and folktales. Moreover, Parry and Lord also "assumed that oral tradition represented a single, unified phenomenon across all cultures, eras, languages, and social contexts. The result was a binary model that restricted verbal art to one or the other of two mutually exclusive categories, which led to the so-called Great Divide concept of orality versus literacy."[22]

---

performers "continue to perform, even when they become literate." Lord, *Epic Singers*, 24.

[19.]Niditch, *Oral World*, 9.

[20.]Lord, *Singer*, 129, quoted in Carr, *Writing on the Tablet*, 6; emphasis original.

[21.]Carr, *Writing on the Tablet*, 6–7.

[22.]Foley, "Plenitude and Diversity," 104.

The Scandinavian School

Within a few decades of the publication of Gunkel's work on oral tradition a group of biblical scholars—the so-called Scandinavian School[23]—linked by geography, but also by methodology,[24] began to articulate an alternative narrative for the role of oral tradition in the history and development of the Hebrew scriptures, which stood in direct contrast to the narrative represented in the work of Gunkel, Wellhausen, and others who drew a hard line between an oral and literate stage.[25] Nielsen, Nyberg and others wanted to affirm a more complex relationship between the oral tradition and its literary expression. For example, Nyberg acknowledges the existence and influence of writing throughout pre-exilic Palestine, but doubts "whether it was used for purely literary purposes to any great extent."[26] Instead, he argues,

> Writing was principally employed in practical matters, for contracts, covenants, monuments—in these cases doubtless also with magical significance—probably also for official registers and lists, and, above all, for letters. Annals were modeled on the Assyrian annals; legal texts of major importance were possibly

---

[23.]For example, Ivan Engnell, Eduard Nielsen, H.S. Nyberg, and Sigmund Mowinckel.

[24.]"It must be observed, first of all, that the Scandinavian School—as is the case of other "schools"—is not an organized and exclusive body with a unique position and methodology. The name arises because of a similarity in viewpoint taken by a number of scholars in the Scandinavian countries and promulgated most forcefully by them. Their uniqueness lies in their use of the materials they have at their disposal and their application of the concept of oral tradition to an overwhelming extent." Zink, "Scandinavian Oral Tradition," 249.

[25.]"The readers of Gunkel and Lods will doubtless agree that these two scholars are right in this, that even the cycles of legends must originate in oral tradition. But the attentive reader cannot escape the impression that another problem arises, the problem of the legitimacy of that literary criticism for which both these scholars stand, faithful as they are to the tradition of Old Testament research. In other words, we are faced with the question of drawing a well-defined line between a literary and a pre-literary stage, belonging to a literary and an oral culture respectively." Nielsen, *Oral Tradition*, 12.

[26.]Quoted in Nielsen, *Oral Tradition*, 24.

committed to writing also. But the actual tradition of history, the
epic tales, the cult-legends, doubtless generally the laws too,
must in the main have been handed down orally.[27]

For those associated with the Scandinavian school—unlike Gunkel,
Parry, and Lord—the presence of writing and the existence of writing
technology does not necessitate the end of oral tradition.

Eventually, of course, the tradition shifts toward the written
medium. With implicit reference to Gunkel, Nielsen posits, "The change
from oral to written literature does not take place because cultural
summits have been reached, nor because the ability to read and write
has become common property, but because the culture itself is felt to be
threatened—from within by syncretism, and from without by political
events."[28] Here Nielsen is drawing on the work of Nyberg and
Engnell—while anticipating some conclusions Walter Ong will make,
which will be discussed in the following section—in pursuit of an
answer to the question "Why have traditionists, poets and reciters made
use of writing, and what consequences does this involve?"[29] Their
conclusion was that the move to write down the tradition "is linked with
a general crisis of confidence. At some time faith in the spoken word
began to waver, and it was thought necessary to write down the
traditions."[30] One implication of this shift is purely technical in nature:
"the inauguration of a different method of transmission."[31] But for
Nielsen et al., more is at stake than simply committing to written form
what had previously existed only in spoken word and memory.
"[S]omething new has happened.... [A]n impersonal intermediary link
has been introduced between the bearer of tradition and the receiver."[32]
The introduction of this "impersonal intermediary" accomplishes a level
of permanence and consistency unachievable by (if not foreign to)

---

[27] Quoted in Nielsen, *Oral Tradition*, 24.
[28] Nielsen, *Oral Tradition*, 60.
[29] Nielsen, *Oral Tradition*, 32.
[30] Nielsen, *Oral Tradition*, 33.
[31] Nielsen, *Oral Tradition*, 34.
[32] Nielson, *Oral Tradition*, 33–34.

memory and oral tradition, but introduces the possibility of the document becoming divorced from the living community's memory and therefore cut off from its interpretive tradition.

Orality vs. Literacy: Walter Ong, Jack Goody, and the Character of Oral Cultures

These larger challenges flagged by Nielsen, Nyberg, and Engnell are analogous to the concerns addressed in Walter Ong and Jack Goody's work on the relationship between oral and literate cultures. Ong,[33] Goody,[34] and others[35] focused much of their research on the character of oral and literate societies; the social and cultural implications of the interaction between the two, or isolation of one from the other; and how persons formed by each type of society experience and process reality. Each scholar has emphasized the dramatic *differences* between societies steeped in writing and literacy, and that of oral-aural cultures both past and present. This particular assumption—the strong dichotomy they assume between oral and literate societies, sometimes called the "great divide thesis"[36]—was inherited in part from Parry and Lord,[37] and has come under strong criticism over the past decade or so.[38]

Although Ong and Goody have been rightfully criticized for arguing for too sharp of a break between oral and literate societies, their insights on the ways orality and textuality influence people who are formed by societies with strong emphases in one or the other are nevertheless helpful. Therefore, in this section, I will summarize some of their contributions, which have shifted our understanding of the character of oral cultures and have thereby enabled greater insight into the cultural context in which the biblical traditions were developed, and out of which the Hebrew Bible arose. The following description of the

---

[33.]See, esp. Ong, *Orality and Literacy and Literacy*.

[34.]Goody Watt, "Consequences;" Goody, *Interface*.

[35.]E.g., Havelock, *Preface to Plato*; and Havelock, *Muse Learns to Write*.

[36.]Person, "Orality Studies," 56.

[37.]See, e.g., Ong, *Orality and Literacy*, 27–28.

[38.]See Levtow, "Text Production," 111–39, but esp. 113–17 and citations listed in notes; also de Vries, "Views of Orality," 145–48.

characteristics of an oral culture, drawn from the work of Ong, Goody, and others, will not apply in every way to every oral culture in every time and place. Rather, acknowledging that each culture is unique and complex, what follows is a sketch of the characteristics that reflect a basic profile of the dynamics of an oral culture, including ancient Israel.[39] Careful consideration of Israel's orality will contribute to a fuller understanding of the *Sitz im Leben* which produced the Bible. By this I refer not to the specific social or cultural event which the text supposedly points to, but the larger cultural context in which the Bible came into being over many centuries.[40]

In *Orality and Literacy: The Technologizing of the Word*, Ong's central concern is a comparison of "primary oral cultures" (composed of persons "totally unfamiliar with writing"[41]) and modern, Western culture (which is "deeply affected by the use of writing,"[42] and has been transformed by the technology of print and now digital media). Though his focus is on this stronger contrast, he nevertheless demonstrates awareness and insight into what Marcel Jousse termed *verbomoteur* cultures—particularly ancient Israel and its neighbors—"which knew some writing but remained basically oral and word-oriented in lifestyle rather than object-oriented."[43] "Verbomotor" cultures have been called *primarily* oral,[44] as an indication that orality was the dominant cultural force, yet writing technologies and the resulting literate elements existed.

At the most elemental level, according to Ong, the spoken word creates and sustains an oral culture. "Because in its physical constitution as sound, the spoken word proceeds from the human interior and manifests human beings to one another as conscious interiors, as

---

[39.]Rhoads, "Performance Criticism—Part I," 121.

[40.]Roland Boer has noted that *"Sitz im Leben* has been released from Gunkel's original straightjacket and applied to a whole range of biblical phenomena, *finding its most natural applications in studies of a text's production* rather than being linked to the context of the genre in question." Boer, "Introduction," 3; emphasis added.

[41.]Ong, *Orality and Literacy*, 6.

[42.]Ong, *Orality and Literacy*, 1.

[43.]Ong, *Orality and Literacy*, 67.

[44.]Cf. Person, "Orality Studies," 56.

persons, the spoken word forms human beings into close-knit groups."[45]
In oral cultures, *sound* creates and sustains reality. It is the most
essential component for any meaningful interaction. Communication in
oral cultures is inherently relational and personal because it requires the
physical presence of those who are communicating. "Oral societies are
collectivist cultures in which the focus is on group identity and on
individuals only in so far as they are embedded in groups and
situations."[46] This was certainly true for Israel.[47] Social interactions are
shaped by empathy and participation. Learning is accomplished through
apprenticeship and discipleship as opposed to study.[48] Without the
influence of writing, thought and language remain close to the human
life-world and are therefore concrete and contextual. Oral cultures are
typically conservative or traditionalist in which elders or sages hold
great authority and the knowledge they hold in their bodies forms the
link between the past and the present, the tradition and the formation of
a new generation. There is, however, room for innovation within the
tradition, as new experiences invoke new tellings of the community's
narrative history, which is allowed to speak a fresh word and to create a
fresh response to an old story.[49] Words themselves acquire meaning not
from a dictionary (that is, defined by *other words*), but "from their
always insistent actual habitat," which includes "gestures, vocal
inflections, facial expression, and the entire human, existential setting

---

[45] Ong, *Orality and Literacy*, 73.

[46] Rhoads, "Performance Criticism—Part I," 121.

[47] On this point, see Joel Kaminsky's treatment of the communal nature of the
covenant's relationship with Israel's corporate responsibility in Kaminsky, *Corporate
Responsibility*, esp. 30–54.

[48] In his fascinating study of the cultural and institutional transformations that took
place in Medieval Europe between the eleventh and twelfth centuries with the rise of
the university movement, C. Stephen Jaeger describes the importance of the "real
presence" of the teacher or instructor in oral cultures. Truth is understood as existing
in "the immediate presence of a model human being. His personality, his conduct, his
bearing is the thing itself, is what study and learning are about. He himself, and not
books and texts, is the lesson." Jaeger, *Envy of Angels*, 189.

[49] Ong, *Orality and Literacy*, 41–42.

in which the real, spoken word always occurs."[50] Words and their meanings are always situated in the lived experiences of the community, and are an essential bond that connects the members of the community to each other.

The formative influence of the spoken word impacts not only the way people in oral cultures relate to each other, but also the way they relate to time. Instead of a strictly linear view of time in which "the past" is understood as the time preceding the present, the time that is now "over and done" and is therefore inaccessible and unrepeatable, for people formed in an essentially oral environment, the past, like the spoken word itself,[51] exists dynamically and fleetingly *in the present moment*. Ong articulates the difference in the starkest of terms:

> People whose world view has been formed by high literacy need to remind themselves that in functionally oral cultures the past is not felt as an itemized terrain, peppered with verifiable and disputed 'facts' or bits of information. *It is the domain of the ancestors, a resonant source for renewing awareness of present existence*, which itself is not an itemized terrain either. Orality knows no lists or charts or figures.[52]

"The past" for an oral culture functions as an empowering force for life in the present. It does not exist outside of the bodies, voices, and memories of the people.

Hans Walter Wolff, in his *Anthropology of the Old Testament*, argued a similar point. With particular reference to "the Deuteronomic

---

[50.]Ong, *Orality and Literacy*, 46–47.

[51.]"All sensation takes place in time, but sound has a special relationship to time unlike that of the other fields that register in human sensation. Sound exists only when it is going out of existence. It is not simply perishable but essentially evanescent." Ong, *Orality and Literacy*, 32. An important caveat to this is the observation that the "existence" of sound is infinitely recoverable; it only exists in the present moment, as Ong says, but it exists every time someone speaks.

[52.]Ong, *Orality and Literacy*, 97; emphasis added.

preachers,"[53] Wolff argued that time is centered around the experience
of the spoken word in the present moment. "[T]he man who lives
vigilantly today is, as a member of the people of God, firmly
incorporated in the events that preceded his generation, and also in what
is to come. But *it is in his hearing of the word that is proclaimed* today
and in his contemplation of the history of the fathers, that man's decision
is made about his future life."[54] For Wolff, as for Ong, the past is the
period of time populated by the ancestors, which comes to life in the
present when the stories are remembered and told, an experience that
influences the "future life" of the people.[55]

It is not only "the past" that is understood differently in a primarily
oral culture, but the related term "history" as well. In his consideration of
the implications of oral tradition on the interpretation of the Bible, Carroll
Stuhlmueller, quoting Fr. Gelin, writes, "History . . . is not an inert matter,
a past thing. It is always totally *present* to Israel. It is a patrimony by
which they live, almost a *mystery* in which they are actually involved."[56]
This is, of course, not to suggest that the people living during the time of
king David thought Noah or Moses were still walking around living their
lives. Rather, it is to suggest that the Hebrew people felt a deep connection
between the time of the ancestors and the time of the present. In oral
cultures, including Israel, both "history" and "the past" are realities that
live in the bodies and memories of the people. The intimacy and
immediacy facilitated by communities bound primarily by speech has a
profound effect on the way each member relates to the other members of
the community—past, present, and future.

One example of this is the genealogy. There are a number of
genealogies in the Hebrew Bible.[57] Ong and Goody both argue

---

[53] His comments come in his section on the book of Deuteronomy in his chapter
on "The Old Testament Concept of Time" in Wolff, *Anthropology*, 83–92, esp. 86–
88.

[54] Wolff, *Anthropology*, 88; emphasis added.

[55] Vestiges of this remain up to the present moment in various religious traditions.
A particularly strong remnant of this is the Catholic Eucharist.

[56] Stuhlmueller, "Influence of Oral Tradition," 311; emphasis original.

[57] See, e.g., Gen 5; 11:10–30; Ruth 4:18–22.

persuasively that for oral cultures genealogies are neither mere lists of names nor proof of pedigree, but descriptions of personal and real relations framed in a narrative context.[58] Further, genealogies in the Bible are framed around specific *actions*, namely begetting.[59] "[T]he persons are not immobilized as in a police line-up, but are *doing* something."[60] For Israel, the genealogies created a connection between the past and the present; each uttered name was a link on a chain connecting the listening community to its ancestors, and through them to God, the *ultimate* "resonant source for renewing awareness of present existence."

By contrast, according to Jack Goody and Ian Watt, in literate societies *texts* form the primary link between the past and the present. They argue that when the link ceases to be located in the bodies and collective memory of the people and is replaced by and abstracted in a document, it creates distance and the possibility of objective reflection[61]—as Eduard Nielsen had warned a decade earlier through his caution about texts as "impersonal intermediaries." It is this movement toward abstraction that concerned Ong and inspired his spirited critique of the past as being reduced to "lists, charts or figures" for cultures formed primarily by the written word and digital media.

---

[58]Ong, *Orality and Literacy*, 42–43, 97–99; Goody, *Interface*, 175.

[59]In the three genealogies listed in n.52, the Hiph'il form of ילד ("to beget, cause to bring forth") appears sixty four times.

[60]Ong, *Orality and Literacy*, 98; emphasis added.

[61]"Writing establishes a different kind of relationship between the word and its referent, a relationship that is more general and more abstract, and less closely connected with the particularities of person, place and time, than obtains in oral communication. There is certainly a good deal to substantiate this distinction in what we know of early Greek thought.... [I]t is surely significant that it was only in the days of the first widespread alphabetic culture that the idea of "logic"—of an immutable and impersonal mode of discourse—appears to have arisen; and it was only then that the sense of the human past as an objective reality was formally developed." Goody and Watt, "Consequences," 321.

John Miles Foley

As the founding editor of the academic journal *Oral Tradition*, which he edited until shortly before his death in 2012, and through a number of published works on issues related to oral tradition, John Miles Foley's work has intersected with Hebrew Bible studies in constructive ways. For example, Foley has helped biblical studies move beyond a strict dichotomy between oral and literate cultures, an emphasis which can be traced back through the entire genealogy this chapter has identified. Ong and Goody, Nielsen and the rest of the Scandinavian School, Parry and Lord, and Gunkel himself all in their own way and to varying degrees assumed a strict break between the period of oral transmission and the succeeding era of literacy and written transmission, what has been called the "great divide" theory. Foley, on the other hand, shifted the conversation in the direction of an interplay between the oral and literate elements within a single society. He developed the phrase "oral-derived text" to describe "works that reveal oral traditional features but have reached us only in written form."[62] Or, said another way, "oral-derived texts" are "works of verbal art that either stem directly from or have roots in oral tradition."[63] In this way Foley acknowledges an ongoing relationship of influence between texts and performances in a single culture, an insight Susan Niditch picked up on and developed with particular focus on the world of ancient Israel, which I will discuss in the following section. Additionally, Foley developed four mutually reinforcing and interpenetrating categories in his important books *Immanent Art* and *The Singer of Tales in Performance* that have been fruitfully applied to biblical studies. These four categories are traditional referentiality, metonymy, performance arena, and register.

Traditional referentiality refers to the intricate web of interconnectedness that exists between an oral telling of a given part of the tradition, and the manifold contexts and meanings that each telling invokes. As Foley explains it, traditional referentiality

---

[62.]Foley, *Immanent Art*, 15.

[63.]Foley, *Immanent Art*, xi; quoted in Rodríguez, *Oral Tradition*, 10.

entails the invoking of a context that is enormously larger and more echoic than the text or work itself, that brings the lifeblood of generations of poems and performances to the individual performance or text. Each element in the phraseology or narrative thematics stands not simply for that singular instance but for the plurality and multiformity that are beyond the reach of textualization.[64]

Because of this elaborate system of "echoes" between each telling of the tradition and the totality of the tradition itself, the meaning of any particular story is always larger and more expansive than the individual performance can grasp or express. This system of references "can by its very nature never be wholly captured by textual fossilization; no matter how long or detailed the exposition, any one performance or text will remain only a partial record of the oral tradition at work."[65] Foley here expresses a concern about textualization that is closer to Eduard Nielsen's critique than it is to Walter Ong's. He is less concerned with the loss of the oral mindset in a culture with the advent of literacy (Ong) than he is with the inability of written documents to capture the fulness of an oral performance of a portion of the tradition (Nielsen). Written texts, according to Foley, are inherently incomplete, peppered with "gaps" and inconsistencies that would perhaps arise when they became disconnected from their traditional moorings in the community's collective memory.

Foley offers traditional referentiality as a method for interpreting these "gaps of indeterminacy" in the text, "those blank spots in the textual map that require the reader's own imaginative contribution. . . . [I]n the case of the oral traditional text the bridging of gaps is accomplished by recourse to extratextual meaning."[66] In addition to the communally held tradition to which each performance refers, and from which it draws in order to make meaning, speak a fresh word, or shock

---

[64.]Foley, *Immanent Art*, 7.

[65.]Foley, *Immanent Art*, 10.

[66.]Foley, *Immanent Art*, 45.

the audience into paying attention,[67] "extratextual meaning" also implies a mode of communication inherent to speech but largely inaccessible through the written word. I am referring primarily to the reality of nonverbal communication, including gesture, posture, tone of voice, facial expressions, eye contact, and much more. Each of these elements communicates meaning, sometimes determinatively,[68] and all contribute to the effectiveness of any verbal communication. As Althea Spencer-Miller has said, "Orality is so much more than speech."[69] In an oral performance, performers would rely heavily on nonverbal cues to tell the story, and the community would listen with their eyes as well as their ears. The "tradition" to which each telling of a story referred was composed over generations, as each individual performance brought "the lifeblood of generations of poems and performances to the individual performance or text,"[70] which increased the "echoic" depth and breadth of every performance.[71]

---

[67]·"The skilled biblical author, at home in the oral world and aware of the audience's expectations within the tradition, can quite consciously invoke traditional patterns to manipulate them in recognizably less than traditional ways in order to shock and to make those who receive the message take notice." Niditch, *Oral World*, 22–23.

[68]·E.g., the difference between a statement that is intended to be taken literally and a statement that is satirical and intended to be interpreted as a joke is primarily a matter of tone of voice and facial expression. The way the words are spoken give the listener the (culturally bound) clues as to how to interpret what is said. In literature, it is possible that some of these issues are resolved through effective use of genre. For example, the same line which in a tragedy an astute reader would (correctly) interpret seriously, could be (correctly) interpreted as a joke in a comedy.

[69]·Spencer-Miller, "Rethinking Orality," 40. It is for precisely this reason that Peter Perry recently suggested "face-to-face" as a preferred label over and against "oral" because, as Perry states it, "'oral' or even 'spoken' abstracts too much from the bodily experience of communication, as if the voice was separable from the body before the days of audio recording devices." Perry, *Insights From Performance Criticism*, 46.

[70]·Foley, *Immanent Art*, 7.

[71]·Although she is not addressing traditional referentiality explicitly, Spencer-Miller's insight is instructive here. She adds that, for communities like Israel in which the oral mindset was dominant but writing nevertheless existed, "[o]rality, as a cultural mode, encompasses all of that moment when the written is performed and *the unspoken codes and experiences of the community determine the specific textual*

An example of how traditional referentiality may bridge a "gap of indeterminacy" comes from the story of the binding of Isaac in Gen 22:1–19. The climactic scene takes place in verses 9–11 when Abraham binds Isaac, places him on the altar, and then hovers over him, knife in hand, preparing to slit his throat. The tension is broken by the Angel of the Lord who cries out "Abraham! Abraham!" and succeeds in stopping Abraham from slaughtering his son. After the Angel's speech concludes, Abraham looks up and sees a miracle: a ram is stuck nearby in a thicket. Abraham goes and gets the ram and offers it on the altar instead of his son. The narrative reads smoothly to the eye, but there exists a significant gap that would be both identified and clarified in the *telling*[72] of the story—how does Isaac get off the altar? The storyteller(s) would need to decide how to accomplish this in preparation for the performance, and would be aided in the interpretive task by the tradition of performances of this story, which we do not have access to today.[73] But by the application of imagination and through an attempt to recreate the scene, a logical and theologically significant possibility becomes apparent. Isaac cannot remove himself, for he is bound. Abraham is the only other human character present, who also has a vested interest in getting Isaac off of the altar now that God has changed God's mind about the sacrifice. Is it not likely that Abraham would take the knife— which he was a moment ago holding to Isaac's neck—and use it to cut Isaac's bonds? This simple and logical choice has the additional benefit of communicating a consistent theological theme throughout the

---

meaning in the particular performance." Spencer-Miller, "Rethinking Orality," 41; emphasis added.

[72.] The word "telling" here does not merely imply speech, but the entire enacted and embodied performance. In other words, like all performance, it involves both telling *and showing*.

[73.] Indeed, Foley articulates the problem facing exegetes in the modern world: "If the connection between text and tradition, that is, between metonym and extratextual meaning, is severed, the work that depends so vitally on that connection cannot be realized." But all is not lost. He continues, "If, however, one attends or learns to attend to the special logic and dynamics of the traditional idiom, then the complex realities subsumed in the simple forms will emerge." Foley, *Immanent Art*, 59–60.

Hebrew Bible, namely, the reversal.[74] By using the knife to cut Isaac free, the knife is transformed from an instrument intended to cause death and destruction to an instrument of life and liberation.[75] This action or gesture, latent in the text, is made accessible by an imaginative, embodied re-telling of the story. It is not that this insight would be completely inaccessible to the silent reader; it is simply the acknowledgement that it would require a seriously attentive and imaginative reader to stop and wonder how Isaac got off the altar, whereas the act of performing the story raises the question and *requires* the interpreter to consider it. Much of the remainder of this book is dedicated to developing a methodology to support and guide the

---

[74.]There are a variety of ways reversals are expressed in biblical narratives. For reversals that come at the end of a narrative and change the way you understand the story, see Amit, "Endings," 213–226. For an analysis of reversal as a symbolic, prophetic undoing of the rational, expected order of things effecting a "world turned over" or "upside-down" world, see Kirova, "Eyes Wide Open," 85–98. For the role of reversal understood *not* as a "sudden change in the action of the narrative or unexpected consequences of a character's actions . . . but to the inversion of culturally endorsed norms and worldviews" see Kuhn, *Heart of Biblical Narrative*, 53–54. Kuhn sees the reversal functioning as an invitation to the reader to see differently, which is accomplished by creating an affective response that is facilitated by the development and release of tension within the story. An Old Testament colleague of mine, Dr. Tom Boogaart, has developed a perspective on "dramatic irony" rooted in the retributive worldview of the people of Israel ("you reap what you sow") that is less a literary technique as it is the narrative working out of the biblical cosmology. Spectacular examples of this would be Goliath killed and dismembered by the one he intended to kill and dismember (1 Samuel 17), Daniel's opponents eaten by the lions they intended to eat him (Daniel 6), and Haman hung on the gallows he built to hang Mordecai (Esther 7). There are also "softer" versions of this in which the "intended means of destruction" are transformed by God's power into "means of liberation." Examples would include the fire burning the ropes that bound Shadrach and his companions (Daniel 3), Abraham's knife cutting Isaac free (Genesis 22), and numerous examples of the insignificant or powerless thing being transformed into the powerful, saving thing, such as Gideon's jugs and torches (Judges 7), Eglon's excrement (Judges 3), and the meal the king of Israel serves the Aramean army that puts an end to war between the two nations (2 Kings 6:8–23).

[75.]I am grateful to my colleague Tom Boogaart for this insight.

interpretive process I am describing here, and to demonstrating the fruit of such a method when applied to the biblical narratives.

Foley's second category, metonymy, is closely related to traditional referentiality.[76] As a figure of speech, metonymy describes the way in which a part stands for the whole of the thing being referred to, such as "Washington" as a reference to the United States government. Foley uses the term to describe a "mode of signification" in which "a text or version is enriched by an unspoken context that dwarfs the textual artifact, in which the experience is filled out—and made traditional— by what the conventionality attracts to itself from that context."[77] Its meaning will perhaps become clearer through an example.

Susan Niditch applied Foley's concept to help explain the connections between three instances of "to see and it was good" in the Hebrew Bible, found in Gen 1, 49:14–15, and Exod 2:2 respectively.[78] Her example demonstrates the contribution of Foley's notion of metonymy while also showing how similar metonymy and traditional referentiality are. Niditch first argues that the refrain "God saw that it was good" in Gen 1 is echoed in the moment after Moses' birth when his mother "saw that he was good" in Exod 2:2. Niditch does not argue, however, that "the tale in Genesis 1, in its written form, is being quoted" in Exod 2:2. This claim would presume that a written version of Genesis 1 predated Exod 2, a chronology that would be found problematic by "those who would assign these passages to a sixth-century *P* source and a tenth-century *J* source respectively."[79] Instead of understanding this repetition to have its roots in a literary connection between the two passages, Niditch proposes that the passages are connected metonymically. She suggests that "the creation account of Genesis 1, whatever its origins in writing or speech, was known, was popular, had

---

[76.]Indeed, Foley refers to traditional referentiality at a number of points as "metonymic referentiality" throughout both *Immanent Art* and *The Singer of Tales in Performance*. See, e.g., Foley, *Singer of Tales*, 28. He even refers to it as "immanent referentiality" in *Immanent Art*, 95.

[77.]Foley, *Immanent Art*, 7–8.

[78.]Cf. Niditch, *Oral World*, 18–19.

[79.]Niditch, *Oral World*, 18.

become a part of the culture, and that the author of the birth story of
Exodus 2 had available the words of world-creation to introduce a new
creation."[80] Perhaps the refrain "it was good" had become a part of the
tradition to which the story of Moses' birth referred metonymically.

Perhaps the same is also true with respect to the third example
Niditch cites, Jacob's blessing over Issachar in which he "saw a resting
place that it was good," found in Gen 49:15. The connection between
Gen 1 and Exod 2 suggests a theme of beginnings, a theme borne out in
Jacob's speech, which is "a founding myth" of Issachar's people settling
in their ancestral land.[81] The phrase "to see and it was good," therefore,
likely has to do with "creation, procreation, and beginnings. Exodus 2
need not be reliant on Genesis 1 or vice-versa, but all three passages
may reflect the sort of metonymic or traditional referentiality that so
aptly described the workings of epithets."[82] Metonymy and traditional
referentiality offer not only a way to consider the connections between
passages, but also—and more importantly for the present study—help
to clarify the means whereby these connections were developed and
sustained, namely, through communal oral performances, a topic which
I will take up more directly in the next chapter.

The third category Foley articulated that is constructive for biblical
studies is performance arena. "The performance arena designates the
locus where the event of performance takes place, where words are
invested with their special power."[83] He continues,

> this arena names a site (or sites) distinct from the locales in
> which other kinds of discourse are transacted. It marks the
> special area in which performance of a certain kind is keyed—
> by the speaker and for the participating audience—and in which
> the way of speaking is focused and made coherent as an idiom
> redolent with preselected, emergent kinds of meaning.[84]

[80.] Niditch, *Oral World*, 18.
[81.] Cf. Gen 49:14–15.
[82.] Niditch, *Oral World*, 19.
[83.] Foley, *Singer of Tales*, 47.
[84.] Foley, *Singer of Tales*, 47.

In other words, the performance is "framed" in a particular kind of way, both by the location in which it is presented and by the tacit agreement between performer and audience that establishes the space and words spoken as unique from everyday discourse. In the performance arena, performer and audience communicate through culturally shaped assumptions about how meaning is made in the time and space in which the tradition is performed. The dynamics of traditional referentiality and metonymy are actualized in the performance arena. The location may not be the same for every performance, but consistency of location would add to the echoic complexity of a performance as the tradition to which it referred expanded to include not only the words, embodied in all of the non-verbals of oral performance, but also a particular location that facilitated multiple performances of the tradition.

Let me illustrate the significance of location within performance arena by drawing an example from my own institutional context that, mutatis mutandis, may apply to other contexts as well. Over the past ten years, a culture of scripture performance has developed during daily chapel services at Western Theological Seminary in Holland, Michigan, where I teach. Sometimes biblical narratives from the Hebrew Bible are performed, in Hebrew, as a dramatic Bible reading by one of the Hebrew classes. Sometimes a narrative is read in English while a group enacts various scenes in freeze-frames to animate the narration and anticipate the movements of corporate prayer. Other times a single voice recites the passage dramatically. Each of these services takes place in the same chapel in which the community daily gathers around Table and Font and pulpit to hear a word from the Lord. The past ten years of performances have developed a growing tradition that each new performance contributes meaning to and draws meaning from, sometimes purposefully and sometimes not. The physical space itself can even facilitate a connection as a particular scene is staged in the same location as a different scene was staged previously, both scenes drawing on each other to expand the meaning of each. Some of these connections were severed by a recent renovation to the chapel in which the entire interior was completely re-envisioned. However, the redesigned space is now much more conducive to generating metonymic references between performances in part because the renovated chapel has become the preeminent place in which the community gathers to offer itself to God in worship and receive God's presence through prayers, psalms, songs, sermons, and the sacraments. Before the renovation, chapel could be held in one of three locations. Now it has become the singular performance arena of the community, and every gathering in that location recalls every other gathering there, which establishes the tacit agreement between leader and congregation, between performer and audience that infuses the words spoken and gestures enacted within that space with "special power." It is upon this agreement that traditional referentiality is built.

The final category to consider from Foley is register. Register is understood as "an idiomatic version of the language that qualifies as a more or less self-contained system of signification specifically because it is the designated and sole vehicle for communication in the act of traditional oral performance."[85] Raymond Person clarifies Foley's definition by adding that register describes "the special grammar of a tradition that acts as the medium within individual oral performances for conveying meaning from the performer to the audience."[86] In other words, register describes the characteristics in a corpus like the Hebrew Bible, or even the narratives contained within the Hebrew Bible, that demonstrate a consistent mode of communication. Susan Niditch applies register to the Hebrew Bible this way:

> While biblical works cannot be proven in any instance to have been orally composed, the written works of the Hebrew Bible evidence traits typically associated with ascertainably orally composed works. They belong somewhere in an "oral register." This phrase refers not to modes of composition but to the style of compositions whether the works were created orally or in writing, whether they are performed or read to oneself.[87]

---

[85] Foley, *Singer of Tales*, 15.
[86] Person, "Foley and the Study."
[87] Niditch, *Oral World*, 10.

She goes on to associate "oral register" with "the patterns of content that are the plots of biblical narratives" as well as "various recurring literary forms, employed by a range of biblical authors" such as Robert Alter's studies of biblical type scenes, even though Alter "never associates biblical modes of composition with an oral style."[88] According to Niditch, in the Hebrew Bible the oral register is expressed in three primary ways. First, through the "presence of repetition in one passage, particularly in narrative but in other forms as well,"[89] which is not simply a "mnemonic device for the illiterate performer"[90] but "a means of metonymically emphasizing key messages and moods in a work of literature," such as the repetition of divine speech or the phrase "it was good" in Gen 1.[91] Second, the use of "formulas and formula patterns to express similar ideas or images throughout the tradition,"[92] such as the epithet "bull of Jacob" throughout the Hebrew canon.[93] And finally, the "use of conventionalized patterns of content that recur throughout the tradition"[94] such as the victory-enthronement pattern.[95]

These four categories—traditional referentiality, metonymy, performance arena, and register—are, as was said above, mutually reinforcing, overlapping, and interpenetrating categories that cannot be easily divided or parsed out in isolation from one another. One could say, for example, that register is the communicative medium that enables metonymic resonance between the performer, the audience, and the tradition, in the context of a performance arena. John Miles Foley's groundbreaking work in the area of orality studies revealed new layers of complexity that has allowed biblical scholars like Niditch and others to develop a clearer understanding of the ways in which the oral world interacted with the written word throughout the biblical period.

---

[88] Niditch, *Oral World*, 10.
[89] Niditch, *Oral World*, 10.
[90] Niditch, *Oral World*, 11.
[91] Niditch, *Oral World*, 13.
[92] Niditch, *Oral World*, 11.
[93] See Niditch's treatment in *Oral World*, 15–17.
[94] Niditch, *Oral World*, 11.
[95] See Niditch's treatment along with explanation in *Oral World*, 21–24.

Susan Niditch and the Oral World of Ancient Israel

Perhaps no Old Testament scholar has had as significant or as fruitful of an impact in applying the methods and insights of orality studies to the study of the Hebrew Bible as Susan Niditch. Her monograph *Oral World and Written Word*, published in 1996, remains a standard text within scholarly discussions of orality in ancient Israel and the nature of biblical literature. As Raymond Person recently noted, one of the most enduring impacts of her work was to apply the insights of John Miles Foley and Ruth Finnegan to the world of the Old Testament by advocating compellingly for an "interplay between the oral and written" within Israelite society.[96] Niditch rejected the false dichotomy of oral versus written assumed by Gunkel, Parry, Lord, and to a lesser extent Ong. The Scandanavian school began moving toward the notion of an interplay, but never gave up the strong distinction between oral and written. Niditch went further than all of them by proposing a more nuanced and complicated position that assumes a dynamic interaction between the oral and written elements in a society. Her rejection of the dichotomy of her predecessors did not, however, result in a rejection of their contributions, for each scholar's work advanced the field's understanding of the ancient world and they made the best use of the tools and data available to them. Niditch's work is certainly not the final word on the subject. She did advance the conversation in a number of important directions, however, such as advocating for an interplay between oral and written in ancient Israel, clarifying the definition of literacy in the ancient world, and developing her insights through a number of compelling examples from the Hebrew Bible.

Niditch was not the first scholar to advocate for an interplay between the oral and the written. John Foley and Ruth Finnegan's work on orality and literacy shaped Niditch's thought, leading her to argue that "[o]ral literature does not cease to exist once people read or write, and the oral aesthetic continues to be manifest even in written works. At the same time, even those who do not have a full range of skills in literacy find

---

[96.]Person, "Foley and the Study," 7. Cf. Niditch, *Oral World*, 4, 81, and esp. 99–107.

themselves around writing."[97] The spoken word and the written word
existed together in a mutually reinforcing relationship. Writing was an
ever-present reality in the people's lives. They encountered it in the
marketplace, and on memorials and monuments. And some, such as
"artisans, traders, a variety of government employees, and others" had
limited, basic facility with letters, which gave them a set of basic skills
for reading, "and, to a lesser degree, for writing certain kinds of
messages."[98] But this minimal facility with the alphabet does not
contradict "the assertion that Israelites lived in an essentially oral
world."[99] This conclusion is based on the reality that both the oral and
the written elements of society exist as part of a "continuum,"[100] and that
"literacy in a traditional culture is very much informed by the
worldviews and aesthetics of orality, even while writing increasingly
becomes a useful tool in many facets of Israelite life."[101]

An example of the "interplay" between orality and textuality in the
Hebrew Bible comes near the beginning of Moses' first speech in the
book of Deuteronomy, in the passage known as the *Shema*.[102]

> [4]*Hear, O Israel, the Lord our God, the Lord is one.*

> [5]*And you will love the Lord your God with all of your
> heart, with all of your life, and with all of your strength.*

> [6]*And let these words, which I am commanding you today,
> be on your heart.*

[97.]Niditch, *Oral World*, 44.

[98.]Niditch, *Oral World*, 44.

[99.]Niditch, *Oral World*, 44.

[100.]Frank Polak has referred to this, with reference to Marc Amodio, as the "oral-
literate nexus." Polak, "Language Variation," 322.

[101.]Niditch, *Oral World*, 45.

[102.]Deuteronomy 6:4–9. This passage is called the *Shema* because *shema* (שְׁמַע) is
the passage's first word in Hebrew, meaning "hear, listen". The passage is central for
both Jews and Christians and articulates the fundamental trajectory of both religions:
the highest form of worship is to "love the Lord your God with all of your heart (לְבָב,
levav), with all of your soul (נֶפֶשׁ, *nephesh*), and with all of your might (מְאֹד, *me'od*)"
(v. 5).

Moses connects Israel's undivided love of God (with "all . . . all . . . all,"
v. 5) with the command to "Let these words that I am commanding you
today *be on your hearts*" (v. 6). The logical connection between verse 5
and verse 6 is that an essential way Israel lives out its love of "the Lord
[its] God" is to hold God's words *in their hearts*. If Israel fails to do this
it is likely they will fail to remember any of what the Lord has done for
them, and will forsake him when they are settled in the land promised
to their ancestors (see Deut 6:10–15). It is not enough for those listening
to Moses on the plains of Moab to write "these words" on their hearts;
they are instructed to "repeat" the words to their children when they are
in their homes and when they are on a journey, when they lay down and
when they rise (v. 7). All of these commands assume *oral* interactions
between the people and the tradition, whether mediated by Moses or
parents or elders or priests. But verses 8–9 demonstrate the supportive
and metonymic[103] role played by texts in this dynamic transmission
process. The written words—whether placed in an amulet of some kind
and wrapped on the arm or forehead, carved onto a doorframe or gate,[104]
or inscribed on a scroll—stand as "signs," "symbols"[105] and reminders
of the tradition held in the heart. The written words are "symbolic, a
witness, iconic like the sacred tablets of ten 'words' themselves. The
words, moreover, are to be *repeated* and *spoken*."[106] According to Edgar
Conrad, "'books' in the Old Testament are for the *ear*, not for the eye
of the silent reader; unlike the proverbial child, they are to be heard and

---

[103.]Niditch, *Oral World*, 100.

[104.]Mircea Eliade offers a fascinating insight into the symbolic significance of door
frames and gates, which informs our understanding of the role they played in this
portion of the *Shema*. Doors and gates are thresholds, which "*show* the solution of
continuity in space immediately and concretely; hence their great religious
importance, for they are symbols and at the same time vehicles of *passage* from one
space to the other." The words carved into or placed on these thresholds therefore
function symbolically as "guardians" which protect and facilitate their passage from
one place to another, from outside to inside, from wilderness to city, from chaos to
cosmos. Eliade, *Sacred*, 25; emphasis original.

[105.]The NRSV translates the Hebrew word טֹטָפֹת (*ṭoṭaphot*) as "symbol," though
the exact referent is uncertain.

[106.]Niditch, *Oral World*, 100; emphasis added.

not seen."[107] In the case of the *Shema*, the written words would not have been read, even if they could have been.

Hearing dominant[108] cultures in antiquity approached the written word with an "oral mentality."[109] Niditch identifies five traits that such a mentality includes:

> (1) writing [is] frequently used for short, pragmatic messages; (2) magical, transformative qualities attributed to writing; (3) preserved writings [are] perceived as monumental or iconic rather than a means of keeping records for administrative purposes or for scholarly consultation; (4) the possibility of managing well in life without skills of modern literacy; (5) great reliance on oral communication and hints of orality even in written texts, so that the written text is not fully appreciated or understood without knowledge of the oral world.[110]

The second item on this list, perhaps, strikes the modern intellect as being rather odd, and points to a fundamental difference between the way those who live in "an essentially oral world" approach the written word, and how those who live in a world of deep literacy do. William Schniedewind offers the following explanation: "Writing was not used, at first, to canonize religious praxis, but to engender religious awe. Writing was a gift of the gods. It had supernatural powers to bless and to curse. It had a special place in the divine creation and maintenance of the universe."[111] In such a context it is not unusual to find that the Egyptian god Thoth was not only the god of writing and scribes, but of

---

[107.]Conrad, "Heard But Not Seen," 59. Similarly, Jon Levenson has caught the irony in a common phrase: "The basis of religion in biblical times was not a Bible: the religion *in* the Book is not the religion *of* the Book." Levenson, "Unexamined Commitments," 24.

[108.]This is the phrase used by John Walton to refer to primarily oral cultures in Walton and Sandy, *Lost World of Scripture*, 17.

[109.]Niditch, *Oral World*, 44.

[110.]Niditch, *Oral World*, 44–45.

[111.]Schniedewind, *Bible Became a Book*, 24.

magic as well.[112] The written word captures and intensifies the power of the spoken word because writing is permanent; whereas speech is ephemeral, writing is immortal.

The Bible itself contains allusions to the numinous power associated with writing. Num 5:16–30 describes the practice for determining the authenticity of a husband's accusation against his wife of adultery, which involved writing the accusation down—likely on a potsherd—then washing the ink off in "the water of bitterness," which the woman then drinks. If she gets sick from the mixture, she is guilty; if not, she is innocent. The text clearly displays a patriarchal bias, but beyond that, it reveals an understanding of writing's inherent power. Schniedewind interprets the ritual: "The writing in the water gives the water a magical property. The magic water now can discern whether the jealous husband is right in his accusation. The ritual testifies to the power and magic of *written* words."[113] Niditch interprets the evidence similarly. In discussing a somewhat lengthy curse, found at Horvat 'Uza in the eastern Negev she remarks, "it is clear that this text ... is rich in traits of writing as employed in oral cultures. *The text makes more permanent the curse and ensures its execution.*"[114] In other words, the efficacy of the curse is guaranteed by the transformation of the word spoken to the word written.

The United States of America in the twenty first century is, in many ways, far removed from the oral culture of the Ancient Near East, yet vestiges of our own oral past nevertheless remain. The original document of the United States Constitution has an analogous function to written texts in antiquity. It is kept in a protective box and put on display in a secure building. People come from all around to *look* at it. The point is not to read it, and those who make the pilgrimage to the National Archives in Washington do not spend their time reading the words. Rather, the point is to celebrate the significant cultural and historical role the document played—and continues to play—in shaping

---

[112.]Schniedewind, *Bible Became a Book*, 27.

[113.]Schniedewind, *Bible Became a Book*, 29; emphasis original.

[114.]Niditch, *Oral World*, 48; emphasis added.

the identity of the nation. The document therefore holds considerable symbolic power. And, though it is regularly invoked by pundits and politicians, most Americans do not even consider reading it outside of what may be required in school.[115]

The interplay between the oral and the written that Niditch discerned throughout the entire Hebrew Bible led her away from the dichotomous thinking that informed the work of Parry, Lord, and Gunkel. Unlike Parry and Lord, who attempted to determine the presence and influence of oral composition in written documents on the basis of formulaic language among other things, Niditch adopted a more cautious posture toward parsing out the oral and textual elements within documents. Raymond Person summarizes her approach:

> [W]ithin ancient Israelite literature there is "an interplay be-
> tween the oral and written" so much so that all ancient Israelite
> literature reflects an oral aesthetic and, because of this observa-
> tion and the tremendous varieties of oral aesthetics known from
> living oral traditions, we cannot adequately distinguish between
> "oral" and "written" styles in ancient Israelite literature.[116]

In her own words, Niditch concludes:

> [O]rally composed works can be long or short, created by people
> who can read and write or by those who can read but not write.
> Written traditional-style literature can be meant to be read aloud
> while orally composed works are set in writing by means of
> dictation or recreated in writing through memory. Writers can

---

[115.]A recent survey conducted by James Madison's Montpelier Center for the Constitution found that only 28% of survey respondents had read the Constitution in its entirety at some point in their life. "2010 State of the Constitution," Center for the Constitution, accessed 10 May, 2014. Susan Niditch offers the example of the Vietnam War Memorial, which illustrates that monuments, even in our own time, "are not so much meant to be read word for word to obtain information or to verify a date as to point to, verify, and eternalize an event in a more holistic and symbolic fashion." In Susan Niditch, *Oral World*, 55.

[116.]Person, "Foley and the Study," 7.

imitate oral style. Written works, their plots and characters, enter
the oral end of the spectrum and vice versa. Once writing and
reading are available in a culture or nearby, even if only
practiced by elites, the two ways of imagining and creating
literature influence one another and belong on a sliding scale or
continuum as Ruth Finnegan has shown.[117]

Foley seems to take this one step further, suggesting "abundant evidence
has accumulated to show that these two (supposedly) mutually
exclusive verbal technologies [orality and literacy] can and do exist
within the very same person."[118] Niditch attempts to avoid the
dichotomy inherent in the pursuit of identifying a particular passage as
being derived either from an "oral" or "written" context by
understanding that all passages include both an oral and a written
mindset, but each generally weighs more heavily toward one or the other
end of the spectrum.

The Egyptologist Miriam Lichtheim has identified literature from
ancient Egypt that resonates with the conclusions of Niditch. She opens
her three volume study *Ancient Egyptian Literature*[119] with a discussion
of what she terms the "orational" style,[120] which is in-between poetry
and prose, and is marked by formalized language primarily expressed in
parallelisms. Kevin Robb applied her ideas to his study of Heraclitus
and discovered resonance between the two. Both Lichtheim and Robb
identify the biblical books of Proverbs and Job as biblical examples of
the "orational" style. According to Robb, "Heraclitus composed and
communicated under essentially the same conditions of protoliteracy
which obtained in all cultures of the ancient Near East, one in which
popular survival meant that an author had to anticipate and linguistically

---

[117.]Niditch, "Hebrew Bible and Oral Literature," 8.

[118.]Foley, "Plenitude and Diversity," 106.

[119.]Lichtheim, *Ancient Egyptian Literature*.

[120.]Lichtheim, *Ancient Egyptian Literature*, 3–12, esp. 11–12.

provide for the fact that his composition would be primarily heard and memorized."[121]

A final contribution Susan Niditch made was to suggest the need for a new way of thinking about ancient literacy. She advocated for an understanding that did not make the jump from the existence of an alphabetic script and broad evidence of rudimentary writings on potsherds throughout the land of Israel to the conclusion that all of Israel was largely literate by the late monarchic period. She cites two prominent archeologists who advocated precisely this view. First, from Amihai Mazar: "The ostraca and simple inscriptions on potsherds and pottery jars as well as the abundance of seals are evidence that, at least during the last two centuries of the Monarchy, the knowledge of writing was wide-spread."[122] And this, from Gabriel Barkay: "The increasing number of inscriptions uncovered in excavations at Iron Age II–III sites in the Land of Israel, as well as the content of the inscriptions, testify that by the end of the eighth century Israelite society as a whole was literate."[123] Other scholars apply different methods but nevertheless arrive at this same conclusion.[124]

The question Niditch poses in the face of these conclusions is as fundamental as it is relevant: "What is literacy?"[125] She understands that the way "literacy" is defined and understood is determinative of one's conclusion with respect to the extent of literacy in ancient Israel.

[121.]Robb, "The Linguistic Art of Heraclitus," 178. Robb's description of the relationship between the oral and written, and between the storytellers and their content resonates with the work of Niditch, and anticipates the work of Carr (below), with one very important distinction: the biblical storytellers were not "authors" in the same way that Heraclitus was. Robb argues that Heraclitus *wrote* for the ear. The argument I am building and will eventually make is that the biblical narratives began with oral performance and were put in written form later on, over the course of a long time that likely became final during the exile when the structures and culture that supported the performance tradition was destroyed.

[122.]Mazar, *Archeology of the Land*, 515; quoted in Niditch, *Oral World*, 39.

[123.]Barkay, "Iron Age II–III," 349; quoted in Niditch, *Oral World*, 39.

[124.]See the helpful summary and critique of these methods in Young, "Israelite Literacy, Part I" 239–253.

[125.]Niditch, *Oral World*, 39.

Following Rosalind Thomas' work on literacy in ancient Greece, Niditch cautions against anachronistic definitions of literacy, drawn from the modern world and applied to the ancient world. "'Literacy' is not necessarily as we would define it."[126]

Epigraphists have considered the ancient evidence as well, and drawn similar conclusions as Niditch and Thomas. For example, Ian Young has persuasively argued that the evidence, in fact, gives "no hint that the 'ordinary' Israelite had any literate abilities at all. . . . the vast majority of the population should be expected to have been illiterate throughout the biblical period."[127] Christopher Rollston recently came to the same conclusion in his helpful survey of the epigraphic evidence throughout Israel during the Iron Age[128] titled *Writing and Literacy in the World of Ancient Israel*. Rollston concludes:

> the Old Hebrew epigraphic data and the biblical data align and reveal that trained elites were literate and there is a distinct dearth of evidence suggesting that non-elites could write and read. Those wishing to argue for substantial amounts of non-elite literacy can do so, but it is a perilous argument without much ancient or modern support.[129]

[126.]Niditch, *Oral World*, 40. Miller, in what seems like an attempt to clarify the issue, actually adds confusion to it by suggesting that "although we should rightly call Israel and Judah from the seventh century BCE on literate societies, the 'literature' of both was predominantly oral." Miller, "Performance of Oral Tradition," 183.

[127.]Young, "Israelite Literacy, Part II," 419. See also Carr, *Writing on the Tablet*, 115–116, "A closer look at the oft-cited biblical texts indicates that they do not testify to general literacy in ancient Israel. In addition, the evidence for literacy is concentrated in the late pre-exilic period and is connected to artisans and professional functionaries"; and Niditch, *Oral World*, 59, "[A]ll of these examples of literacy in ancient Israel do not in the least overturn the suggestion that Israelites live in a world heavily informed by the oral end of the continuum."

[128.]The Iron Age began in roughly the twelfth century BCE and extends throughout the biblical period.

[129.]Rollston, *Writing and Literacy*, 134.

Rollston allows for the simultaneous presence of orality and literacy within ancient Israel, but draws a strong distinction between the two along social lines, locating literacy within the elite classes and "illiteracy" among the vast majority of the Israelite populace.

As I implied above, a complicating factor in this argument appears to be the fundamental differences in how "literacy" is defined and understood. I am persuaded by Rollston's definition, which was composed with scholars such as Barkay and their conclusions about ancient literacy in mind. The following is Rollston's "working description of literacy":

> the possession of substantial facility in a writing system, that is, the ability to write and read, using and understanding a standard script, a standard orthography, a standard numeric system, conventional formatting and terminology, and with minimal errors of composition or comprehension. Moreover, I would affirm that the capacity to scrawl one's name on a contract, but without the ability to write or read anything else is not literacy, not even some sort of "functional literacy." Rather, those with this level of eptitude should be classed as illiterate.[130]

To this I would add David Carr's helpful consideration, "The 'literacy' that was the focus of most ancient education went far beyond mastery of the alphabet to a more extensive oral/cognitive mastery of a cultural tradition."[131] Very few in Israel had the opportunity to reach this level

---

[130] Rollston, *Writing and Literacy*, 127. Schniedewind makes a helpful (corrective) distinction between "illiterate" and "non-literate." He argues it is more accurate to describe people "who belong to societies where writing is either unknown or restricted" as non-literate because illiterate "is a pejorative term used in societies that have widespread literacy." Schniedewind, *Bible Became a Book*, 25.

[131] Carr, *Writing on the Tablet*, 116.

of literacy, and ancient cultures like Israel and Greece "simply did not have the cause to invest the resources"[132] universal literacy required.[133]

The epigraphic evidence as Rollston and Young have interpreted it implies what Niditch, along with a growing consensus of biblical scholars and historians are affirming: the vast majority of ancient Israelite society lived in a world "heavily informed by the oral end of the continuum."[134] Though there is debate about the precise numbers, by many estimates the literacy rate during the Roman era in first century Palestine at the time of Jesus was around 5% or less.[135] It is generally agreed that the literacy rate was lower even than this in ancient Israel.[136] Taken as a whole, Israel's relationship with words was mediated primarily by the ears as opposed to the eyes.

Recent Developments in Orality and the Hebrew Bible

The last ten to fifteen years have seen a flurry of activity around issues of orality, the formation of the Hebrew Bible, and the relationship between oral tradition and the documents collected in the Hebrew Bible.[137] Two scholars in particular have further developed a number of

---

[132.]Carr, *Writing on the Tablet*, 116.

[133.]See the recent essay by Christopher Rollston describing the elaborate and complex "scribal curriculum" that literate scribes were required to undergo to develop the requisite skills for the profession. Rollston, "Scribal Curriculum," 71–101.

[134.]Niditch, *Oral World*, 59.

[135.]Bar-Ilan, "Illiteracy in the Land of Israel," 46–61.

[136.]Dever, *Did God Have a Wife?*, 28. See also Niditch, *Oral World*, 39–-40; and Schniedewind, *Bible Became a Book*, 25. For an argument in favor of various levels of Cuneiform literacy (Functional, Technical, and Scholarly Literacy) in the pre-biblical Ancient Near East, see Veldhuis, "Levels of Literacy," 68–89.

[137.]See, e.g. (in order of date of publication): Schniedewind, "Orality and Literacy," 327–332 for a review of a number of books written throughout the 1990s related to issues of orality and the Hebrew Bible; Ben Zvi and Floyd, *Writings and Speech*; Reed Lessing, "Orality in the Prophets," *Concordia Journal* 29, no. 2 (April 2003), 152–165; Schniedewind, *Bible Became a Book*; Horsley, "Origins of the Hebrew Scriptures, 107–134; Carr, *Writing on the Tablet*; Doan and Giles, *Prophets, Performance, and Power*; Doan and Giles, "Performance Criticism," 273–286; Doan and Giles, *Twice Used Songs*; Weissenrieder and Coote, *Interface of Orality and*

Niditch's insights. David Carr took Niditch's conclusion about an interplay between the oral and the written and applied it to the relationship between orality and textuality in educational systems throughout the Ancient Near East.[138] Carr nuances Niditch's conclusions by suggesting that written texts played an important but *subordinate* role in the life of Israel and its neighbors. Written texts were used to support and sustain the community's memory and were therefore employed in the service of *oral* transmission. Texts facilitated the process of "inscribing a culture's most precious traditions *on the insides of people*,"[139] that is, on their hearts. According to Niditch, however, both Carr and William Schniedewind do not sufficiently incorporate the oral character of Israelite life into their articulation of the transmission process and subsequently preserve the text-dominant paradigm. She suggests that their "notions about ancient Israelite education and the centrality of elites in the composition of the Bible . . . seem to open the door to new misconceptions that regard biblical traditions as reflecting a rather fixed virtual canon."[140] Moreover, they "seem to be resisting a new paradigm, instead tucking notions of orality more safely under some of the old assumptions about documents and intertextuality."[141] Although the critique is subtle, and she mostly agrees with Carr (though perhaps a bit less so with Schniedewind), for Niditch it is a matter of emphasis. For example, Schniedewind, in *How the Bible*

Writing; Carr, *Formation of the Hebrew Bible*; Miller, *Oral Tradition*; Polak, "Book, Scribe, and Bard," 118–140; Mathews, *Performing Habakkuk*; Polak, "Language Variation;" Spencer-Miller, "Rethinking Orality;" Walton, *Lost World*; Person, "Orality Studies;" Schmidt, *Contextualizing Israel's Sacred Writings*.

[138.]More recently he further nuanced the traditional binary of orality and literacy by arguing for memory as a "third pole" of the transmission process that is related to yet distinct from the other two, and in some ways is the essential link between them. "[T]hese different forms of variation point to *three* not *two* major poles in ancient textual transmission: the written text, the oral performance reception dimension, *and the medium of memory*. Furthermore, in many contexts these three poles are integrally interrelated." Carr, "Orality, Textuality, and Memory," 168–69; emphasis original.

[139.]Carr, *Writing on the Tablet*, 6; emphasis added.

[140.]Niditch, "Hebrew Bible and Oral Literature," 7.

[141.]Niditch, "Hebrew Bible and Oral Literature," 8.

Became a Book, is primarily concerned with the process that culminates in the final, textual expression of biblical tradition, as the title of his book implies. Niditch, on the other hand, is "interested in how *unlike* a book the Bible is, even in its written preserved form,"[142] because, in her estimation, it "reflects an oral world mentality."[143]

Beyond these quibbles about the fixedness of the canon during the biblical period, what is of significance for the present chapter is Carr's claim that Israel's primary concern was "accurate recall of the treasured tradition."[144] It is important not to assume that "accurate recall" meant the same thing to ancient primarily oral cultures as it would mean today in the text- and print-oriented culture of the modern West. Today texts have largely replaced memory, but for primarily oral cultures, texts played a supportive role to memory.[145] As Jack Goody has shown, in oral cultures performances of the same text are rarely, if ever, *exactly* the same: "It is possible that exact repetition is not given the same value as in many written cultures."[146]

Raymond Person argues a similar point with respect to the practice of producing and copying texts in ancient Israel. According to Person, "the ancient Israelite scribes did not slavishly write the texts word by word, but preserved the texts' meaning for the on-going life of their communities in much the same way that performers of oral epic re-present the stable, yet dynamic, tradition to their communities."[147] The scribes "performed" rather than "copied" the texts. Person bases this conclusion, in part, on the resonance between the the definitions of the

---

[142.]Niditch, "Hebrew Bible and Oral Literature," 8; emphasis added.

[143.]Niditch, "Hebrew Bible and Oral Literature," 7.

[144.]Carr, *Writing on the Tablet*, 7.

[145.]Carr has said more recently: "At least up through the Second Temple period of Jewish scribalism, writing was not *opposed* to memory, but served it." Carr, "Orality, Textuality, and Memory," 169. Similarly, Eduard Nielsen quotes Plato's *Phaedrus* on the relationship between texts and memory. Plato argues the only gift of a written manuscript is as an aid to memory, to "treasure up reminders for himself, when he comes to the forgetfulness of old age." Nielsen, *Oral Tradition*, 34, n.2.

[146.]Goody, *Interface*, 168.

[147.]Person, "Scribe as Performer," 602.

word for "word" in Serbo-Croation (oral) communities and the Hebrew word *dabar* (דָּבָר).

> Within Serbo-Croatian epic, a word is understood as a line, a stanza, or even the entire epic. The semantic range of the Hebrew word *dabar* can be translated as "word" but also "speech" and "utterance." Thus, what the ancient Israelites understood as a "word" included much more than what we moderns typically understand as a "word." Even if the scribes did not copy their texts "word for word" from our perspective, from their perspective they very well may have copied them "word for word."[148]

In addition to the cultural and semantic evidence that supports a different understanding of "accurate recall" than verbatim repetition, David Carr has shown how memory played a primary role in transmission by drawing attention to the presence of "memory variants"[149] in the received text. Examples of memory variants range from "substitution of synonymous terms," to "radical adaptation of the tradition."[150] Memory variants are created "when a tradent modifies elements of text in the process of citing or otherwise reproducing it from memory, altering elements of the text, yet producing a meaningful whole ('good variants') amidst that complex process that Bartlett termed the 'effort after meaning'."[151]

The presence of dual versions of the same stories in both the Samuel-Kings and Chronicles cycles offers an array of examples that strongly point to the role of memory creating the variant in the textual transmission process. Carr lists a number of examples in his chapter titled "Documented Cases of Transmission History: Part 2."[152] One

---

[148.]Person, "Orality Studies," 58. See also Foley, *Singer of Tales*, 2–3.

[149.]Carr, *Formation of the Hebrew Bible*, 17.

[150.]Carr, *Formation of the Hebrew Bible*, 17.

[151.]Carr, *Formation of the Hebrew Bible*, 17–18. See also Carr, "Orality, Textuality, and Memory," 164–70.

[152.]Carr, *Formation of the Hebrew Bible*, 37–56.

example will suffice here. First Samuel 31:9 and 1 Chr 10:9 both report the story of Saul's demise. Both versions "describe how the Philistines cut off Saul's head and stripped him of his weapons, but they describe the events in different order and in different words."[153] First Samuel 31:9 reads: "and they cut his head and stripped his weapons," while 1 Chr 10:9 reads: "and they stripped him and lifted his head and his weapons."[154] The presence of variants like these, created through memory as opposed to scribal error, suggest there was a "mix of oral and written dynamics" at work in the transmission process, particularly throughout the First and most of the Second Temple period, up to around the late second or early first centuries BCE, when "verbatim precision" became not only a priority but also a possibility.[155] "Yet our existing evidence for scribal transmission for earlier periods, both within Israelite-Judean contexts and further afield, overwhelmingly suggest that such precision was not characteristic of scribal transmission in the Second Temple period and before."[156] With respect to Carr's phrase "accurate recall," what seems to be of primary significance is, first, the fact that the tradition is recalled, and second, the means whereby it is recalled: through oral performance, delivered from memory.[157]

An oral performance of an ancestral story did more than simply recall the treasured tradition; it reawakened it, recreated it. Building on the work of the German Egyptologist Jan Assmann on cultural memory, Carr suggested that for Israel and her neighbors, the "past is never 'past' in the way we might conceive it but stands in the ancient world as a potentially realizable 'present' to which each generation seeks to

---

[153.]Carr, *Formation of the Hebrew Bible*, 60.

[154.]Carr, *Formation of the Hebrew Bible*, 60.

[155.]Carr, *Formation of the Hebrew Bible*, 114.

[156.]Carr, *Formation of the Hebrew Bible*, 114.

[157.]See also Gregory Nagy's comments on the term *mouvance*, which he uses to describe the evidence of "certain textual variations" in passages that "reflect the potential for actual variations in performance" in Medieval manuscript traditions. Nagy, *Poetry as Performance*, 9. Nagy prefers the term precisely because it presumes a link between the textual manuscript and the oral tradition. Nagy, *Poetry as Performance*, 9–13.

return."[158] This resonates with the conclusion of Walter Ong with respect to an oral culture's relationship to the past, which he saw as "the domain of the ancestors, a resonant source for renewing awareness of present existence."[159] John Miles Foley understood traditional referentiality to accomplish a similar effect in which the division between past and present dissolves as part of the tradition is performed. "Since it may thus be said that the traditional metonymic signals do not 'repeat' but rather *recreate*, the networks of inherent meaning enrich the momentary with the timeless, the situational with the all-pervasive, the story-specific with the traditional."[160] Each performance "re-creates" the event it recalls, as the gathered community's commitment to and understanding of the present is renewed through its encounter with the past.

Reconsidering Gunkel: The Seeds of Performance

As the beginning of this chapter argued, at the turn of the twentieth century Hermann Gunkel universalized the notion in biblical studies that an oral tradition existed behind the written documents contained in the Hebrew Bible. I intentionally overlooked a portion of his work at the beginning of the chapter because it seemed to fit better here as a transition into the body of my argument, which will begin in the following chapter. Although some of his assumptions and conclusions have rightly suffered criticism over the last century, including in the present chapter, his work endures as a testament to his perception and rigor. Indeed, perhaps he appreciated the oral dimensions of the received text more fully than he generally gets credit for. For example, in *The Legends of Genesis*, Gunkel demonstrated a great sensitivity to the dynamics of oral narration that dovetail with the work on oral performance Foley would do over sixty years later. Gunkel understood there was—to borrow Foley's term—"extratextual" meaning in the biblical text that required attentiveness to oral performance in order to access the full meaning latent within it.

[158.]Carr, *Writing on the Tablet*, 11.

[159.]Ong, *Orality and Literacy*, 97

[160.]Foley, *Immanent Art*, 10; emphasis original.

We must recall at this point that we are dealing with orally recited stories. Between narrator and hearer there is another link than that of words; the tone of voice talks, the expression of the face or the gestures of the narrator. Joy and grief, love, anger, jealousy, hatred, emotion, and all the other moods of his heroes, shared by the narrator, were thus imparted to his hearers without the utterance of a word. Modern exegesis is called to the task of *reading between the lines* the spiritual life which the narrator did not expressly utter. This is not always such a simple matter. We have in some cases gotten out of touch with the emotions of older times and the expressions for them.[161]

Gunkel's insight points to performance as an interpretive method to access both meaning and a whole range of emotions inaccessible to the literary scholar reading silently, isolated inside an office. Recent research on orality likewise points to performance as a primary means of transmission of the biblical traditions. However, performance has been almost entirely overlooked by the field of Hebrew Bible/Old Testament scholarship until only very recently.

In the concluding chapter of *Oral World Written Word*, Susan Niditch made a number of tentative suggestions about various ways the Hebrew Bible may have come together. Her suggestions are framed by her observation that, instead of thinking of "the Bible as a book, we do well to think of the Bible as a library."[162] This image allows for much greater flexibility in considering how the various traditions, which represent various and sundry perspectives on Israel's history and contain differing theologies and even markers of different locations and dialects were all collected into the Hebrew Bible, particularly in light of the "interplay between the oral and the written" that marks her research and is expressed through what she calls the "oral-literate continuum."[163] The manifold types of literature in the Hebrew Bible suggest many

---

[161.]Gunkel, *Legends*, 62; emphasis added.

[162.]Niditch, *Oral World*, 116.

[163.]Niditch, *Oral World*, 116.

sources, and there is no doubt the formation of the Hebrew Bible is steeped in mystery. However, as Niditch demonstrates, enough information is known to make educated guesses about elements of the formation process.

Her chapter contains four models, but I will discuss only the second model because it is directly related to the narrative portion of the Hebrew Bible, which is the focus of this study. This model, titled "Oral to Written and Written to Oral—The Pan-Israelite Story"[164] deals with "longer narrative compositions that provide a slice of essential Israelite myth, the stories of ancestors, heroes, and the formation of the early history of the group that help to express and formulate Israel's self-definition."[165] In other words, the narrative corpus in the Hebrew Bible. Her suggestion is that "portions of these traditions were performed to audiences, taking basic shape in content and theme in response to the audiences who hear the performances."[166] Her model allows for both performer and audience to play a shaping role in the formation of the tradition. The performance tradition was influenced by writing and visa versa. Some of the performances were likely eventually either dictated to a scribe by a skilled performer, or written down by a "gifted writer who like most Israelites knows how the stories go."[167] Perhaps, also, some of the longer performances were supported by written notes aiding the performer's (or, performers') memory, creating a context in which not only oral becomes written, but written also becomes oral and then is sometime later recommitted to writing in an elaborated form.[168]

[164.] See her full treatment of this model in Niditch, *Oral World*, 120–125.

[165.] Niditch, *Oral World*, 120.

[166.] Niditch, *Oral World*, 120.

[167.] Niditch, *Oral World*, 120.

[168.] Niditch, *Oral World*, 120. Recently Robert Miller argued the same line of reasoning: "We are concerned here with more than the literature's emergence, but with its performance in a culture that was not merely 'primarily oral' but oral-and-written. Written texts circulated in spoken form by recitation long after they were committed to writing. And those recited forms begat oral forms that were not in writing, or were not put in writing for some time afterwards. Oral texts that circulated from bard to audience or bard to bard could be recorded in writing, could be consulted by writers,

This tradition, transmitted over a number of generations, even centuries, primarily through oral performances that were variously supported by and committed to writing did not sustain itself. The most likely candidates to carry out such a significant cultural and religious task would have been the Levites, who were "traditionally considered the teacher clan, more portable and less territorially bound than the members of other tribes (Joshua 14:3, 4; 18:7), more vulnerable in the view of the author of Deuteronomy 12 and 1 and 2 Chronicles (Deut 12:12, 18, 19; 14:27; 16:11; 26:11)."[169]

The full "job description" of the Levites is not clear from Scripture. Second Chronicles and Nehemiah, both late biblical works, ascribe the Levites with the role of "singing praises to the Lord" (2 Chr 29:30) and being "in charge of the songs of thanksgiving" (Neh 12:8) along with playing instruments (Neh 12:27–28).[170] This insight ought not lead one to the conclusion that the Levites were Israel's bards, their "singers of tales in performance," to borrow the title of Foley's book. However, as Niditch insightfully explains, "even songs of praise and thanksgiving that have been preserved in the tradition frequently do include renditions of key threads in essential Israelite myth."[171] She cites 1 Chron 16:14–22, which parallels Ps 105:1–15, and how both Pss 105 and 106 recite Israel's history—the former positively and the latter negatively—with explicit reference to a number of patriarchal stories from the Torah.[172] In each of these psalms and others, "an essential outline of Israel's founding myth is found albeit with variations. The songs of thanksgiving and praise performed by Levites can thus have much in common with the narratives in Genesis through Numbers."[173]

---

and could be consulted by bards of other stories." Miller, "Performance of Oral Tradition," 182.

[169.] Niditch, *Oral World*, 122.

[170.] Niditch, *Oral World*, 122–23. Further, Miller has proposed that narrative performances would have been accompanied by music. Miller, "Performance of Oral Tradition," 188.

[171.] Niditch, *Oral World*, 123.

[172.] Niditch, *Oral World*, 123.

[173.] Niditch, *Oral World*, 123.

The case of Neh 8:8 is an interesting one. Ezra reads aloud to the people from "the book" (בַּסֵּפֶר *vassepher*), from "the Torah of God" (בְּתוֹרַת הָאֱלֹהִים *vattorat ha'elohim*), after which the Levites taught and interpreted the words to the people. It is unclear what exactly is referred to by the term "Torah."[174] Perhaps it refers to "the law," as the NRSV translates it. But, as Niditch points out, it would also make sense at a ritual gathering such as Neh 8 (and Deut 31) describes, for an occasion "to tell of the history of the people, to reinforce essential myth, the narrative context for Torah."[175] Either way, "[t]here is no way to know for certain what the term 'Torah' means in these passages."[176] Niditch concludes,

> We consider it at least a possibility that Levites are cast in these teaching, tradition-delivering, and preserving ways by authors of the second temple period because they were the preservers and promulgators of the tradition even in the first temple period. It is for this reason that 2 Chron. 17:7–9 portrays the southern king Jehoshaphat as sending Levites throughout the cities of Judah to teach among the people. . . . Traditions concerning the Levites as composers of psalms, the founding-myth content of several extant examples, and traditions about the Levites' teaching among the people combine to suggest an Israelite parallel to Nagy's model.[177]

[174.]Cf. Deut. 31:11–12 in which Moses gathered the people and read to them from "the Torah" and instructed them to "fear the Lord your God and to observe diligently all the words of this Torah."

[175.]Niditch, *Oral World*, 124.

[176.]Niditch, *Oral World*, 125.

[177.]Niditch, *Oral World*, 125. Nagy develops the model Niditch refers to here in Nagy, *Greek Mythology and Poetics*, 36–43. Niditch summarizes it in Niditch, *Oral World*, 120–22. Nagy's model attempts to explain two phenomena: the means whereby Homer and Hesiod's poetry achieved pan-Hellenic status, and how they were transmitted before they were definitively committed to writing by the time of Herodotus in the fifth century B.C.E. His starting point is "the historical fact that the medium of transmitting the Homeric and Hesiodic poems was consistently that of performance, not reading" (Nagy, 38). Nagy sees the poetry of Homer and Hesiod "as

If Niditch is right, and the narrative corpus of the Hebrew Bible was sustained through a combination of oral performances of texts and performances that were eventually committed to writing, and if this tradition was overseen and maintained by the Levites, then a more careful consideration of the role of performance and its implication for biblical interpretation must be considered. It is my contention that Niditch is right, or at least partly right, and that more attention needs to be given to the context of performance.

Conclusion

This chapter traced the development of the reality of orality as an essential dynamic in the transmission process of biblical tradition in

---

strongly evidencing the traits of oral composition as laid out by Lord and Parry" (Niditch, 120). As such, it "becomes reality only in performance," and is affected strongly by "the poet's interaction with his audience" (Nagy, 39). He postulates that Homer and Hesiod's poetry achieved pan-Hellenic recognition and acceptance through performances at pan-Hellenic festivals, such as the eighth century B.C.E. Olympic Games and other similar events, and that through "countless such performances for over two centuries, each recomposition at each successive performance could become less and less variable. Such gradual crystallization into what became set poems would have been a direct response to the exigencies of a pan-Hellenic audience" (Nagy, 42). This performance tradition was sustained by rhapsodes, "who by the time of Plato were not oral poets composing and performing simultaneously but performers who inherited oral traditions and participated in their systematization" (Niditch, 120–21). Throughout this period of "rhapsodic transmission" the written texts of their poems "could have been generated at any time—in fact, many times" (Nagy, 41). Although Nagy argues, appropriately, for a continual movement toward more "fixed" tradition, characterized by "mnemonic techniques that had been part of the oral tradition" (Nagy, 41), by which he means not only words, but also meter and syntax, Niditch points out that "this is not the case with extant Israelite literature. When writing of systematization and the gradual fixing of the tradition, we refer to essential contours of content and character and to frequently used expressions for the pieces of content" (Niditch, 121). She concludes: "Even allowing for these nuances and differences, Nagy's model is an excellent one for the Israelite case, allowing for the traditional style of the material, helping to explain the particular pan-Israelite interests of the narratives and the way in which once disparate traditions coalesced into the people's story" (Niditch, 122).

modern Western scholarship, beginning with Hermann Gunkel at the turn of the twentieth century. The motif of a genealogy drew attention to the way scholarship is always embedded in a context that is historical, cultural, and generational: each successive generation of scholars is dependent upon the previous generation, but is also free to take their scholarship in directions unforeseen to their forebears. And, just as it is with families, not each "child" in a given generation agrees with all of their "siblings" or their "ancestors," but no one is free to claim they are autonomous or truly original. Such is certainly the case with biblical scholarship that has engaged the topic of orality in ancient Israel. Gunkel's insight into the oral history—and the strict dichotomy he saw between the oral and the written—was reinforced and developed by Parry and Lord a few decades later, although the strict dichotomy was challenged around the same time by a group of biblical scholars in the so-called Scandinavian school. Walter Ong and Jack Goody, in the next generation, applied their knowledge as cultural anthropologists to the cultural differences between text- and print-based societies and those formed primarily by the spoken word. John Miles Foley nuanced the work of Parry and Lord to be less dependent on the strict dichotomy that had characterized Parry and Lord's work, and developed new applications of orality studies to the Old Testament, a task which Susan Niditch took up with powerful results. Others have followed her footsteps, such as David Carr and Raymond Person, adding new layers to her seminal insight of an "interplay between the oral and the written," and laying the building blocks upon which the remainder of this project is built.

In the following chapter, therefore, I will attempt to take the next step beyond where this genealogy of scholarship has led me. This process of moving forward will begin with a reconsideration of the narratives from the perspective of form criticism. In some sense this will mean starting again back at the beginning with Hermann Gunkel and form criticism. But in another sense it will not, since we will return to form criticism in light of the generational journey of the present chapter, and with a clearly defined path to take. This path will involve a reconsideration of the genre of the narratives in light of the evidence provided in Chapter 1 concerning the formative influence of orality and the "oral mindset," and will lead to the suggestion of drama as the best genre designation for the stories contained in the Hebrew Bible. Some of the implications of this designation will be developed with reference to performance theorists whose work has begun to intersect with biblical studies in generative ways. Following this, Chapter 3 will examine the methodological implications involved in interpreting the stories as dramas.

CHAPTER 2
DRAMA AND PERFORMANCE: THE GENRE OF THE BIBLICAL NARRATIVES RECONSIDERED

Introduction

This chapter will build on the foundation laid in the previous chapter by considering what implications Israel's orality may have on how we determine the genre of the biblical stories, and what methodology (or, methodologies) we employ to interpret them. I will argue that the narratives collected in the Hebrew Bible are dramas, scripts of ancient performances. Recognizing this calls for a paradigm shift in biblical studies from a text-orientation to a performance-orientation. This paradigm shift will change the relationship between the scholar and the story and will open up new interpretive possibilities inaccessible to the silent reader.

The Changing Face of Form Criticism

In 2003 Ehud Ben Zvi and Marvin Sweeney published a series of essays collected mostly from papers presented during two special sessions during the 2000 annual meeting of the Society of Biblical Literature on "The Changing Face of Form Criticism in Hebrew Bible Studies." The eleven papers presented there gave attention to the role of form criticism with respect to the Pentateuch, the Deuteronomistic History, and the Prophets, and were supplemented by other solicited essays to create the volume *The Changing Face of Form Criticism for the Twenty-First Century.*[1] The essays vary in terms of their assessment of the present state of form criticism and its viability for the future. In one incisive declaration a contributor concluded that form criticism does, in fact, have "a future—if its past is allowed a decent burial."[2]

---

[1] Ben Zvi and Sweeney, *Changing Face of Form Criticism.*
[2] Campbell, "Form Criticism's Future," 31.

The past that is in need of burial began with Hermann Gunkel. Gunkel, as we saw in the previous chapter, inaugurated form criticism and defined the terms by which it was conducted for a century. According to Ben Zvi and Sweeney, "Throughout most of the twentieth century, [form criticism] has been conceived as an inherently historical or diachronic discipline that focuses on the identification and analysis of typical patterns of language that appear and function within and give shape and expression to the overall form of a text."[3] The two primary purposes toward which form critical analysis applied itself was to identify the genre of the text, and through that identification to discern the *Sitz im Leben*. One way the "face" of form criticism has changed of late is the decoupling of *Sitz im Leben* from the genre question. According to Roland Boer,

> *Sitz im Leben* has been released from Gunkel's original straightjacket and applied to a whole range of biblical phenomena, finding its most natural applications in studies of a text's production rather than being linked to the context of the genre in question.[4]

This decoupling of *Sitz im Leben* from genre has much to commend it. There is, perhaps, one significant drawback. It is possible that this decoupling has contributed to perpetuating an oversight within form criticism and other approaches that have begun concerning themselves with genre. The oversight I refer to relates to the fundamental assumption concerning the singularly *textual* character of the biblical passage being studied. This oversight applies equally to the question of genre, which is universally taken to mean *literary* genre.

Ben Zvi and Sweeney's conclusion—after the papers were presented and the subsequent essays were collected—was that form criticism is in the midst of a season of considerable, if not radical, change in which the moorings upon which it was built are shifting.

---

[3] Ben Zvi and Sweeney, *Changing Face of Form Criticism*, 1.

[4] Boer, "Introduction," 3.

This is a time bubbling with activity in form-critical studies, of emerging patterns of substantial methodological change and conceptual reshaping of what form criticism either is or should be about. It is therefore an opportune time to reexamine form-critical methodology and to consider its conceptualization and potential for future research.[5]

The change form criticism is undergoing will (and must) include the emergence of new directions for and applications of form criticism; it will require flexibility and openness to new possibilities. I will suggest in this chapter that a promising possibility lies in *re-coupling* genre with a redefined and expanded notion of *Sitz im Leben*, which follows Boer's suggestion of taking into consideration the cultural context in which the texts were produced, discussed in the previous chapter. I will suggest a particular way of pairing diachronic (historical) and synchronic (literary, textual) analysis, which would help to mitigate the textual bias of much modern, Western biblical scholarship.

My conclusion will be a suggestion that the stories collected in the Bible are ancient dramas, the scripts of ancient performances. The implications of this reconsideration will point beyond form criticism[6] to

---

[5] Ben Zvi and Sweeney, *Changing Face of Form Criticism*, 5.

[6] James Muilenburg famously inaugurated rhetorical criticism as a distinct approach to Old Testament research "with eminent lineage" (69) in form criticism in his 1968 presidential address to the Society of Biblical Literature conference titled "Form Criticism and Beyond." Muilenburg, "Form Criticism," 1–18. Muilenburg identified certain weaknesses and excesses of form criticism as it was being practiced, and suggested greater emphasis needed to be given to the received text *as a text* ("What I am interested in, above all, is in understanding the nature of Hebrew literary composition, in exhibiting the structural patterns that are employed for the fashioning of a literary unit" (57)). He offered rhetorical criticism as a way of moving "beyond" the limitations and exclusive application of form criticism. I am making a suggestion of a similar sort. Form criticism provides essential tools in the task of biblical interpretation through the identification of genre. But it has not adequately taken into account the pervasive influence of Israel's orality on the texts collected into the Bible today. Therefore, it is necessary to move "beyond" form criticism, but not to abandon it. Rhetorical criticism—and its close relative narrative criticism—also have failed to adequately account for the historical context that produced the biblical stories.

the emergence of a new methodology called biblical performance criticism. Biblical performance criticism constitutes a paradigm shift from a text-orientation to a performance-orientation. But the road to biblical performance criticism begins with form criticism.

Form Criticism and Genre

Form criticism helped the field of Hebrew Bible/Old Testament studies understand the significance of genre identification as an essential part of the process of interpreting a biblical passage. Reflecting on this legacy, John Barton asserted, "it is not too much to say that it is impossible to understand any text without at least an implicit recognition of the genre to which it belongs."[7] Barton implies here that genre is in some way a carrier of meaning, its intention is to communicate meaning, and that the full range of meaning—or perhaps even the plain sense meaning—is not accessible to the interpreter without at least some basic apprehension of the genre. Also implied in Barton's comment is the obvious yet profound statement of Michael Goldman: "the first function of genre is that it be recognized."[8] The task is not as easy as it might appear, however.

In general, form criticism has understood genre to exist at the point of intersection between the setting (*Sitz im Leben*) a particular passage implies or points to, and the structure (form) created by the language and content of the passage. The language is generally treated as a window backwards into the (historical) setting.[9] Rolf Knierim has adequately demonstrated the challenges inherent in this approach in his

---

Subsequently, form criticism, rhetorical, and narrative criticism have developed purely textual/literary methodological approaches to interpreting the stories. I am suggesting the field of biblical studies take the next logical step "beyond" form *and* rhetorical criticism to biblical performance criticism.

[7.] Barton, *Reading the Old Testament*, 16.

[8.] Goldman, *On Drama*, 8.

[9.] And yet, paradoxically, as Antony Campbell has shown, the historical preoccupation of Gunkel and Gressman resulted in an anti-historical approach: "Intrinsic to form criticism is a focus on text before event." Campbell, "Form Criticism's Future," 19.

1973 article "Old Testament Form Criticism Reconsidered."[10] According to Knierim, form criticism operated on the basis of two assumptions. First, it assumed a "hermeneutic of language according to which life and language corresponded to one another: life creates language, and language reflects—societal, customary—life and its meaning."[11] Secondly, it assumed the setting was constitutive of the genre. "In other words, the setting is assumed to provide or produce the matrix to which typical linguistic units owe their existence."[12] The two assumptions are interrelated and interdependent. For example, according to this model, the life setting (corporate worship or the public square, say) dictates what language is used (complaints in the first person plural or hyperbolic and shocking language to decry injustice), and attentiveness to the language reveals the genre (corporate lament or prophetic oracle). Knierim points out that, although this approach has many merits to it,[13] it is also problematic, particularly with respect to these two assumptions. The first assumption is perhaps true, but not the whole truth; and the second is commonly true, but not necessarily true in every instance. Further, and perhaps most fundamentally, "we are no longer so clear as to what exactly a genre is. More pointedly: it is doubtful whether this has ever been clear."[14]

Drawing on the work of the structuralist anthropologist Claude Lévi-Strauss, Knierim suggests the insights of structuralism can contribute to an understanding of genre, despite the fact that the word hardly appears in structuralist literature. The structuralist's attempt to uncover "the unconscious structure underlying each institution and each

---

[10.]Knierim, "Form Criticism Reconsidered," 435–68.

[11.]Knierim, "Form Criticism Reconsidered," 436.

[12.]Knierim, "Form Criticism Reconsidered," 446.

[13.]"The question concerning us here, however, is precisely this programmatic assumption that genres are constituted by their setting. In other words, the setting is assumed to provide or produce the matrix to which typical linguistic units owe their existence. *To be sure, this assumption can be ascertained with regard to a great many forms, formulas, and genres in the Old Testament.* Thus the problem is not whether generic language can depend on setting but whether this has to be assumed always." Knierim, "Form Criticism Reconsidered," 446; emphasis added.

[14.]Knierim, "Form Criticism Reconsidered," 436.

custom"[15] connects to the discussion about genre because it assumes that "the variable patterns of linguistic expression and human behavior are received in already structured forms from the patterns and schemata conceived by the collective consciousness on its prelinguistic level."[16] According to this model, genre is more an expression of unconscious structures that underlie human expression generally—both linguistic and societal—than the direct and inevitable expression of a particular setting in life. This helps to complexify the first assumption above.

Genre in the structuralist framework is akin to grammar. "Grammar is the invisible infrastructure of a language."[17] It guides the ways words connect to make meaning that is comprehensible to others who share the language. Grammar generally operates at an unconscious level, as a structure that guides thought, expression, meaning, and interpretation. It is expressed unconsciously or tacitly, and it is also received and processed unconsciously.[18] It is both the unconscious operation of grammar and the mutual comprehension of meaning that connects grammar to genre. In the same way that grammar operates invisibly and is unconsciously "recognized" in the act of effective communication, so too genre generally operates beneath the level of consciousness as it is recognized intuitively by members of a society due to shared cultural formation.[19] It is the work of critical analysis to elevate the operations of genre to the level of conscious awareness—just like literary analysis

---

[15.] Knierim, "Form Criticism Reconsidered," 439.

[16.] Knierim, "Form Criticism Reconsidered," 440.

[17.] West, *Biblical Hebrew,* 63.

[18.] The primary exception to this is when grammatical structures are violated in speech, whether intentionally or inadvertently (as when a child says "He goed to bed"). The violation draws attention to what is otherwise taken for granted, and presents an opportunity for the parent to instruct the child in the operations of grammar so that, as the child grows, it will speak according to the rules of the language naturally, intuitively, communicating meaning without drawing undue attention to the *way* the meaning is communicated.

[19.] People intuitively read the newspaper differently than a novel or a poem, for example. This is so not because of something inherent in the genre, but because members of the culture have been formed to do so, and the operation becomes "natural" or intuitive, unconscious.

must evaluate the particular operations of grammar in a given work—in order to achieve faithful interpretation.

One beneficial contribution of a structuralist approach to genre is that it moves away from definitional or classificatory approaches, which have historically characterized form-critical scholarship. These approaches "are now seen as not representing well the functions of genre in human communication."[20] Alastair Fowler has offered a memorable and witty corrective of the classificatory approach, turning another scholar's comment on its head. Graham Hough argued that "in abstraction the theory of kinds is no more than a system of classification. It is given content and positive value by filling each of its pigeon holes with adequate description and adequate theory."[21] Fowler retorts: "in reality genre is much less of a pigeonhole than a pigeon."[22] This is critical for Fowler whose approach prioritizes the way in which genres are dynamic in that they adapt and change through a continual process of "metamorphosis"[23]—like each successive generation of pigeons, which are similar yet different from their predecessors—instead of remaining static and unchanging as a pigeonhole.

Carol Newsom perceptively develops Fowler's insight about genre metamorphosis through Mikhail Bakhtin's "notion of texts as utterances in dialogical relationship to one another. Not only is every utterance unique but also must be conceived of as a reply to what has gone before. Thus every instance of a genre can be understood as a reply to other instances of that genre and as a reply to other genres, whether or not self-consciously conceived of as such."[24] Preserved in each "reply," however, are the consistent, stable "elements of the *archaic*."[25] Thus Bakhtin identifies the inherently paradoxical nature of genres, which remain

[20] Newsom, "Spying Out the Land," 20.
[21] Quoted in Fowler, *Kinds of Literature*, 37.
[22] Fowler, *Kinds of Literature*, 37.
[23] Fowler, *Kinds of Literature*, 23.
[24] Newsom, "Spying Out the Land," 28.
[25] Bakhtin, *Problems of Dostoevsky's Poetics*, 106; emphasis original.

rooted in a tradition through a process of continual renewal.[26] Bakhtin called this process "genre memory." According to Bakhtin, "A genre lives in the present, but always *remembers* its past, its beginning."[27]

Fowler's understanding of the constant reinvention of genres and Bakhtin's paradoxical notion of "genre memory" resonate deeply with the continual process of development and modification inherent in the performative nature of the oral transmission process discussed in the previous chapter. Each new telling of the tradition is simultaneously—and paradoxically—rooted in the tradition and a fresh word to the gathered community who hears the story "again, for the first time."

To briefly summarize what we have covered so far, Knierim argued that the constitutive relationship assumed between setting and genre by form critics was built on a shaky foundation, further complicated by an oversimplification of the relationship between a life setting and specific language appropriate to that setting. He offered the structuralist understanding of the unconscious, underlying structures that are culturally formed and guide both expression and interpretation as a helpful way of reframing the discussion about genre. Alastair Fowler and Mikhail Bakhtin spoke of the way each successive expression of a genre is rooted in a tradition while at the same time modifying and changing the tradition by way of "metamorphosis" or "genre memory." All of this suggests that genres are dynamic rather than static, are culturally conditioned, and ultimately have to do with communication.

This final point is developed further by Fowler. He argues "genre primarily has to do with communication. It is an instrument not of classification or prescription, but of meaning."[28] In other words, the point of considering the genre of a particular work is not to classify it and name it as such, but to facilitate *interpretation*, to access the meaning being communicated through a combination of language,

---

[26.]Bakhtin, *Problems of Dostoyevsky's Poetics*, 106; Newsom, "Spying Out the Land," 28.

[27.]Bakhtin, *Problems of Dostoyevsky's Poetics*, 106; quoted in Newsom, "Spying Out the Land," 28.

[28.]Fowler, *Kinds of Literature*, 22.

formal features, and context. Recognizing the genre enables one to access meaning, and puts the interpreter on surer interpretive footing.

The classic form-critical approach was to identify the genre at the intersection of (narrowly defined) internal structures and a specific external setting. I propose an adjustment to these categories in light of the foregoing discussion of the limitations of this approach, and the contributions of Lévi-Strauss, Fowler, and Bakhtin. My proposal would soften the role of a *specific* external setting—which is often conjectural—in the process of determining genre. It would do this first by expanding the notion of *Sitz im Leben* to include the broader cultural identity of the ancient Hebrews, namely, the discussion of orality and performance discussed in Chapter 1. In this re-conceptualization, oral performance before a live audience would be the primary setting-in-life in the light of which genre would be determined.[29] It would also expand the notion of a text's internal structures to include Lévi-Strauss' grammar-like description of pre-linguistic, culturally-conditioned, mutually-held, tacit structures which facilitate all forms of effective communication. The benefit of this addition would be to acknowledge the role that socially constructed understandings of genre play in the recognition process. Further, as Fowler and Bakhtin demonstrated, these formal/genre structures are not fixed, but rather undergo a continual process of modification and development with each new performance.

One important point of clarification may be necessary. The description in the previous paragraph does not include a suggestion to abandon the search for and identification of the more narrowly defined formal structures of a given text, as they are expressed in both the language and content of the passage in question. These formal structures are a critical part of differentiating between genres, and abandoning such considerations would be tantamount to losing a capacity to differentiate between various genres within the Hebrew Bible. What my expansion of the classical form-critical categories intends to do is prioritize orality and

---

[29.] Another way to describe it would be to see orality as a sort of "macro-setting" that establishes the cultural cache on which faithful interpretation of genre depends, and oral performance as the more immediate setting in which the genre is expressed.

the context of oral performance in the genre-determination process, which has hitherto been characterized by a prioritization of texts and textuality to the exclusion of orality and performance.

I am not the first to suggest prioritizing orality and performance over textuality and texts. Tom Boogaartv also sees Israel's orality playing a critical and formational role in framing the people's reception of the tradition through performance. With subtle reference being given to the way performance has been overlooked (due to a textual bias), Boogaart argues that performance is a logical context in which to understand the biblical narratives.

> That the structure of the biblical narratives implies performance should not be surprising to us. Performance is exactly what we would expect from a culture like that of the ancient Israelites. The vast majority of the Israelite people could not read or write, and they would have absorbed their traditions through their participation in the various rituals that constituted public worship at their sanctuaries—not only seeing the performances of the narratives, but also singing the songs of faith, reciting the law, eating meals together at the Lord's table, uttering prayers of lament and praise, etc.[30]

Similarly, in the New Testament context, David Rhoads likewise expands the definition of setting and concludes that the oral culture itself is the "context for performance."[31] A benefit of expanding the scope of *Sitz im Leben* in this way is that the more speculative settings in life that have characterized form-critical analyses would be downplayed by contrast to the less speculative (though much more general) setting of orality and oral performance. In the following section I will offer some comments on the internal formal structures of the narratives that suggest the genre of the narratives is drama.

[30.]Boogaart, "Arduous Journey," 4.
[31.]Rhoads, "Performance Criticism—Part I," 121.

Evidence for the Narratives as Dramas

The clearest structural evidence for drama as the genre of the stories collected in the Bible is the consistent presence of dramatic structure guiding each story from establishing the setting, to introducing the central conflict, through its development to its eventual resolution, and a concluding dénouement. The plot, which follows this fundamental story arc, progresses through scenes. Scene shifts are indicated by a change of location, the introduction of a new character, or a shift in the temporal flow[32]—or, often, a combination of these. Each scene progresses primarily through dialogue between two or three characters.[33] Biblical dialogue is not quoted speech, similar to what would be found in a novel or history-writing. In dramatic dialogue characters speak for themselves and to each other, in the present tense.[34] The story is told by a narrator who introduces the dialogue, establishes the setting(s) in which the dialogue and action take place, introduces and describes the characters—in short, the narrator tells the story—using third person verb forms, which suggests that the narrator speaks directly to the gathered audience,[35] and makes reference to the action unfolding on the stage as s/he speaks. The resolution of the conflict often returns to the opening theme so that the drama ends where it began, but in light of the transformation the conflict made possible.

[32.]The shift in temporal flow is often accompanied by a shift in location, and is generally accomplished in one of two ways. Either it is indicated through the use of וַיְהִי (*vayyehi*, "and it happened," cf. 2 Kgs 5:8 as the scene shifts from the palace in Samaria to Elisha's house, וַיְהִי כִּשְׁמֹעַ אֱלִישָׁע, "And it happened / when (he) heard / Elisha" or, more smoothly, "And when Elisha heard"), or the reversal of the typical narrative word order of verb–subject to subject–verb (cf. Jonah 1:4, after Jonah sets sail toward Tarshish, וַיהוָה הֵטִיל, "And the Lord / hurled").

[33.]Boogaart, "Arduous Journey," 3–4.

[34.]This practice has parallels in other ancient contexts. For example, Kevin Robb has shown how Heraclitus, working in the late sixth and early fifth centuries B.C.E. in Ephasus, a "protoliterate society," used "the present tense in describing the activities of long-dead figures: Homer, Hesiod, and Archilochus." Robb, "The Linguistic Art of Heraclitus," 157.

[35.]For more on the role of the narrator in dramatic performance, see Chapter 3.

An example will illustrate the structure's presence. Take the story of Elisha and the unnamed widow from 2 Kgs 4.1–7. Here is the text of this drama, arranged to accentuate its dramatic structure and scenic development. Narration is in roman type and dialogue is in italics.

CONFLICT

Scene 1

[1] A woman, the wife of a member of the sons of the prophets, cried out to Elisha:

> *Your servant, my husband, is dead. And you know that your servant was one who feared the Lord. And the debt collector has come to take away my two children to be his slaves.*

DEVELOPMENT

[2] Elisha said to her:

> *What can I do for you? Tell me, what have you in the house?*

She said:

> *Your servant has nothing in the whole house, except a single jar of oil.*

[3] He said:

> *Go. Borrow vessels from the streets, from all your neighbors. Empty vessels.*
> *Not just a few!*
> [4] *Enter your house and close the door behind you and behind your children. Pour into each and every vessel. When each is full, set it aside.*

CLIMAX

Scene 2

[5]She left Elisha. And she closed the door behind her and behind her children. They were bringing the vessels to her, and she was pouring. [6]When the vessels had all been filled, she said to her son:

> *Bring me another vessel!*

He said:

> *There are no other vessels!*

The oil stopped immediately.

RESOLUTION

Scene 3

[7]The woman went and told the man of God. He said:

> *Go. Sell the oil. Pay off your debt. You and your children will live on what is left over.*

Note the extensive use of dialogue and how it carries the burden of developing and resolving the conflict. Note, too, how the characters speak in the present tense—using present-tense verbs, including imperatives and participles. Each new location indicates a shift in scene. Each scene involves dialogue between two or three characters. This short drama has only three scenes, which take place in three locations: the first and last are undisclosed locations where the woman engages the prophet, and scene two takes place within the woman's house (after she has collected the vessels, ostensibly from her neighbors, which is unnarrated). The conflict is introduced at the very beginning of the drama (the death of her husband and the threat of losing her children, v. 1) and is developed through dialogue and action. The resolution of the conflict returns to the opening theme by way of a dramatic *inclusio* (death to life; crushing debts to financially stable). Variations on this structure can be traced in every drama in the Hebrew Bible, from dramas in Genesis and Judges to the extended dramas of Ruth and Jonah. In general, the shorter the drama the simpler the structure. Longer dramas could have multiple scenes. More than one climax is also possible as interweaving storylines develop and are resolved as the drama moves from conflict to resolution.[36]

A Paradigm Shift in Biblical Studies

The identification of the narratives as "drama" is complicated by a pervasive textual/literary bias in biblical scholarship, both with respect to methodology and the genre question. For example, with respect to methodological assumptions, much of the structural evidence offered above to support the designation of "drama" has been used by literary critics over the last few decades to demonstrate the singular *literary* achievement of the Israelites. Meir Sternberg has highlighted the critical role of the narrator in biblical storytelling,[37] although not from a perspective that takes seriously the oral-performance context in which the art was refined.[38] Robert Chisholm identified the ubiquity of dramatic structure that develops through scenes that shift based on location and narration,[39] and the role of conflict or tension was famously used by Erich Auerbach to illustrate the power of Israel's *literary* achievement (somewhat ironically through comparison to the *dramatic* achievement of Homer's *Odyssey*).[40]

On the one hand, it is not surprising this has occurred. The Bible *is* a text, after all, and all of its component parts are likewise *texts*. As such, they can be productively studied *as texts*. Narrative critics such as Alter,

---

[36.]Dramatic structure, narration, dialogue, and several other features of Israelite drama will be discussed in much greater detail in the following chapter.

[37.]Sternberg, *Poetics of Biblical Narrative*. Sternberg discusses the narrator from many different angles throughout this tome. See index for extensive reference.

[38.]I will return to this theme and comment on it directly in Chapter 3.

[39.]Chisholm, *Interpreting the Historical Books*, 46.

[40.]Auerbach, *Mimesis*.

Sternberg, Dana Fewell and David Gunn; along with rhetorical critics such as Phyllis Trible have demonstrated this time and again with deeply satisfying results. But, on the other hand, they are *more* than texts. They are the scripts of ancient performances.

The difference between the two conclusions about genre (literary or dramatic) is largely dependent upon the assumptions the scholar holds about the nature of the biblical material. As Chapter 1 argued, the textualized versions of the biblical dramas existed for generations, even centuries, alongside the oral performances. *And the written versions existed primarily as a way of sustaining and supporting oral performances of the tradition.* In other words, the oral performances were primary and the written texts were secondary. The written texts grew out of and are reflections of oral performances.

This final point is critical, and clarifies some of the confusion inherent in the intersection of orality, textuality, drama, and genre. Walter Ong states the issue straightforwardly when he laments that we tend to derive our concept of oral performance from what we know of literature, "despite the fact that in actuality it is literature which grows out of oral performance."[41] Michael Goldman concurs. In his insightful book *On Drama*, Goldman argues that a number of the complications and confusions within genre research would be clarified by the simple recognition that drama gave birth to literature.

> Many problems not only in dramatic but literary theory would take on a sharply new perspective if, just to clear the air, let us say, we were to reverse the process and think instead of drama as the most general case of literature, with poetry, the novel, and so forth as specializations. We might do well in fact to imagine drama as the originary literary or artistic form, if only to offset the myth, nowadays unacknowledged because epistemologically incorrect, but nevertheless still dominant, of the literary origins of drama (from choral lyric, narrative, Solonic speeches in the agora, or whatever). Actually, the old

---

[41.]Ong, *Presence of the Word*, 21.

habit of thinking about drama as a genre of 'literature,' a habit seemingly as old as criticism itself, has worked to obscure some important connections between drama and life—especially with some features of life we're likely today to regard as intensely difficult, issues that bear on self and meaning, on persons and texts, on identity and community.[42]

When Goldman suggests drama as "the originary literary or artistic form," one should not conclude he is suggesting that drama is a textual reality. Quite the opposite. He is attempting to shift the conversation away from a genre-as-literature orientation to a medium- or performance-orientation. This shift is inherent in the generic identification "drama." Another extended quote from Goldman will clarify his argument. This quote follows a brief overview of the contradictions and complications embedded in the genre-as-literature conversation, which do not discuss drama or the paradigm shift it introduces into the conversation.

> Still, most of these discussions, certainly the most influential, are deficient in a signal respect. They fail to engage drama fully as an experience, an ongoing moment-to-moment process for audiences or readers. They have in common a tendency to treat genre as a reflective category, a way of classifying and systematizing dramatic texts and performances after the fact. Everything changes, however, if we stop to think of genre as not entirely unlike rhyme, say, or ambiguity, as a feature, that is, whose primary interest for readers or audiences is as something that *happens* to us in a poem or play, *as* it happens.[43]

Goldman, like Fowler, is trying to shift the conversation about genre away from a traditional classificatory approach. But Goldman's experience in the theatre compels him to take a step beyond Fowler, who

---

[42.]Goldman, *On Drama*, 6–7.

[43.]Goldman, *On Drama*, 3; emphasis original.

still considers the point of genre as essentially descriptive, just in a more nuanced way than classificatory approaches have described them. Goldman expands the conversation to include the dynamic *encounter* that is inherent in dramatic performance as an essential part of what constitutes a genre. A genre is not just a carrier of meaning and communication, as Fowler argued, it is something that *happens*, and it happens *in the moment.*

Shimon Levy is an Israeli theatre critic and theatre professor who has been exploring biblical dramas through the lens of theatrical performance for some time. Like Goldman, he was baffled by the genre conversation as it had been conducted, particularly in biblical studies, that focused on the narrative portion of the Hebrew Bible. But, unlike Goldman, who tried to change the conversation by expanding it to include drama, Levy chose to abandon the question of genre altogether:

> Among the literary approaches to the Old Testament, Meir Sternberg's *The Poetics of Biblical Narrative* is a major breakthrough in the field, as well as Robert Alter's insightful *The Art of Biblical Narrative* and Uriel Simon's *Reading Prophetic Narratives*. However, whereas the term 'dramatic' is used in most literary-oriented works mainly to indicate particular structural elements, as well as the prevalence of conflict, dialogue, modes of characterization, and other drama-as-genre elements, this book shifts the focus from a literary genre-oriented discussion to a medium-oriented one.[44]

Terry Giles and William Doan, who have written extensively on the impact of Israel's orality and performance traditions on the works now collected in the Hebrew Bible,[45] came to a similar conclusion as Levy:

[44.] Levy, *Bible As Theatre*, 5.

[45.] In order of publication: Giles and Doan, *Prophets, Performance, and Power*; Giles and Doan, "Performance Criticism," 273–286; Giles and Doan, *Twice Used Songs*; Giles and Doan, *Story of Naomi*.

"'drama' is best understood as an event and not a particular literary form or text."[46]

Two things seem to be clear at this point. First, despite the insightful and constructive research of a number of scholars, Rolf Knierim's conclusion in 1973 still appears to resonate, over forty years later: "we are [still] no longer so clear as to what exactly a genre is."[47] This is particularly true with respect to drama, which has a textual element (the script) and can be fruitfully analyzed as literature, but is fundamentally an event, an experience, something that *happens* between audience and actors on a stage. Secondly, whether genre is conceived of as a singularly literary category, or more akin to "ambiguity" or "rhyme," as Goldman offered, the narratives in the Hebrew Bible exhibit a distinctly dramatic character and, given the culture out of which they arose it would be profitable to explore ways of interpreting them that resonate with this inherent dramatic nature. The implications of this are implied in David Rhoads' insightful application of a familiar axiom: "[T]he medium is part of the message, if not the message itself. Studying these texts in an exclusively written medium has shaped, limited and perhaps even distorted our understanding of them . . . Taking oral performance into account may enable us to be more precise in our historical re-constructions and more faithful in our interpretations."[48] Biblical performance criticism is an emerging methodology in biblical studies which offers a way to do precisely that.

Resistance to the Narratives as Drama

Beyond the textual bias that has characterized most academic approaches to the Bible, there may be yet another reason why biblical scholars have been slow to see the importance of performance in Israel. Namely, an assumption regarding Israel's reticence to represent God in a physical form on stage in light of the commandment against making a graven image of God. In fact, theatre historians such as Gordon C.

[46.]Giles and Doan, *Twice Used Songs*, 86.

[47.]Knierim, "Form Criticism Reconsidered," 436.

[48.]Rhoads, "Performance Criticism—Part I" 126.

Bennett and modern Israeli theatre professors such as Shimon Levy argue against a dramatic tradition in ancient Israel precisely on this assumption: the Israelites would have never dared represent an embodiment of God. Bennett argues the point this way:

> Unlike the Egyptians and Greeks and some early Eastern civilizations, the Hebrews made little use of drama. Indeed, they dabbled very little in art since they were forbidden by Exodus 20:4 to make "any likeness of anything that is in heaven above, or that is in the earth beneath, or that is in the water under the earth."[49]

Bennett's assertion that the Hebrews largely rejected "art" because of the second commandment is demonstrably false. Shortly after the Ten Commandments are delivered God carries on for several chapters providing detailed and imaginative descriptions of the craftsmanship God desired for the Tabernacle.[50] Not only so, but God called two artists *by name* (Bezalel and Oholiab[51]) and filled Bezalel, the leader, with the Spirit of God (רוּחַ אֱלֹהִים, *ruach 'elohim*[52]) in order to empower him to fulfill God's calling on him to fill the Tabernacle with art. Indeed, the Tabernacle itself—and the Temple after it—was a work of art. Bezalel and Oholiab were not the only artists in Israel; they were set in leadership over many craftsmen. Israel had a rich artistic tradition.

Bennett's earlier point concerning the Hebrew's avoidance of drama is made more explicitly and compellingly by Shimon Levy, with reference to the same verse in Exodus. Levy argues "the very notion of presenting the Almighty in a corporeal fashion is strongly opposed to the second commandment."[53] A closer look at the biblical evidence, however, suggests otherwise. The second commandment has to do with fashioning idols and preventing idolatry, the worship of human-made

---

[49.] Bennett, *Acting Out Faith*, 15; quoted in Boogaart, "Drama and the Sacred," 39.
[50.] Cf. Exod 25–40.
[51.] Exod 31:2, 6.
[52.] Exod 31:3.
[53.] Levy, *Bible as Theatre*, 6.

images. It does not prohibit a human—who is described in Gen 1 as a *representative* of God (God's *image*) on earth—from standing in God's stead to represent God's presence, to manifest God's actions, or to speak God's words to a gathered congregation. Scripture is full of humans speaking God's words to the people of God (this was the vocation of the prophet[54]), and of humans both mediating God's presence to the gathered people and bringing their concerns before God (this was the vocation of the priest[55]). Prophets and priests used their bodies and voices not only to communicate God's words and intentions to the people of Israel, but to mediate God's physical presence in their midst as well.

That the stories were told before live audiences is a relative certainty. And whether the stories were performed by a single storyteller or by a cast of actors, both types of performance require the audience to "see" the stage and "see" the action as the actors incarnate it on the stage. There is no question that God is a character in many dramas in Scripture. God is the subject of verbs that describe concrete actions, such as "seeing,"[56] "speaking,"[57] "hearing,"[58] and even actions like "hurling;"[59] God speaks for Godself. When God speaks (as in Gen 22:2), God's words create the framework in which the entire drama is set.[60]

[54.]Cf. "[P]rophecy as a communication between God and humanity dates back to the very beginning of human history." *NIDOTTE*, s.v. "Prophecy."

[55.]"Perhaps the central concept of priesthood is mediation between the sphere of the divine and the ordinary world. A priest through his ritual actions and his words facilitates communication across the boundary separating the holy from the profane. *The priests represented God to the people* in the splendor of their clothing, in their behavior, and in oracles and instruction, while in sacrifice and intercession they represented the people to God." *NIDOTTE*, s.v. "כָּהַן."

[56.]Cf. Exod 2:25.

[57.]Cf. 1 Kgs 3:5.

[58.]Cf. Gen 21:17.

[59.]Cf. Jonah 1:4.

[60.]Another classic example of this is the book of Jonah. God is even more active and physically located in Jonah. The story of Jonah also begins with God's speech, and God's words create the framework by which Jonah's actions will be measured ("Get up! Go! Cry out!"). But God is also physically located in (or immediately above) Nineveh, which is explicitly referenced a number of times by different characters, and

It is conceivable that the speech, actions, and presence of the God-character in the dramas was somehow achieved without a specific actor—or actors—performing them visibly and audibly on stage. I do not find this argument compelling, however, given the way the stories themselves are told, and the unique way that God is presented *as a character* in many of the dramas. Israel maintained a prohibition against graven images *and* told their ancestral stories in the way they did. They did not see the two as incompatible, nor should we. In other words, the force of the biblical material itself ought to drive our conclusions about it. The scripts themselves raise the question and point toward the conclusion that representing God in some way[61] is not only acceptable

---

is the backdrop for the scandal of God's mercy demonstrated in the drama. God locates himself in Nineveh to Jonah: "their [Nineveh's] evil *has come up before my face*" (Jonah 1:2); the narrator also implies this several times by describing Jonah's actions in traveling *toward* Tarshish as moving "away from the face of YHVH" (Jonah 1:3, 10), thus establishing a horizontal axis between Nineveh and Tarshish, with God in Nineveh and Jonah moving toward Tarshish. Establishing this horizontal axis is a crucial backdrop for one of the drama's primary theological affirmations: God is in Nineveh because God is *everywhere*; you cannot flee "away from the face of the Lord," no matter how hard you try or how far you go, you will always be running *toward* the face of YHVH (the psalmist's metaphors find concrete expression in Jonah's tale: "Where can I go from your spirit? Or where can I flee from your presence? If I ascend to heaven, you are there; if I make my bed in Sheol, you are there. If I take the wings of the morning and settle at the farthest limits of the sea, even there your hand shall lead me, and your right hand shall hold me fast" (Ps 139:7–10)).

[61.]There are a number of different ways this could be explored, each of which would offer a different insight into Israel's understanding of God. Certainly one option is simply to have a single actor represent God in the same way another actor represents Abraham, and another Isaac. Another possibility would be to have a male and a female actor both portray God, given that Gen 1:27 male and female together as constituting God's image. The narrator could also adopt the role of God, as the narrator, by virtue of his/her omniscience and unique mediating role, is a more logical choice for that role than any other character within the drama. A final example is drawn from an especially powerful performance of God in the Binding of Isaac that a group of musically-inclined students developed a few years ago. Given ancient societies' connection with music (and the many references to it throughout the Hebrew Bible), it is entirely possible these performances were accompanied by singing, instrumentation, or some kind of drumming. These students chose to utter God's lines in a three-part chant,

but beneficial. This suggests that the stories can be studied to understand more deeply how the people of Israel rendered God. What was permissible? What crossed the line into idolatry? Biblical performance criticism opens up this very important conversation and offers new insights and directions for future consideration.[62]

Further resistance is made against a dramatic tradition in pre-exilic Israel on the basis of a two-fold lack of concrete archeological and artifactual evidence. Namely, the absence of theaters in ancient Israel, and the lack of a continuous performance tradition sustained throughout the intertestamental period as Judaism emerged into the first century CE and beyond—especially given the negative perspective on pagan theatrical performances by the rabbis.[63] In his 2005 dissertation on the Hellenistic Jewish author Ezekiel the Tragedian's first century BCE play L'Exagoge, Pierluigi Lanfranchi remarks that this work is an exceptional instance of Jewish theatre in the ancient world; the only one of its kind from that era. L'Exagoge is a theatrical retelling of the Exodus story. But apparently it did not catch on, for "historians set the

---

composed of the actor representing God, along with the Angel and the narrator. For God's line in Gen 22:2 Abraham slept center stage. The three actors gathered in a semi-circle behind him, facing the audience. God began the line alone, slowly chanting the words. After a few words the Angel and narrator joined in three-part harmony. When they arrived at the critical word in the line, וְהַעֲלֵהוּ (veha'aleihu, "and you will offer him up"), they broke the harmony and introduced dissonance, which persisted throughout the remainder of the line, creating a very uncomfortable ethos, which not only played out visually as they surrounded Abraham, but aurally as the dissonant tones manifested the theologically dissonant command. It is impossible to know how God as a character in the dramas was represented; perhaps various traditions or communities had different ways of rendering God, and perhaps some were more inclined to do so than others. Regardless of the specific way it was done, it seems clear to me that God was presented in some way, and biblical performance criticism offers the scholar tools to explore this theological and theatrical dynamic further.

[62.]The foregoing discussion should not be interpreted as a denial or rejection of the fact that a tradition developed within Judaism against physical representations of God that resulted in the relative absence of a continuous theatrical tradition. But it is to say that appeals to Exod 20:4 are not satisfying as justification for a rejection of a dramatic performance tradition in ancient Israel.

[63.]Lanfranchi, L'Exagoge, 8.

birth of a true Jewish theater in the XVII century when the Ashkenazi communities of northern Italy developed an original form of spectacle based on the medieval tradition of the Purim Spiel."[64]

The absence of theaters in Israel is *not* evidence against a rich dramatic tradition in pre-exilic Palestine. Perhaps the discovery of ancient theaters in Palestine would have made my argument easier to make, but we must not equate the absence of Greek-style theatrical stages in Israel to a lack of a performance tradition. Indeed, the *absence* of such is precisely what we would expect to find (or, rather, *not* find). This is because Israel's dramatic tradition did not serve the purposes of secular entertainment. It was grounded in Israel's ritual and worshiping life. The performance arenas of the biblical dramas would not have been divorced from their places of worship and community gatherings, for the performances served the explicit purpose of connecting the community to each other and ultimately to God through their ancestors.[65] Indeed, Peter Brook's famous opening line in *The Empty Space* was no doubt as true in ancient Israel as it is now: "I can take any empty space and call it a bare stage. A man walks across this empty space whilst someone else is watching him, and this is all that is needed for an act of theatre to be engaged."[66] The "empty spaces" in Israel were likely the courtyard of the Tabernacle, or Temple, or wherever local communities gathered for formal and informal worship, to pass on tradition, living into the psalmist's words in Ps 145:4: "One generation shall laud your works to another, and shall declare your mighty acts."[67]

It is perhaps true that what is today known as the "true Jewish theater" began among Ashkenazi communities in northern Italy in the seventeenth century, but it is also likely that this theatrical tradition was not the first one to grow out of a Jewish (or, more accurately, their ancient Israelite forebears') context.

---

[64] Lanfranchi, *L'Exagoge*, 7.
[65] See Chapter 1 for a fuller treatment of this.
[66] Brook, *Empty Space*, 9.
[67] NRSV.

What is Meant by "Performance"?

I have used the term "performance" a number of times already. It is not
easy to define. Over the last few decades the term has received extensive
critical reflection across a vast array of disciplines—including the
humanities, social sciences, and fine arts.[68] Richard Schechner
demonstrates the complicated ways in which the word "performance" is
used today through a list he titles the "Eight Kinds of Performance."[69]
According to Schechner, "performances occur in eight sometimes separate,
sometimes overlapping situations:

1. in everyday life—cooking, socializing, 'just living'
2. in the arts
3. in sports and other popular entertainments
4. in business
5. in technology
6. in sex
7. in ritual—sacred and secular
8. in play."[70]

In light of this profound diversity, performance has been described as
"an essentially contested concept."[71] Marvin Carlson and other
performance critics view this as a positive development. This is because
the inherent lack of consensus serves a generative academic function,
namely, to stimulate critical dialogue toward the end of attaining "a
sharper articulation of all positions and therefore a fuller understanding
of the conceptual richness of performance."[72] In the pages that follow I
attempt to contribute to "a sharper articulation" of the concept of
performance as it relates to ancient Israel.

---

[68] Giles and Doan, *Twice Used Songs*, 141.

[69] Schechner, *Performance Studies*, 31.

[70] Schechner, *Performance Studies*, 31.

[71] Carlson, *Performance*, 1.

[72] Strine, Long, and Hopkins, "Research in Interpretation," 183; quoted in Carlson,
Performance, 1.

Victor Turner, the trailblazing interdisciplinary cultural anthropologist, made an early contribution to the discussion around the definition of performance by drawing on the etymology of the word itself, which is helpful in that it narrows the scope of the word from its ubiquitous application across various disciplines to describe a particular process. The English word "performance" is borrowed from Old French, and is the composite of *par*, "thoroughly," and *fournir*, "to furnish." Turner explains that to "thoroughly furnish" does not suggest "the structuralist implication of manifesting form, but the processual sense of 'bringing to completion' or 'accomplishing'."[73] If this etymological definition is situated in the context of a primarily oral culture like Israel in which the sundry textual tradition serves to sustain the community's memory, performance speaks of the process whereby the reality latent in both text and memory is manifested—"furnished," or "brought to completion"—before a gathered community through the bodies, movements, voices, and silences of performers.

This is precisely the context David Rhoads had in mind when he offered his own definition of performance as it relates to the biblical tradition. Although Rhoads was speaking particularly about the New Testament context, his description is equally as accurate for the Old Testament context. According to Rhoads, performance refers to "any oral telling/retelling of a brief or lengthy tradition—from saying to gospel—in a formal or informal context of a gathered community by trained or untrained performers—on the assumption that every telling was a lively recounting of that tradition."[74]

This final claim—"that every telling was a lively recounting of that tradition"—is the most important addition to Turner's etymology because it describes *how* performance "thoroughly furnishes" a tradition or a story, whether it is drawn from text or memory. What Rhoads means by "a lively recounting" includes much more than merely words spoken to an audience. "It includes intonation, movements, gestures, pace, facial expressions, postures, the spatial relationships of the imagined

---

[73.]Turner, *From Ritual to Theatre*, 91.
[74.]David Rhoads, "Performance Criticism—Part I" 119.

characters, the temporal development of the story in progressive events displayed on stage, and much more."[75] In short, a "lively recounting" is a dramatic performance.

To say a performance "brings to completion" is to imply a state of incompleteness prior to performance. Max Harris states this fact straightforwardly: "Dramatic texts are incomplete works of art."[76] An analogy to music is suggested in the conclusions of both Turner and Harris. Consider, for example, the Brandenberg Concertos by J. S. Bach. It would not make sense to simply study the score and consider each note as it was written on each page. Certainly, careful attention to the score is helpful and important, and provides the violinist with a fuller sense of the patterns, repetitions, and trajectory of the concerto, but the score was composed in order to be performed, and until it is performed it is, in a real sense, incomplete. The performance (the "lively recounting" of the score through the dynamic encounter between the musicians' bodies and skills, their instruments, the music they create, the space and its acoustics, and the gathered audience) brings the composition to its fullest expression—the expression for which it was written. Certainly, some performances are better than others (compare the Philharmonic Orchestra to a local middle school symphony), but each performance actualizes the latent dynamism of the score and projects it into space and time, creating a shared experience that is dependent upon—and greater than the sum of—all the parts.

It is the same with the biblical dramas. They do not reach their fullest expression until they are embodied and voiced by a performer, or a group of performers, who present the drama to a gathered audience. Modern stage performance views the script of the play in the same way. "From the performative perspective, stage production is, in a sense, the final cause for the writing of plays, which are fully realized only in the circumstances for which they were originally intended: theatrical performance."[77] An important caveat to the comparisons I am making

---

[75.]Rhoads, "What Is Performance Criticism?" 89.

[76.]Harris, *Theater and Incarnation*, 1.

[77.]Worthen, *Shakespeare*, 4.

between biblical dramas and, either a Bach concerto or a Shakespearean play, is to note that both Bach and Shakespeare *wrote* a piece that was intended to be performed. In other words, the writing came first and the performance was the fulfillment of the script. The biblical dramas were first *told*, and then written as a way to support and sustain the community's memory. But the text did not replace the performance (at least not initially[78]); the two existed together for a long time before the performance tradition faded. The analogies with Bach and Shakespeare are apt, but orality and the performance event takes an even more prominent role in the historical process with the Bible.

To conclude this section I offer the following definition of "performance," built on the definitions above, as well as a definition of "drama" and "theater," as I use them. "Performance" refers to the public event for which all of the preparations—script, memorization, blocking, rehearsal, gathering of the audience, etc.—are intended. Further, and building on Victor Turner's etymology, the event manifests a latent potentiality in the script—bringing it to completion—in a way that no other engagement with the text can adequately accomplish, and in a way that resonates with the original context and purpose of the script. "Drama" and "theatre" are very similar terms, and I will occasionally use them interchangeably. According to William Doan, professor of theatre at the Pennsylvania State University, "drama occurs when one or more human beings, isolated in time and space, present themselves in imagined acts to another or others."[79] And "theatre" is nearly identical to drama, except it refers to "the larger framework for acts of presentation" of which drama is a part.[80]

[78.] It is impossible to know precisely when this happened, but it would likely have coincided with an event that threatened the preservation of the tradition through memory, and that prevented the community to continue to gather in order to remember. The most likely explanation is that the performance tradition declined during the exile even as the desire to commit the tradition to writing increased.

[79.] Giles and Doan, *Twice Used Songs*, 141.

[80.] Giles and Doan, *Twice Used Songs*, 143.

Dramatic Implications: Insights from Theatre
and Performance Theorists

So far this chapter has engaged the issue of genre, what the text and the context suggests about the nature of the biblical narratives, and the elusive term "performance." If I am right, and the narratives are dramas, scripts of ancient plays, then a methodological paradigm shift is needed to approach the dramas in a way that is faithful to their basic character. This section will take a closer look at the performance event itself—the event that constitutes the shift from a textual-orientation to a medium- or performance-orientation—and will draw on performance theorists and other biblical performance critics in order to understand more fully what the paradigm shift involves. This section will also lend credibility to my argument by corroborating with and further developing the insights of cultural anthropologists, orality scholars, and biblical performance critics offered above and in Chapter 1.

What *happens* in a performance? Many things, in fact. Performances are complex and multi-layered events, with various implications for how we approach biblical dramas today. Performances complicate a linear view of time by exhibiting a "ghostliness" to past experiences or past events *in the present*. Performances are powerful encounters which can transport and even transform actor and audience alike. They consist of elevated actions, interactions, and speech occurring in spaces that are framed to communicate that something unusual is happening and normal definitions of reality do not apply. Finally, performances involve self-reflexivity, embodiment, process, and re-enactment.

"Ghostliness"

Marvin Carlson identified the "ghostly" character of performance as "the common coin of theatre everywhere in the world at every period."[81] He defines this sense of "ghostliness" this way: "The retelling of stories already told, the reenactment of events already enacted, the reexperience of emotions already experienced, these are and have

---

[81.]Carlson, *Haunted Stage*, 3.

always been central concerns of the theatre in all times and places."[82] Put another way, the ghostly character inherent in theatre, drama, and performance is captured in descriptions of performance that begin with the prefix "re." Elin Diamond explains that "the terminology of 're' in discussion of performance, as in *re*member, *re*inscribe, *re*configure, *re*iterate, *re*store" points to the way performance constitutes a "repetition within the performative present, but 'figure,' 'script,' and 'iterate' assert the possibility of something that *exceeds* our knowledge, that alters the shape of sites and imagines new unsuspected subject positions."[83]

All performances occur at the intersection of the past (the "re") and the present (the "enactment"). This is particularly true of performances that take history—understood as the stories that constitute a community's identity—as their subject matter. In *Performing History* Eddie Rokem suggests that "the repressed ghostly figures and events from that ('real') historical past can (re)appear on the stage in theatrical performances. The actors performing such historical figures are in fact the 'things' who are appearing again tonight in the performance. And when these ghosts are historical figures they are in a sense performing history."[84]

The dynamic experience of time that Carlson, Diamond, and Rokem describe as characterizing the theater—which could be called "performance time"—resonates with the nonlinear notion of time common to oral cultures, discussed in Chapter 1. Tom Boogaart has considered how this understanding of time was expressed in Israel's dramatic tradition with respect to the ancient custom of honoring the ancestors. According to Boogaart, the lives of the ancestors

> bore meaning, and the events of their lives were potentially sacramental. The performance of a narrative probed this deeper meaning in the lives of the ancestors and made it accessible to their descendants. In the moment of a narrative performance, the

---

[82.]Carlson, *Haunted Stage*, 3.
[83.]Diamond, *Writing Performances*, 2; quoted in Carlson, *Haunted Stage*, 2–3.
[84.]Rokem, *Performing History*, 6.

barriers of time and space were overcome, and the people were caught up in the drama—in the same way people today are caught up in the performance of a drama. The people of Israel heard again the words of their fathers and mothers, and they saw again their deeds. In this way, they honored their ancestors as a source of wisdom and guidance in the ways of the Lord.[85]

During oral performances of Israel's dramatic tradition, the tradents of the tradition "became" the ancestors of Israel who "appeared again here tonight."[86]

Gregory Nagy describes an analogous experience in the traditions of Homeric performance with the term mimesis, or, re-enactment.[87] According to Nagy, the narration of Homer's works, as well as the speech of heroes and gods

> are not at all representations: they are the real thing.... Further, and this is crucial for the argument at hand, when the rhapsode says "tell me, Muses!" (*Iliad* 2.484) or "tell me, Muse!" (*Odyssey* 1.1), this "I" is not a *representation* of Homer: it *is* Homer. My argument is that the rhapsode is re-enacting Homer by performing Homer, that he is Homer so long as the mimesis stays in effect, so long as the performance lasts.[88]

My argument is essentially the same. In performance—particularly performances in ancient Israel—time and memory conspire to collapse the distance that normally divides the awareness of the past from the experience of the present. In performance the past and the present overlap. And the continual overlapping of past and present in performance maintains each generations' connection to the past and opens up new possibilities and new interpretations as they encounter unforeseen circumstances. This is an example in "real life" of what

---

[85] Boogaart, "Arduous Journey," 4.

[86] A line from Shakespeare's *Hamlet*, quoted in Rokem, *Performing History*, 6.

[87] Nagy, *Poetry as performance*, 83.

[88] Nagy, *Poetry as performance*, 61.

Bakhtin and Fowler described in genre theory, namely, Bakhtin's notion of "genre memory"[89] and Fowler's "metamorphosis."[90]

Similar to Nagy, Jeanette Mathews uses the term re-enactment to describe this "ghostly" dynamic that characterizes performances. According to Mathews, all performances are seen as being "based on pre-existing models, scripts or patterns."[91] She also notes the interchange between tradition and innovation that occurs each time a past performance is re-enacted in the present, which is always accompanied by the "knowledge that change will come about in the re-enactment."[92]

Transportation and Transformation

The change that results from this overlapping of past and present is achieved, in part, by the power of performance to "transport" and "transform."[93] Each participant—actors and audiences alike—is *taken* somewhere in a performance, transported to another place, another time, something like another dimension where different possibilities or emotions or experiences become possible than what "normal" everyday living typically allows. Transportation is a common denominator among various types of cultural performance. In theatrical performance the actors experience transportation by temporarily "leaving" themselves in order to "be fully 'in' whatever they are performing."[94] The transportation actors experience in performance provides the context for Schechner's famous term "double negative." He defines it this way: "In theatre, actors onstage do more than pretend. The actors live a double negative. While performing, actors are not themselves, nor are they the characters. Theatrical role-playing takes place between 'not me . . . not not me.'"[95] It is the actors' ability to be transported "into" their roles that

---

[89] Bakhtin, *Problems of Dostoyevsky's Poetics*, 106.

[90] Fowler, *Kinds of Literature*, 23.

[91] Mathews, *Performing Habakkuk*, 33.

[92] Mathews, *Performing Habakkuk*, 34.

[93] Schechner, *Performance Studies*, 72.

[94] Schechner, *Performance Studies*, 72.

[95] Schechner, *Performance Studies*, 72. Cf. Carlson, *Performance*, 49.

enables the audience's transportation "out of" their world and "into" the world of the story unfolding through the performance. Transportation can serve purposes both secular and sacred; they can entertain and affect change.

Transformational experiences, according to Schechner, either mark or actually facilitate a shift of identity and are, therefore, much less common than transportation experiences. "Transformational" performances are something like modern rites of passage—religious conversion, becoming a shaman or medium, for example.[96] Schechner suggests that people are generally transformed only once or twice in a lifetime—some never—but transportation experiences could happen much more often.

For the people of Israel it is likely these two experiences had considerably more overlap than Schechner allows with respect to modern theatrical performances. Israel did not have a theatrical tradition focused on entertainment, but on transformation. Israel's tradition, rather, was grounded in the worship and ritual life of the people. The intention was to facilitate a connection between the gathered people and their ancestors, to ground each successive generation in the traditions of Israel as a people, to continually transform the people (back) into the people of God, and to sustain the ancestors' memory and their way of life into the unknown future.

Framing

How does an audience member or actor know when a performance has begun or ended; how does one know when one is experiencing the dynamics of performance? Schechner notes that a performance is simply "whatever takes place between a marked beginning and a marked end."[97] This marking is called "framing." It is distinctive to the type of performance and also to the culture in which the performance takes place. In modern theatre the beginning is framed by a dimming of the lights and the curtain being opened. Similarly, the end is framed by

---

[96.]Schechner, *Performance Studies*, 72.
[97.]Schechner, *Performance Studies*, 240.

the bows of the actors, the closing of the curtain, and the lights coming back on.[98] In between those two frames actor and audience agree to set aside the normal conventions of human interaction and together enter into performance time. A frame need not be a formal convention such as the opening and closing of a curtain; it can happen in myriad informal ways, such as a group of people unexpectedly gathering around a street performer, or a child shouting "Mommy, look at me!" Framing is a way of establishing a boundary that defines the difference between typical interactions and the operations of performance. Framing constitutes part of the difference between people acting strangely in public, and performers transporting and possibly transforming themselves and an audience. Recognition of the frame is critical to appropriate interaction with and interpretation of the performance, and is, like the operations of genre, culturally constructed. Performances in Israel may have been framed by any number of elements, from the gathering of people into the performance space (whether the Temple or a local gathering place, like a city gate, perhaps) to a worship leader introducing or setting up the performance, to the communal singing of a psalm that made reference to the historical event(s) that would be returned to explicitly in a dramatic performance.[99]

Self-Reflexivity[100]

Self-reflexivity involves the recognition that performance makes culture "conscious to both the performer and the viewer."[101] It is related to Schechner's "double negative" in that it involves the awareness that the actors are not the characters they are portraying, but is larger, and

---

[98.]Schechner, *Performance Studies*, 240.

[99.]E.g., Ps 135:8–9 with reference to the exodus, or Ps 136, which references God's actions throughout many events of Israel's sacred history.

[100.]The next three elements are borrowed and expanded from a list of "five performance themes" in Jeanette Mathews' *Performing Habakkuk* that she identified to demonstrate elements of performance studies that are relevant for the scholarly dialogue between biblical studies and performance studies. Mathews, *Performing Habakkuk*, 27–35.

[101.]Mathews, *Performing Habakkuk*, 27.

includes the way performances impact culture by rendering the cultural exchange explicit and conscious to both actor and audience through the mutual acknowledgement and acceptance of "'pretence'—a pretence on the part of the performer that the interaction is somehow other than it actually is and an awareness on the part of the observer that pretence is occurring."[102] Framing, discussed above, helps to communicate the presence of pretense. Some forms of performance are particularly self-reflexive. Among these are "theatrical devices that heighten the nature of a play such as addresses to the audience."[103] The biblical dramas draw heavily on this heightened element of self-reflexivity through the operations of third person narration in which the audience would be constantly addressed directly by the narrator, drawing them not only into the story, but into the cultural exchange the performance is facilitating.

Embodiment

Text-oriented epistemologies are challenged by performance studies' emphasis on embodiment. Dwight Conquergood, the late professor of theatre at Northwestern University, compared propositional, abstract, and objective knowledge (what he called "map") with participatory, practical, and embodied knowledge ("story"), and argued that both kinds of knowledge are necessary, and must interact— especially within academic institutions in which "map" knowledge has predominated to the exclusion of story. According to Conquergood, performance studies uniquely fosters this overlap or cross-fertilization within the binary divisions that prevail in the academy. "Performance studies struggles to open the space between analysis and action, and to pull the pin on the binary opposition between theory and practice.... Performance studies brings this rare hybridity into the academy, a commingling of analytical and artistic ways of knowing."[104] The real presence of human beings together in space and time is an essential

---

[102.]Mathews, *Performing Habakkuk*, 27.

[103.]Mathews, *Performing Habakkuk*, 27.

[104.]Conquergood, "Performance Studies," 145, 151; quoted in Mathews, *Performing Habakkuk*, 31.

element of performance. The elevation of embodiment as an equally important way of knowing ("the view from a body"[105]) offers a necessary corrective for the disembodied, text-centric approach that predominates in biblical studies ("the view from above"[106]), and its inclusion will help narrow the cultural gap that exists between modern interpreters and ancient actors and audiences. I will return to this theme again below when discussing the implications of performance on scholars and scholarship.

Process

Process refers not only to the various steps involved in leading up to and including the performance event, but also the cultural exchange that happens between actors and audience in the midst of a performance, particularly in performances that purpose to affect change. Richard Schechner draws a helpful distinction in performance between efficacy and entertainment. Efficacious and entertaining performances are not "binary opposites" but "the poles of a continuum."[107] "No performance is pure efficacy or pure entertainment," but they do lean in one direction or the other, and the difference between them "depends mostly on context and function."[108] Performances that lean toward the "entertainment" end of the spectrum do not intend primarily to affect change within the audience or the larger culture. Performances that lean toward the "efficacy" end, however, do desire to make a lasting impact. Examples of efficacious performances would include public protests, and (sacred or religious) rituals.[109] Mathews suggests one emphasis of a performance approach is a reminder that "the focus in performance is acting in/upon the world and the dynamic relationships between social, political and cultural spheres."[110] Efficacious performances "shape and

---

[105.] Conquergood, "Performance Studies," 146.
[106.] Conquergood, "Performance Studies," 146.
[107.] Schechner, *Performance Studies*, 79.
[108.] Schechner, *Performance Studies*, 80.
[109.] Cf. Mathews, *Performing Habakkuk*, 33.
[110.] Mathews, *Performing Habakkuk*, 32.

define the values and beliefs of cultures."[111] The performances of Israel's sacred tradition, of the ancestral stories, would undoubtedly lean toward the "efficacy" end of Schechner's spectrum. As Erich Auerbach so poignantly remarked, in comparing biblical narrative to Homeric epic, "the Scripture stories do not, like Homer's, court our favor, they do not flatter us that they may please us and enchant us—they seek to subject us, and if we refuse to be subjected we are rebels."[112] In other words, biblical performances intended not only to transport the audience to the world of the ancestors (or vice versa), but sought continually to transform the gathered people (back) into the people of God.

Implications of Performance on the Scholar

Calling the narratives "dramas" calls for a paradigm shift in biblical studies from text-oriented to performance-oriented approaches. This paradigm shift has significant implications for how scholars conduct research of the Bible, as well as the way scholars relate to the material they interpret. The preceding section on performance studies has anticipated some of these implications, and indeed the paradigm shift will be facilitated in part by biblical exegetes' willingness to engage the literature and practitioners of performance studies to learn from their unique combination of "analysis and action."[113] It will also require a willingness to adopt and learn new methods that incorporate both analytical and embodied ways of knowing.

Some biblical scholars have already begun to do this. David Rhoads is one such biblical scholar. He observes that although "we can never recover a first century performance event . . . we can experiment with twenty-first century ones.... If the biblical writings were composed for performance, then we certainly should use performances to interpret these writings."[114] He continues, more emphatically:

[111.]Mathews, *Performing Habakkuk*, 32.

[112.]Auerbach. *Mimesis*, 11–12.

[113.]Conquergood, "Performance Studies," 145.

[114.] Rhoads, "Performance Criticism—Part II," 173.

Performance criticism involves a paradigm shift. It will not do simply to take the methodologies we have developed for analyzing print and apply them to oral composition. Performance in an oral culture presents serious challenges to biblical scholars trained in written texts. We need to accompany the media shift with methodological shifts and the development of new methods, skills, and models.[115]

Rhoads is, in effect, calling on the community of biblical scholars to develop the skills of oral performance as a way of refining their capacity to interpret the Bible *as a scholar*. This is a call to change the definition of what it means to be a scholar, and the way the interpreter relates to the biblical text.

Rhoads identifies two insightful ways the scholar can relate to the biblical passage to facilitate this shift in perspective. First, "the exegete

---

[115.]Rhoads, "Performance Criticism—Part II," 180–81. Cf. James Maxey: "[P]erformance challenges earlier models of communication and requires new methods for appreciating the epistemological shift involved in this mode of communication." Maxey, "Biblical Performance Criticism," 7. Diana Taylor makes the same argument from the perspective of performance studies. She compares the "repertoire"—the collection of "embodied practice/knowledge (i.e., spoken language, dance, sports, ritual)"—to the "archive"—the "supposedly enduring materials (i.e., texts, documents, buildings, bones)." Taylor, *Archive and Repertoire*, 19. Mirroring Rhoads' argument, Taylor suggests performance studies can confront the overarching focus in the humanities on the "archive" by offering a new "way of rethinking the canon and critical methodologies. For even as scholars in the United States and Latin America acknowledge the need to free ourselves from the dominance of the text—as the privileged or even sole object of analysis—our theoretical tools continue to be haunted by the literary legacy. . . . It's imperative now, however overdue, to pay attention to the repertoire. But what would that entail methodologically? It's not simply that we shift to the live as the focus of our analysis, or develop various strategies for garnering information, such as undertaking ethnographic research, interviews, and field notes. Or even alter our hierarchies of legitimation that structure our traditional academic practice (such as book learning, written sources, and documents). *We need to rethink our method of analysis*." Taylor, *Archive and Repertoire*, 27; emphasis added.

can interpret from the position of being part of the audience."[116] New methods are needed to accomplish this. Namely, scholars "will need to learn listening skills as we have traditionally learned reading skills—becoming empathetically involved, identifying with characters, being aware of our own emotions and reactions, discerning the cognitive challenges of a narrative, suspending judgment."[117] Critical reflection on the performance is also helpful, as is experiencing multiple performances of the same script, so conclusions are not based on a single experience alone.[118]

"Second, the exegete can interpret by taking on the role of a performer."[119] The exegete is generally thought of as a "recipient," not unlike a music or drama critic who attends a performance to gauge its critical value and meaning, as opposed to being a performer herself. Rhoads suggests that if the two roles were combined the exegete's exploration of and access to the meaning in the passage is expanded through both listening and performing. "Becoming the "voice" and the "embodiment" of a narrative or letter places the exegete in a relationship with the text that is quite distinctive from hearing a performance. It represents a different medium."[120] Again, this calls for developing new skills, new methods. The position and location of the exegete's body in space has interpretive implications, physically moving from place to place within the story frame on the stage, discerning the interactions between characters, "recounting the narrative world from the narrator's perspective and standards of judgment," etc.[121]

Both of the implications Rhoads identifies suggest the act of interpretation in performance requires not only the *personal* engagement of the interpreter, but *embodied* engagement. This line of reasoning was anticipated in the "embodiment" section above. Performance invites the scholar to bring her entire self into the

---

[116.]Rhoads, "Performance as Research," 169.

[117.]Rhoads, "Performance as Research," 169.

[118.]Rhoads, "Performance as Research," 170.

[119.]Rhoads, "Performance as Research," 170.

[120.]Rhoads, "Performance as Research," 170.

[121.]Rhoads, "Performance as Research," 170.

interpretive process, not only her mind and her capacity to analyze. Embodied interpretation is not only—or even primarily—conducted by the scholar isolated in her office, reading the text silently. Rather, performance beckons her to abandon her office in favor of a more open space, preferably joined by colleagues or students who are researching the text with her in community. Biblical performance criticism calls for a (re)joining of analysis and practice, as Conquergood said above.[122] Peter Perry, who has also been influenced by Conquergood, recently suggested biblical performance criticism accomplishes this in part by understanding that "the performer is an analyst and the analyst is a performer."[123] The binary assumed between critical or objective engagement with a text on the one hand, and practical or emotional engagement with the text on the other is overcome. "Performance criticism offers a way to reunite analysis and practice."[124] In other words, the scholar relates in both objective (reading, analysis) and subjective (embodied engagement) ways to the biblical passage on the way to an interpretation.

Lesslie Newbigin, the British theologian, missiologist, and bishop in India, though neither a Bible scholar nor an advocate of biblical performance criticism, articulated the move toward acknowledging and embracing the subjective elements of interpretation that performance beckons. He offers his perspective by way of a critique of approaches which, regardless of the depth of their analysis, emphasize objective engagement with the text to the exclusion of the subjective.

> It is possible to undertake the most exhaustive and penetrating examination of the biblical text in a way which leaves one, so to say, outside it. The text is an object for examination, dissection, analysis, and interpretation from the standpoint of the scholar. This standpoint is normally that of the plausibility structure which reigns in her society. From this point of view she examines the text, but the text does not examine her.... [M]ost

---

[122.]Conquergood, "Performance Studies," 145.

[123.]Perry, *Insights From Performance Criticism*, 31.

[124.]Perry, *Insights From Performance Criticism*, 32.

biblical study as currently conducted is protected from that interruption. The text is examined, so to say, from the outside.[125]

Newbigin's point, of course—as a priest and a missiologist—is that to examine the text "from the outside" by maintaining an objective distance from it is not consonant with the nature of the text itself, which he understands to be sacred Scripture, a text that makes demands on those who read it and seek to interpret it. My argument, in addition to Newbigin's, is that it is not consonant with the text because the text is, in fact, a dramatic script.

Scripts that are not performed are incomplete. Dramatic scripts invite entrance; they are interpreted by being enfleshed, incarnated through both body and voice. Peter Brook, an internationally acclaimed director and theatre critic, though not a Christian, nevertheless articulates a perspective on modern theater that also uses the language of incarnation. Brook names an essential aspect of theatre the Holy Theatre, which he defines as "The Theatre of the Invisible—Made—Visible."[126] The holy theatre manifests the invisible reality that is always present but rarely seen. In reflecting on a small theatre company in Poland led by Jerzy Grotowski, Brook relates the actor to a priest and the audience to a worshiping congregation.[127] "The priest performs the ritual for himself and on behalf of others. Grotowski's actors offer their performance as a ceremony for those who wish to assist: the actor invokes, lays bare what lies in every man – and what daily life covers up. This theatre is holy because its purpose is holy."[128] That holy purpose is bound up with the fact that holy theatre does not exist for itself; it is a means to an end, and a primary end is to offer "a possibility of salvation."[129] It is in making visible what is so often invisible that the holy theatre connects with the deep "hunger"[130] of the audience to offer

---

[125.]Newbigin, *Gospel in a Pluralist Society*, 97–8.
[126.]Brook, *Empty Space*, 42.
[127.]Brook, *Empty Space*, 59.
[128.]Brook, *Empty Space*, 60.
[129.]Brook, *Empty Space*, 59.
[130.]Brook, *Empty Space*, 44.

"salvation." Brook's understanding of salvation is decidedly secular, but his insight resonates deeply with the performance tradition of the Bible, and the telos of performance criticism of the Bible. As the actor(s) enter the "script" and incarnate the biblical drama on stage the audience is confronted with the sacred in the form of the beloved ancestors who plead with them to return to YHVH and remind them of the consequences of not doing so.

Biblical performance criticism offers a way for scholars to enter the script. Or, to return to Newbigin's language, to examine the text "from the inside." It offers not only an opportunity for the scholar to examine the Bible, but also for the Bible to examine the scholar. The exegete's relationship with the passage is changed through performance, but the exegete herself is often changed by the act of performance as well. James Maxey acknowledges that biblical performance criticism "celebrates" the inclusion of subjective engagement with the text into the interpretive process. "Biblical performance criticism cannot support a position of objectivity or neutrality on the part of anyone involved in translation, a performance, or its evaluation. In performance, the performer is the medium. And people are not neutral."[131]

In the remainder of this chapter I will lay out the steps involved in applying biblical performance criticism to an Old Testament drama. This will build on the methodological work of David Rhoads and others, but will largely be drawn from the experience I have gleaned over the last decade of developing, refining, and practicing biblical performance criticism with hundreds of students at Western Theological Seminary, under the tutelage of my colleague and mentor, Dr. Tom Boogaart.

Oral Text, Oral Approach: Biblical Performance Criticism

Three decades ago Meir Sternberg made a considerable contribution to the development of narrative criticism, which was just maturing beyond its infancy in 1987 with the publication of his tome *The Poetics of Biblical Narrative*. His opening chapter, titled "Literary Text, Literary

---

[131.]Maxey, "Biblical Performance Criticism," 10.

Approach"[132] laid the groundwork for his pursuit of the poetics undergirding and expressed through biblical narrative. The logic was that, since the text was fundamentally literary in character, the most appropriate way to discern its meaning is by applying the tools and skills of professional readers, a case Robert Alter had likewise made some years earlier in *The Art of Biblical Narrative*.[133] This volume is narrower in scope and scale than the likes of Sternberg's and Alter's classic volumes, but a similar logic informs the present study: biblical performance criticism is an oral approach to an oral text.

Biblical performance criticism is a relatively "young" approach to interpreting the Bible. In 2006 David Rhoads called it an "emerging methodology" in his field of Second Testament studies.[134] It has been developing at an even slower rate in First Testament studies. However, the last ten years since he published his two-part essay "Performance Criticism: An Emerging Methodology in Second Testament Studies" has seen an explosion of research into both the orality of Israel and performance traditions in ancient Israel and first century Palestine. For example, there are presently fourteen volumes published in the Biblical Performance Criticism series by Wipf and Stock (Cascade) of which David Rhoads is the series editor—recently joined by Kelly Iverson and Holly Hearon. Most of the books in the series deal with New Testament issues, but the Old Testament is the subject of growing emphasis.[135]

[132.]Sternberg, *Poetics of Biblical Narrative*, 1–57.

[133.]Alter, *Art of Biblical Narrative*.

[134.]Rhoads, "Performance Criticism—Part I" and "Performance Criticism—Part II." James Maxey notes the publication of these two essays as the moment the method "began to gain traction" in the academic community. Maxey, "Biblical Performance Criticism," 2.

[135.]Of the fourteen books, only one so far deals directly with Old Testament narratives by treating the book of Ruth. Several deal with issues related to orality in either ancient Israel or first century Palestine—or both. Some deal primarily with issues of translation and the impact of performance on that practice. And a number of the volumes deal directly with New Testament texts, or the New Testament world. The fourteen books in the series are as follows, in order of publication date (I have included the year of publication only here in this list for ease of reference and comparison): Hearon and Ruge-Jones, *Bible in Ancient and Modern Media*, 2009; Maxey, *From*

Terry Giles and William Doan have published several articles along with three full-length books (one of which is in the series just mentioned) that all focus on the Old Testament, treating the prophets,[136] songs situated within narratives,[137] and the story of Naomi/the book of Ruth,[138] respectively. Tom Boogaart has published two essays offering insights from performance on the Binding of Isaac in Gen 22:1–19,[139] and Elisha and the Bands of Aram in 2 Kgs 6:8–23.[140] Jeanette Mathews's exploration of performance with the prophetic book of Habakkuk has been well received.[141] Performance critical approaches to the Psalms of Ascent and the book of Lamentations are being pursued by doctoral students around the world.[142]

Biblical performance criticism can be fruitfully applied to many different genres in both the Old and New Testaments, as the brief survey above illustrates. The methodology I have been describing, and describe in greater depth below, is primarily applicable to the narrative corpus.

Orality to Orality, 2009; Clark Wire, *The Case for Mark*, 2011; Miller, *Oral Tradition*, 2011; Botha, *Orality and Literacy in Ancient Israel*, 2012; Maxey and Wendland, *Translating Scripture for Sound and Performance*, 2012; Loubser, *Oral and Manuscript Culture in the Bible*, 2013; Dewey, *Oral Ethos of the Early Church*, 2013; Horsley, *Text and Tradition*, 2014; Iverson, *From Text to Performance*, 2014; Boomershine, *The Messiah of Peace*, 2015; Weissenrieder and Coote, *Interface of Orality and Writing*, 2015; Giles and Doan, *Story of Naomi*, 2016; Oestreich, *Performance Criticism of the Pauline Letters*, 2016.

[136.]Giles and Doan, *Prophets, Performance, and Power*.

[137.]Giles and Doan, *Twice Used Songs*.

[138.]Giles and Doan, *Story of Naomi*.

[139.]Boogaart, "Arduous Journey," 3–21.

[140.]Boogaart, "Drama," 35–61.

[141.]Cf. Val Billingham, review of *Performing Habakkuk*, *Colloquium* 45, no. 1 (May 2013), 111–13; Lee A. Johnson, review of *Performing Habakkuk*, *The Catholic Biblical Quarterly* 76, no. 3 (July 2014), 532–34.

[142.]E.g., Melinda Cousins recently completed a dissertation incorporating performance to interpret the Psalms of Ascent through Charles Sturt University in Sydney, Australia. It is titled "Pilgrim Theology: Worldmaking through Enactment of the Psalms of Ascents (Pss 120–134)." Heather Pillette is a PhD student at Trinity Evangelical Divinity School in Chicago, and is interested in issues related to performance and the book of Lamentations.

The method will look different when applied to the psalms or prophetic texts, for example. Indeed, as a discipline that is still in its infancy, biblical performance criticism is not practiced in a uniform way, even when applied to similar genres of biblical material. Mathews identifies three different ways that biblical performance criticism is presently practiced among the scholars who apply it to both testaments. In the first place, some see performance as a metaphor for the task of theological reflection,[143] or for the practice of discipleship that takes the Eucharist as the focal point of Christian performance.[144] For example, Sam Wells used the metaphor of improvisation as the central theme of his theology of ethics.[145] In the second place, scholars like Mathews herself use performance criticism to uncover "intrinsic performative aspects in the texts as they stand."[146] This approach, what Mathews calls "finding performance *in* biblical traditions,"[147] is generally applied in one of three ways: "(1) those who focus on particular aspects of performance theory and apply them to a text; (2) those who see the traditions themselves as having been deliberately composed as dramas; and (3) those who illuminate the intrinsic performative qualities in the text."[148]

The third approach, what Mathews calls the "performance *of* biblical traditions," in which "the scholars are interested in the performance *of* the material"[149] is the kind of approach I have been advocating for, and describe in detail below. I offer this description of biblical performance criticism with the understanding that it has its own integrity as a critical methodology, and yet it is in constant dialogue with many other disciplines, most notably narrative criticism.[150] On the path to

---

[143.]E.g., Balthasar, *Theo-Drama*; VanHoozer, *Drama of Doctrine*.

[144.]Lash, *Theology on the Way to Emmaus*.

[145.]Wells, *Improvisation*.

[146.]Mathews, *Performing Habakkuk*, 57,

[147.]Mathews, *Performing Habakkuk*, 57.

[148.]Mathews, *Performing Habakkuk*, 57.

[149.]Mathews, *Performing Habakkuk*, 54.

[150.]For a helpful overview of the way the way performance criticism (understood as the performance *of* biblical traditions) interacts with other criticisms in mutually-affecting ways, see David Rhoads' insightful essay, already referred to in this chapter: Rhoads, "Performance Criticism—Part II," 164–184.

performance, form criticism was the trailhead; historical, social-scientific, cultural, rhetorical, liberationist, and other approaches are signposts; and narrative criticism is the primary landmark that eventually leads the scholar-pilgrim to the performance itself.

A Medium-Oriented Methodology: Steps to Interpretation

Select/Translate the Script

The first step is to choose which drama is to be performed. Will it be the binding of Isaac, the coronation of Saul, or Jael's murder of Sisera? This decision will be informed by a number of factors: the performance context, the length of time available, the performance space, number of actors and number of characters, as well as other considerations. Once the drama is selected the boundaries of the script must be determined. Every drama has a beginning, middle, and end, but it is not always clear where those boundaries lie, and sometimes the imposed framework of chapters and verses do not align with the true boundaries of the drama. Narrative criticism can help to establish these boundaries with its careful attention to these textual details. When the boundary is defined, the next decision relates to translation. In my own practice I generally do not perform the dramas in English translation; choosing instead to perform them in the original Hebrew, using the Masoretic Text as it appears in *Biblia Hebraica Stuttgartensia*. Even when the performance is in Hebrew, however, an English translation is always read beforehand to (re)familiarize the audience with the story, since no one in the audience is fluent in Biblical Hebrew.

Whether the English translation is read aloud (which, of course, is a kind of performance) before an ensemble[151] performance in Hebrew, or

---

[151.]I will discuss this later on, but the performances I generally participate in involve an ensemble cast as opposed to a single storyteller. The inclusion of several "cast members" significantly increases the interpretive potential of performance by allowing for features like simultaneous action, as well as visibly creating space on stage between characters or locations on stage, which opens the possibilities for symbolic representation. For example, in a performance of the healing of Naaman in 2 Kgs 5, the king of Aram and the king of Israel sit on thrones on opposite sides of the

is the version performed, I prefer to use my own translation over any modern translations. I attempt to accomplish several things in a translation. I try to keep intact idiomatic expressions in the Hebrew that imply concrete actions. For example, in 2 Kgs 5:1 the narrator describes Naaman, the protagonist, as being "highly respected" (NASB), "highly regarded" (TNIV), or "in high favor" (NRSV). The Hebrew phrase is וּנְשֻׂא פָנִים (unsu' phanim), which means "his face was lifted up." Rather than translating for meaning accessible to a silent reader (e.g. "highly respected"), I translate this literally, and the meaning is clearly communicated in performance when the king of Aram raises his hand before the face of Naaman, who is kneeling before him, allowing Naaman to stand in the presence of his lord. This example clearly illustrates the veracity of David Rhoads' assertion that live performances are critical to the translation, indeed the performance *is* the translation "in a new medium. Here we would be dealing . . . with noises, gestures, movement, facial expressions, volume and inflection, pace, and so on. Performers would work to bring to expression the explicit and implicit suggestions for performance in the original text."[152] Several other considerations must be made in preparing a translation for performance, but there is not adequate space here to discuss them. Two books by James Maxey discuss the matter in depth, and from a variety of perspectives, with reference to both Old and New Testament issues.[153]

Internalize the Script

Before a biblical drama can be performed it must be internalized by the performer(s). I intentionally do not use the term "memorize" here. Memorization is akin to writing the words on the back of one's eyelids.

---

stage throughout the performance, representing the horizontal axis of power manifested in kingdoms, while Elisha's house is located downstage to represent the vertical axis of power, which comes from service to YHVH and does not participate in the destructive act of taking by force characteristic of kingdoms and seen in the behavior of Naaman first, and Gehazi last (see Chapter 5 for a thorough analysis of 2 Kgs 5).

[152.]Rhoads, "Art of Translating," 33.

[153.]Maxey, *Orality to Orality*; and Maxey and Wendland, *Translating Scripture*.

This reduces the act of internalization to a *visual* exercise ("reading" the words off the eyelids, instead of a page) that maintains objectivity between reader and text.[154] Internalization involves writing the words on the heart. Dennis Dewey also resists the term "memorization," and instead advocates for the phrase "learn by heart." For Dewey, learning "by heart" is a "process that entails deep immersion in the text, the internalization not just of sounds but of feelings, images, complexes of visualizations of setting, character, and narrative structure, all of it 'clothed' with the words of the text."[155] Internalization is engagement with the words to the degree that they become a part of the performer. In the great *Shema* in Deut 6, Moses told the Israelites that the way for them to love the Lord their God with all the heart, soul and strength was to "let these words that I am commanding you today be *on your hearts*."[156] This is subjective engagement, where the script becomes another subject with whom the interpreter/performer has a relationship characterized not just by careful analysis, but by intimacy and love as well. As a Christian scholar, I consider this an essential element. The interpreter still engages the Bible critically, but the Bible also exerts its own influence on the interpreter. Internalization moves in both directions—the script gets inside the scholar so the scholar can get inside the script.

Also implied in the quote from Dewey above is the embodied learning of the script. To internalize the words of the drama is more than a cerebral exercise and implicates the entire body of the interpreter.

[154.]For more on the move away from the term "memorization" in biblical performance criticism, see Perry, *Insights From Performance Criticism*, 39–40; Rhoads, "Performance Criticism—Part I," 125; and Ward and Trobisch, *Bringing the Word to Life*, 70.

[155.]Dewey, "Performing the Living Word," 154. Dewey goes on to relate this level of engagement with a passage to an act of prayer.

[156.]Dennis Dewey has mused that this may "allude to [a] commonly known methodology for the internalization of the texts. Does this reference give us any clue as to a technique for 'keeping the words' in a culture that was essentially oral? We tend to regard this corollary as a quaint figure of speech. But that may be because we who have mastered the technologies of literacy can hardly conceive of living and learning in an oral/aural world." Dewey, "Mnemonics of the Heart," 5.

Internalization of this sort is best done standing up (as opposed to sitting down), and the script should be spoken aloud as it is being learned (listening to a recording of it is also extremely helpful, especially if one is learning it in the original Hebrew). Movements can be helpfully paired with words to make physical, bodily connections between the flow of words. In my experience my body often reminds my brain what the next word is because it remembers the next movement, even when my brain cannot yet recall the next word or phrase. If the drama will be performed by an ensemble cast, it is also extremely helpful, as well as much more fun, to spend some time learning the script together as a group. Games can even be introduced to help create recitation situations more akin to a performance than simply saying the entire passage straight through.[157]

Block the Script

"Blocking" refers to the various staging decisions required to facilitate the performance. It includes the arrangement of the stage itself, the various locations where actors will stand and when they will stand there, when and where they move (and how fast), when they enter or leave the stage, etc. In short, it has to do with the entire physical, spatial

---

[157.]With an ensemble performance each character would speak only their lines. It is one thing to "memorize" all of the words of a biblical drama; it is another thing to be able to anticipate when your character's lines will begin, while also remembering where to stand, where to look, and how to say the line, etc. Theatre games, such as a modified version of the game "zip zap zog" have been helpful in taking the internalized script to the next level, especially when learning in Hebrew. In this game everyone stands in a circle facing inwards. One person begins by reciting the first phrase in the passage, or however length they desire. If the group has developed hand motions to coincide with the recitation, the entire group would do the motions as the individual recites. When they complete a phrase they jump into the air, clap their hands, and as they land point to another member around the circle. The sound and movement act as a distraction that forces deep concentration, preparing each member for the level of focus necessary for the eventual performance situation. The person who is pointed to then provides the next phrase, then jumps, claps, and points to another member of the circle. The game continues for as many rounds through the script (or the portion of the script learned) as is necessary.

dimensions of the staging of the script, but also includes more intangible elements such as tone of voice, dramatic silences or pauses, pacing, etc. All of these elements are done intentionally and should be considered carefully throughout the rehearsal period. It is through this process of blocking the performance that the actors truly begin to "enter" the script as the world of the drama materializes in rehearsal. A term I often use to describe this process is "embodied exegesis."[158]

The type of theatre recommended is "minimalist." This approach does not concern itself with costumes or the creation of a set. Props are kept to a minimum. This is an important point. If props are included, they should be limited to one or two at most. The "less is more" principle applies here: the less props used the greater significance each prop takes on within the performance frame and can help serve to unlock latent meaning in the script. For example, in the binding of Isaac (Gen 22:1–19), if the only prop used is a knife, it builds tension and becomes a focal point of dramatic action, which builds to climax during the sacrifice scene. Further, the meaning, tension, and emotions associated with the knife take on even greater significance when that same knife is used to slit the ram's throat (instead of Isaac's) after cutting Isaac free from his bonds.

The spacing decisions actors are forced to make throughout the blocking process—the orientation of the stage, each character's position onstage relative to the other characters and audience, etc.—grant the interpreter access to layers of meaning latent in the script, and then provide a mechanism whereby these latent dimensions are brought to visible expression. Often this meaning is accessed by identifying "gaps" in the story. Recognition of these gaps often leads to asking interesting questions, questions that otherwise would never have been considered by silent, isolated reading practices, however imaginative. One example, discussed in Chapter 1, is: How does Isaac get off the altar? This question, hardly discussed in the voluminous literature on Gen 22, holds consequential theological and interpretive meaning.

[158.]Embodied exegesis is simply a descriptive term for biblical performance criticism.

Another example from the same drama concerns the blocking of God's initial words to Abraham in Gen 22:2, "Take your son, your only one, whom you love, Isaac. And go to the land of Moriah. And offer him up there as a whole burnt offering, upon one of the mountains about which I will tell you." The first and most fundamental question is: where is God when these lines are delivered? God is clearly a character in the drama, and God's location on (or off) the stage in relation to Abraham has theological implications for how this interaction and God's command to Abraham is received. What is communicated if God is close to Abraham, kneeling over, looking lovingly and compassionately at him while he sleeps? What is communicated if God stands across the stage, straight faced, body rigid, demanding the sacrifice of his beloved child? What is communicated if God is a disembodied voice coming from off stage, the words shattering the fragile safety Abraham had enjoyed with his son up to this point? These questions, and others like them, guide the the performers along the way to discovering layers of meaning embedded within the script, in and between the words, that will come to their fullest expression in performance.

Research the Script

The process of blocking out the script inevitably raises important questions related to culture, social customs, history, and language; it reveals issues related to power, geopolitics, socioeconomics, identity, community, vulnerability, and oppression. Many of these issues cannot be resolved simply by rehearsing them, but nevertheless must be expressed in performance. I have already said that biblical performance criticism has its own integrity as a critical methodology, but is in constant dialogue with the other disciplines. This is the point at which this dialogue becomes essential. For example, in order to block the scene in The Bands of Aram (2 Kgs 6:8–23) in which the king of Aram outlines his plan to ambush the cities of Israel from a base camp (2 Kgs 6:8), research must be conducted into the ancient concept of cartography and how the king may have illustrated the army's movements to his counselors—drawing on the ground with a stick, moving objects on a table to representative sites, pointing to the cities from a high place, etc.? Performances are greatly enhanced when the results of other critical approaches are taken into account. Indeed, it is perhaps not too much to say that the event of performance is the ultimate end toward which these insights were discovered, whether that was the intention of the historical, narrative, or post-colonial critic or not. Discernment will need to be employed when choosing which insights from which other methodologies to include. The blocking process must guide this discernment process. The questions raised along the way will dictate what resources to engage, and which insights to incorporate. Features of space, number of actors, available props, the setting and context of performance (whether it is in worship, its own event, or a mainstage production) will all contribute to guiding the process, and are all relevant filters to use to isolate the most helpful contributions from other critical approaches.

Perform the Script

The performance is, of course, the most important step in the process, and the event toward which every other step is directed. The entire process is oriented toward preparing the performer or ensemble cast for the event of performance; all of the preparations come to bear in this event. Anyone who has participated in a performance and prepared for it through rehearsals knows that the event of performance is fundamentally different from rehearsal, and often is the occasion for new insights to be discovered by the performers *as* they perform. These insights may be initiated by audience participation, such as laughing at an unexpected time (e.g., when Sarah responds to the Angel saying she did not laugh *in Hebrew*, Gen 18:15), or letting out a collective sigh when the tension breaks (e.g., when Naaman rises up from the Jordan River healed, 2 Kgs 5:14). This could also be occasioned by an unexpected moment of eye-contact with someone in the audience, or perhaps when an experience of audience participation that is built-into the performance that was un-rehearsable is more illuminating than anticipated (as in a performance when the audience stood up and waved yellow and red papers in the air when Elisha's servant's eyes are opened to behold the horses and chariots of fire surrounding him and Elisha, 2 Kgs 6:17).

David Rhoads has experienced this through several decades of performing New Testament passages for live audiences. He reflects, "I regularly discover new meanings of a line or an episode or a point of argumentation in the course of preparing for a performance *and in the act of performing itself.* In this way, performances can confirm certain interpretations, can expand interpretive possibilities, and can set parameters on viable interpretations."[159] Not only does the performance often prompt deeper insights into the passage, it can also confirm (or reject) certain interpretive decisions the performers made when blocking it. Multiple performances of the same drama will regulate the interpretation while also continually breathing fresh insight into the passage, thus echoing the very process in which the stories were originally transmitted.

Analyze the Performance

The final step of the process is to critically reflect back on the entire process. If the performance was done by an ensemble cast, it is beneficial to debrief the performance event with the entire cast to complete the loop of engaging the passage as a community of interpreters. This space provides an opportunity for the cast to remember and to process the insights that may have occurred to them during the performance, enriching each member's experience and understanding of the drama. If it is possible, it can be illuminating to debrief the performance with the audience, especially if the performance takes place in the context of corporate worship. Like any form of art, more is communicated than is intended. Reader-response criticism has raised the challenge to historical-criticism's hyper-focus on a single, original meaning by arguing that, to a certain extent, interpretation is in the eye of the beholder. Rhoads proposes shifting the reader-response to

---

[159.]Rhoads, "Performance as Research," 170, emphasis added.

an "audience-response" approach to compensate for the shift from silent readers to participatory audiences that help performers locate and communicate meaning in the drama.[160]

There is also merit to reflecting on performances in writing and through publications. Although the performance is an *event*, and that event is the climax of the interpretive process, and although the performance-as-event cannot be reduced to explanation, and written-reflection perhaps partly reverses the paradigm shift back to textual-orientation, written reflections on the experience can nevertheless be helpful as a way to consolidate what was learned along the way, and to share more broadly and in traditional scholarly circles the insights gleaned into the passage through performance. Emphasis on performance is not a rejection of textuality or the written word. A legalistic commitment to the performance mode will be unhelpful in affecting change in the scholarly conversation concerning biblical interpretation, and about the use of performance toward that end.

Conclusion

This chapter contained three primary sections. The first section reconsidered the genre of the biblical narratives from a form critical perspective that more fully integrated orality and oral performance into the consideration process. My conclusion was that even though the term "genre" has been complicated by a considerable degree of textual bias, the best generic label for the biblical narratives is drama. The second section of this chapter engaged the complex term "performance," providing a definition based on the term's etymology and focusing it to fit with the biblical context. Following this I drew on performance theorists in order to consider more carefully what is at stake in the act of performance. A number of themes brought up in the first chapter were confirmed here, such as the peculiar experience of time created by a performance context in which the past and present coalesce ("ghostliness"), and the importance of "framing" the performance space

---

[160.]Rhoads, "Performance Criticism—Part II," 167.

in such a way as to communicate that something extra-ordinary is going to take place, which is at once connected to and transcends beyond normal, everyday life. Some new insights were also brought up: the inherent self-reflexivity of performance, and the intrinsically embodied nature of performance.

The final section of the chapter was devoted to articulating a methodology that incorporates orality and performance into the interpretive approach. This methodology is suitable for biblical narratives, and is rooted in an ensemble performance approach, instead of a single storyteller, although that approach can also reveal dimensions of meaning in the scripts that silent reading cannot access. There are six basic steps to the methodology called biblical performance criticism when applied to the dramas: 1. Select/translate the script; 2. Internalize the script; 3. Block the script; 4. Research the script; 5. Perform the script; and 6. Analyze the performance.

In Chapter 3 I will identify five essential elements of Israel's dramatic tradition. The five elements are: dramatic structure, the role of the narrator (audience participation), dialogue, point of view, movementand gesture. Each element will be described and explained with examples. These elements provide a picture of the art of biblical performance. Sensitivity to them will lead to deeper readings of the scripts and greater access to meaning otherwise difficult to find.

CHAPTER 3
THE ART OF BIBLICAL PERFORMANCE: FIVE ESSENTIAL ELEMENTS OF ISRAEL'S DRAMATIC TRADITION

Introduction

In his classic and inspired study *The Art of Biblical Narrative*, Robert Alter identified a number of literary conventions employed by the Israelite authors that collectively constitute the artistry of Israel's literary achievement in the genre he labeled "historicized prose fiction."[1] Among the literary conventions Alter identifies are "type-scenes,"[2] "characterization,"[3] and "repetition."[4] Alter's logic is that sensitivity to these literary conventions enables the careful reader of the Bible to make more penetrating analyses of the biblical texts, while also giving the reader the tools to discern narrative gaps in the story and the clues to unlock the possible meaning of those gaps.

In this chapter I will attempt to follow a similar approach to Alter but with an altered trajectory. I will identify five components of Hebrew performance that each contribute something unique and important to the artistry and profundity of Israel's dramatic tradition. The five elements are: dramatic structure, the role of the narrator (audience participation), dialogue, point of view, movement and gesture. I will argue that sensitivity to these elements—and the manifold ways they intersect and overlap—can lead to deeper readings of the scripts, and to identify *and fill in* gaps that have remained inaccessible with other approaches.

The essence of drama is conflict, and each of these five elements provides a window into the tension that drives each drama. As the story unfolds, tension builds and is eventually released. This implies that a

---

[1] Alter, *Art of Biblical Narrative*, 13.

[2] Alter, *Art of Biblical Narrative*, 47–62.

[3] Alter, *Art of Biblical Narrative*, 114–130.

[4] Alter, *Art of Biblical Narrative*, 88–113.

process is at work in the dramas. Various techniques are employed by the composers of Israel's dramas in the service of this process of developing and resolving conflict. The purpose toward which this process works is not entertainment, as Auerbach famously said.[5] The dramas, as sacred scripture, had a formational purpose; they were catechesis, discipleship. They were told to awaken the past into the present by allowing the ancestors to speak again, to re-actualize the transformations they experienced and so to unleash that transforming power on all who gathered to hear and to see their stories told. Paying attention to the elements described in this chapter, in light of the previous two chapters, can contribute to an understanding of this process, just as enacting the dramas today can re-actualize the transformative power of the stories.

If the process by which conflict is developed and resolved is the light a drama shines, these five elements are the five faces of a prism refracting that light in various directions. The prism metaphor is apt, as none of the elements are autonomous; each is a different aspect of a single reality. They can be considered in isolation from one another, but the isolation is heuristic and theoretical. When taken together they demonstrate the theological and dramatic achievement of Israel's dramatists, whom I will refer to as the composer.[6]

Five Essential Elements of Israelite Drama

Dramatic Structure

Dramatic structure was briefly discussed in Chapter 2 as evidence that the narratives are dramas. But there is more to say about this facet of Israel's dramatic tradition. This section will build on that brief description in order to demonstrate its critical role in facilitating the formative encounter between the audience and the story. To summarize briefly, every narrative in the Hebrew Bible follows that pattern

---

[5] "[T]he Scripture stories do not, like Homer's, court our favor, they do not flatter us that they may please us and enchant us—they seek to subject us, and if we refuse to be subjected we are rebels." Auerbach. *Mimesis*, 11–12.

[6] See the section on The Role of the narrator below for an explanation of this term.

common to dramas in any culture and age: conflict, development, resolution.[7] The dramas unfold through scenes composed of interactions between various characters—usually only two or three—in a particular location at a particular time; a change of location or the introduction of a new character introduces a new scene. The conflict is generally introduced near the beginning, it develops throughout the middle, and is resolved near the end. The resolution of the conflict brings about a change in the fortunes of the protagonist, from danger to safety, illness to health, ignorance to knowledge (or the reverse). This is often accomplished through a reversal, which returns to a theme introduced at the beginning and flips it around, and may even cast the rest of the story in a new light.[8]

Exod 17:1–7 will serve as an example to illustrate the component parts of dramatic structure. Below is the script, arranged according to its dramatic structure, in scenes, with narration in roman type and dialogue in bold. The translation is my own, and was developed specifically for a performance of this passage. I have attempted to maintain a close rendering of the word order of the Hebrew wherever possible, and kept the flow of the Hebrew as well, such as the way almost every sentence begins with "and."[9]

[7.]Various schemas have been suggested through the years that add layers of complexity or nuance to this basic structure. Aristotle's insightful and now axiomatic explanation was that a drama consists of a beginning, middle, and an end. In the nineteenth century the German playwright Gustav Freytag articulated a five-act schema for plays, referred to as Freytag's Pyramid: exposition, rising action, climax, falling action, dénouement. The more general three-fold structure of conflict, development, resolution seems to be generous and flexible enough to resonate with biblical dramas, although many dramas do not resolve the tension in a way that satisfies the appetites of modern Western societies raised on a healthy diet of sitcoms and "happily ever after" fairy tales.

[8.]Amit, "Endings," 213–226. See also Tyson, "Who's In? Who's Out?" 546–557; and Kirova, "Eyes Wide Open," 85–98.

[9.]This performance—in both English and Hebrew—is available on YouTube at this   link: https://www.youtube.com/watch?v=UKDOkQDNyUk&index=23&list=PLL6Sl4Od xSvjiOayUtYPS4r3xNE73O60o.

CONFLICT

[1]All the congregation of the children of Israel set out in stages from the wilderness of Sin upon the command of the Lord. They encamped at Rephidim. But there was no water for the people to drink.

DEVELOPMENT

Scene 1

[2]And the people quarreled with Moses, saying,

> *Give us water! Let us drink!*

And Moses said to them,

> *Why do you quarrel with me? Why do you test the Lord?*

[3]But the people thirsted there for water. And the people grumbled against Moses, saying,

> *Why did you bring us up from Egypt, to kill us and our children and our livestock with thirst?*

Scene 2

[4]And Moses cried out to the Lord, saying,

> *What can I do with these people? In a moment they're going to stone me!*

CLIMAX

[5]And the Lord said to Moses,

> *Pass in front of the people and take from [them] the elders of Israel. And the staff with which you strike the Nile, take it in your hand and go. [6]Behold, I will be standing over there, in front of*

*you, on the rock of Horeb. Strike the rock, and water will come
from it, and the people will drink.*

And Moses did this in the sight of the elders of Israel.

RESOLUTION

Scene 3
[7]And he called the name of the place Testing[10] and Quarreling,[11] because
the children of Israel quarreled and because they tested the Lord there
saying,

Is the Lord in our midst or not?

Conflict

All drama is driven by tension, which is an effect generated by the
introduction of conflict. "Conflict is central to drama," writes David
Ball.[12] Biblical performance criticism compels the interpreter to pay
careful attention to the conflict and the tension that results from it. This
requires more than an objective identification and articulation of the
conflict; it involves moving beyond passive recognition to active
connection. The performer must identify with the conflict, connect with
it, and own it in some way personally, bodily. This process involves
careful and focused reflection on the nature and character of the conflict
as it is presented in the "script."

Biblical dramas typically open with a brief description of the setting into
which the conflict will be introduced. Often, this narrated introduction
establishes an initial equilibrium, which will be upset by the conflict, and will
be returned to when the conflict is resolved at the end.[13] The conflict is

---

[10.] מַסָּה, *massah*, "testing," cf. v. 2.

[11.] מְרִיבָה, *meribah*, "quarreling," cf. v. 2.

[12.] Ball, *Backwards and Forwards*, 25.

[13.] Take, for example, the drama involving the Hebrew midwives in Exod 1:15–22.
In vv. 15–16 Pharaoh commands the midwives to kill every Hebrew male on the birth
stool, but to let every female live, thus setting off a conflict that functions on a macro
(demoralization at the violent loss of a generation of male progeny) and micro scale

generally theological in nature (even when God is not a character in the drama or explicitly mentioned at all, as in the Book of Esther) and provides a window through which the people of Israel sought to discern God's presence in the moments of everyday life, whether in feast or famine, city or wilderness, peace or war, the palace of the king or the home of a poor widow. In our example drama from Exod 17, the conflict is introduced in the opening verse: *"there was no water for the people to drink."*

Although Exod 17:1–7 is a relatively short drama, the conflict is multi-faceted. The obvious problem is that the people are stuck in the barren, hot, unforgiving wilderness of the Sinai peninsula without water.[14] If this problem is not remedied, the people, their children, and their livestock will not have long to live.[15] But this physical reality has a theological source: God *led* the people into this situation. Here the narrator is explicit, even if through a subtle idiomatic phrase. The people moved from Sin to Rephidim "upon the

---

(the midwives are caught between their vocation and Pharaoh's command—and the consequences for disobedience). The tension escalates as the midwives enact a remarkable feat of civil disobedience that extends all the way to Pharaoh's throne room (vv. 17–19). The micro-scale conflict resolves as the midwives are blessed by God, but the nation of Israel is plunged (back) into grief by a repetition of Pharaoh's initial edict, but now on a much greater scale: the midwives will not carry out the Pharaoh's male infanticide, his soldiers will (vv. 21–22). The drama ends where it began, but with a tragic twist. Though this specific drama's resolution is less than satisfactory, it is part of a larger story arc, and the tension carries forward into other dramas involving some of the same characters. Nevertheless, even within this drama, though the scale and scope of Pharaoh's edict is increased exponentially, the intervening events reduce its sting somewhat: if God can thwart the mighty Pharaoh's plans through the faithful action of a couple of Hebrew midwives, hope is not yet lost.

[14.]Or, perhaps, without *access* to water. It is conceivable, as Nahum Sarna proposes, that water was available but the Amalekites—with whom the Israelites make war in the second half of Exod 17—prevented their access to the available water sources. Cf. Sarna, *Exodus*, 93. This hypothesis is possible, but there is no mention of external hostility in the story itself, which casts doubt on this suggestion as unnecessary conjecture. Perhaps we can simply take the story at its face value and assume the Lord led the people to a place where there was no water (there is no way to know either way, as the location of Rephidim is uncertain, and water sources have a way of changing over the course of millennia), just as they were led to a place that had no bread or meat in the previous chapter, and God miraculously provided manna and quail (Exod 16).

[15.]Cf. Exod 17:4.

command of the Lord" (v. 1). The Hebrew word translated "command" is פֶּה
(*peh*, "mouth").[16] They travelled "upon the mouth of the Lord," as the Lord
had commanded them to do. The Israelites, as it were, "proceed from the
mouth of the Lord"[17] into the wilderness.

The drama unfolds in a way that indicates the people do not understand
that the Lord has led them to this place. The narrator informs the audience of
this important fact, but there is ostensibly no mention of this to the people
themselves. This introduces the possibility of irony, which is dependent upon
the exclusive knowledge of some played off on the ignorance of others. The
audience is in on the Lord's action from the beginning but the people are left
in the dark. Thus the conflict that develops is multi-layered. Within the
boundary of the drama, the conflict the characters endure is physical (imminent
death by thirst), personal (the people quarrel with Moses), and theological
(God ostensibly abandons Israel to this fate). The tension felt by the audience
is somewhat different, however, because they know of God's participation,
hear God speak to Moses (unlike the other characters), and witness God's
presence and movement within the drama. Perhaps the conflict the audience
endures is the age-old question of theodicy: Why does God allow the people
to suffer in this way when God was present with them the entire time?

Development

The conflict introduced at the beginning intensifies by means of
dialogue, contrasted points of view, movement and gesture. Eventually
the tension builds to a breaking point—the climax—when the tension is
released and the conflict is resolved. This event marks a change in the
fortune of the protagonist, who through it moves from danger to safety,
ignorance to knowledge, sickness to health, captivity to freedom. The
change can move in the other direction as well, from health to sickness,
and so on.

In the present drama, the conflict develops in verses two through
four, and reaches its climax in verses five and six. The dialogue in verses
two through four clearly identifies the expansion and development of
the conflict surrounding God leading the people into a location that

---

[16.]The entire phrase is עַל־פִּי יְהוָה (*'al pi YHVH*).
[17.]Cf. Deut 8:3.

cannot support their lives. A rift is exposed between the people and their leader, a rift that echoes features of the people's complaint over the lack of bread and imminent death by starvation in Exod 16:3.[18] Further, each characters' speech articulates their respective points of view, which intersect violently and render the conflict more explicit. The people equate the present danger with Moses' leadership and hold him at fault (v. 3). Moses interprets their fear and violence as testing the Lord (v. 2). The narrator's descriptions of the people's speeches ("And the people quarreled with Moses," 17:2) also signals the intensification of conflict: in verse two the people "quarrel" or "contend" (ריב, *r-y-b*) with Moses. Their discontent then spreads throughout the camp as insidious murmuring (לון, *l-u-n*, v. 3), which almost culminates in their mutinous assassination of Moses by stoning, revealed in Moses' impassioned prayer to God (וּסְקָלֻנִי, *usqaluni*, "and they will stone me," v. 4). Tone of voice further elevates the experience of the conflict: as the people scream at Moses they betray their desperation and the volume of their voices elevates the audience's emotional and bodily experience of the tension. Movement and gesture likewise combine to reveal the intensity of the conflict as the people approach Moses with stones in their hands, arms cocked and ready to stone him to death. The scene unfolding on the stage confronts the audience with the severity of the people's desperation, which now envelops Moses in its web. The audience leans in, wondering how Moses will get out of this jam; or perhaps they lean back, covering their eyes, not wanting to see the result. Either way, the audience is engaged, drawn into the unfolding conflict by a heightened awareness of the tension expressed through bodies, voices, the use of space, and perhaps props as well (stones).

[18.]Several echoes are present between the two complaints. Both include complaints of Israel being 'brought out" (הוֹצֵאתֶם אֹתָנוּ "you brought us out" in 16:3 and הֶעֱלִיתָנוּ "you brought us up" in 17:3), both reference Egypt; both include accusations of the purpose of the liberation being death (לְהָמִית, *lehamit*, "(in order) to kill"); and both identify the lack of a vital resource as the means of death, identified with the preposition בְּ ("with"): בְּרָעָב (*bara'av*, "with hunger," 16:3) and בַּצָּמָא (*batsamah*, "with thirst," 17:3).

Moses now enters into urgent conversation with God (v. 5). How does he escape the people's violence unscathed? One dramatic possibility is the use of tableaus (freeze-frames). The people freeze in their places—stones in hand—as Moses proceeds to address the Lord, thus maintaining a sense of the urgency of Moses' prayer. Another possibility is that Moses slips away from the pressing mob by creating a separation between him and them. Perhaps he raises his staff, which causes the people to momentarily step back or pause; they know what power his staff holds. Perhaps he throws his staff down in front of them to create a buffer zone—this could explain why God later tells Moses to *pick up* (לקח "take, grasp") his staff after "passing before the people" in verse five. Either way, Moses buys or finds time to pray, which leads to the climax of the drama.

God tells Moses to re-engage the people (who may still have stones in their hands!) and to remove the elders from the people. The elders will witness the miracle, the people will not. Staff in hand, Moses (and presumably the elders with him) are instructed to walk to where God will be "standing . . . upon the rock of Horeb." "Horeb" is often used to refer to Mt. Sinai, but apparently also refers to the region around it. The exact location is unknown.[19] And the exact location of the rock is less important to the Hebrew composer than what happens at the rock. What does it mean that God will be "standing" on the rock? How are we to understand this? Dismissing it as ancient anthropomorphism is not sufficient as it is clearly a stage direction, explicitly identifying not only God's location on the stage but also God's posture. Whether God is presented by an actor or a chorus or a voice, God's presence stands עַל ("upon," perhaps "before" or "beside") the rock which Moses is to strike (הִכָּה, *hikkah*, "strike, smite"). This location and posture explicitly puts God in harm's way: Moses's staff must go through God's presence to reach the rock. A Christian reading of this moment would see in it an anticipation of the self-sacrificial love of God offered in Jesus on the

---

[19.]Sarna, *Exodus*, 14.

cross to save the world.[20] This is certainly how the Apostle Paul interpreted the event in 1 Cor 10:3–4: "[A]nd all ate the same spiritual food, and all drank the same spiritual drink. For they drank from the spiritual rock that followed them, *and the rock was Christ*."[21] A Jewish interpretation would see this as a manifestation of God's Spirit, affirming God's presence in the face of the people's skepticism (v. 7).[22]

With respect to the miracle itself, John Walton is certainly correct to point out that "[s]edimentary rock is known to feature pockets where water can collect just below the surface. If there is some seepage, one can see where these pockets exist and by breaking through the surface can release the collected water."[23] But the composer is unconcerned with a geological explanation. The narrative gap reveals a theological profundity *when it is seen* in performance: God's sacrificial love abounds on the earth, and it can transform a rock into a stream of life-giving water (or, perhaps, multiply the water behind a rock barrier to save an entire nation). Again, the apostle Paul interpreted the story not as a miracle of geology, but of theology: "*and the rock was Christ*."[24]

Moses, along with the elders—and eventually the people as well[25]—drink the water that flows from the rock and all are saved. The climax

---

[20.]See West, "Unseen Grace," 5–8. Cf. 1 Cor 10:4. This was also Max Harris's read on this passage. He argued that the Bible "abounds in smaller instances of such theatricality. That, for instance, the invisible God stood against the rock at Horeb in front of the elders and people of Israel and allowed himself to be beaten with Moses' rod so that water might flow from the rock to assuage Israel's thirst (Ex. 17:1–6) has been interpreted as both an immediate gracious provision for material need and a carefully staged figurative enactment of Jesus' crucifixion and the consequent outpouring of the Holy Spirit (Jn. 7:37–39; cf. 1 Cor. 10:4)." Harris, *Theater and Incarnation*, 9.

[21.]NRSV; emphasis added.

[22.]God's action "is a response to the people's skeptical questioning of God's continued support (v. 7). God's immediate and potent presence will indeed be manifest." Sarna, *Exodus*, 94.

[23.]Walton, Matthews, and Chavalas, *Bible Background Commentary*, 92.

[24.]Emphasis added.

[25.]The drama does not include a reference to the people drinking, but clearly they did, otherwise they would have all died in the wilderness while Moses and the elders drank to their heart's content.

transforms death into life. The climax also facilitates a double reversal. The stones which at first symbolized Moses' imminent death are transformed as the "rock of Horeb" becomes a font of living water, saving Moses from the stones and the people from their thirst. And this is accomplished by Moses's staff—which represents God's life-giving power—being wielded as a weapon to strike (הִכָּה, *hikkah*, "strike, smite") the rock somehow imbued with God's presence. The stick-of-life becomes a weapon through which the stone-of-death pours out life-giving water. Sticks and stones weighing the balance between life and death.

Resolution

The transformation achieved in the climax gives way to establishing a new equilibrium. Often the drama ends where it began (the literary term is *inclusio*) by returning to the opening theme, although the events that have occurred along the way make it impossible to return to "the way things were." The new equilibrium is established in light of the change that took place over the course of the drama, and often mirrors the initial equilibrium. The endings, like the beginnings, are often very short. Occasionally, however, an ending is drawn out through an element in the plot structure called "falling action," in which the outcome of the climax is thrown into doubt for a period. An example of this will be discussed in Chapter 5.

Moses does not name the place "Living Water" or "Spring of Our Salvation," as other place names commemorating revelation or miraculous salvation might lead one to expect.[26] Moses memorializes not God's miraculous intervention, but the people's faithless rebellion, drawing attention to it as the context in which God's presence and sacrificial love was manifested, despite the people's lack of faith.

[26.]Cf. Abraham naming the place of Isaac's near-sacrifice יהוה יִרְאֶה (YHVH *yir'eh*, "The Lord Will Provide") in Gen 22:14; or the well of Hagar's salvation coming to be known as בְּאֵר לַחַי רֹאִי (*b'eir lachay ro'i*, "Well of the Living One Who Sees Me") in Gen 16:14; or Jacob naming the place of his revelatory dream בֵּית־אֵל (*beit-el*, "The House of God") in Gen 28:19.

Similar to the Book of Jonah,[27] this drama concludes with dialogue in the form of a rhetorical question—left unanswered—spoken by a character ("the people") that drips with irony and poignancy. "Is the Lord in our midst or not?" the people cry. This is the justification offered for why Moses called the place Massah and Meribah, instead of Mayim Chayim (Living Water), say. The composer's placement of this line here at the end of the drama—as opposed to the moment in which it was actually uttered in the chronology of the unfolding plot (likely during either the "quarreling" in v. 2 or "murmuring" in v. 3)—is both intentional and profound. Placing it here increases the contrast between God's self-sacrifice and the people's rebellion by demonstrating in stark terms the irony and ignorance of their complaint.

The poignancy—and tragic irony—of the composer's conclusion, and its relation to the conflict surrounding God's presence, is made unavoidably evident through performance. The miracle takes place "in the eyes of the elders," which implies the people do not see it take place. The people, perhaps standing down stage facing the audience (with their back to the rest of the stage), ask if God is even present among them *while God is behind them with Moses and the elders offering Godself in love for their survival*. The God who opens his mouth to lead them into the wilderness (v. 1) now opens his hands to save them from death, but the people do not have the eyes to see or the faith to believe. Seen in its canonical context, God teaches the people of Israel how to trust in divine provision—first for bread and meat (Exod 16), now for water (Exod 17:1–7), and later for security when they face hostile neighbors (Exod 17:8–16)—on their way from Egypt to Sinai; on their way from being slaves to the free, covenant people of God.

Sensitivity to the complex process whereby the tension is built and released attunes the interpreter to important details in the script that might otherwise be passed over, such as the location of God with respect

---

[27.]The Book of Jonah also concludes with God's rhetorical question to the wayward prophet Jonah who preferred his own death over witnessing the miraculous conversion of the Ninevites. "And should I not have compassion on Nineveh, the great city, which has within it more than 120,000 people who do not know their right hand from their left, and many cattle besides?" (Jonah 4:11).

to the rock and Moses' staff (and the theological implications of such a detail), a detail about which God is explicit in God's instructions to Moses. As was clear in the above explanation, the operations of dramatic structure are enmeshed with the other elements of Israel's dramatic tradition in such a way that it is impossible to talk about one without reference to the others. Dramatic structure is the process by which tension is developed and resolved. The other four elements are the specific techniques employed by the composer to facilitate that process.

The Role of the Narrator (Audience Participation)

Two brief points of clarification are necessary before we begin. First, it is essential to clarify that there is an absolute distinction between the narrator and what I have been calling the "composer."[28] The narrator is a character contained within the boundaries of the drama. The narrator is not the "author" of the drama, not the playwright or dramatist, not the Deuteronomistic historian, not the scribe(s) who committed the versions of these dramas now collected in the Hebrew Bible to writing. As was discussed in Chapter 1, the exact timing and process by which these oral performances became written and collected into the Bible involves a long period of time, and is shrouded in mystery. However exactly it happened, I will refer to the individual(s) responsible for the final form of each script as the "composer,"[29] a term much preferred over "author" with its attendant literary and textual connotations. Included in the field of reference of "composer" as I will use it are the generations of oral performers and communities who developed and refined the dramas, and sustained their memory among the people.

[28.]This is a different perspective on the narrator than has been typically discussed by narrative critics. For example, J. P. Fokkelman takes the narrator and the "author" to be the same person: "Whoever writes a story establishes himself as the narrator, choosing the position of narrator." Fokkelman, *Reading Biblical Narrative*, 55.

[29.]I will use the singular "composer," but *by no means* is this to suggest that a single individual was responsible for establishing the final forms of the biblical dramas.

The narrator is a character within the drama itself. It was a purposeful choice made by the composer[30] to tell these stories through the eyes of a narrator. Other choices were certainly possible, but this was the way the stories were told, and that fact bears meaning and invites new reflection in the light of my thesis that these stories are dramas and were performed in some way.[31]

Second, the narrator is a wholly unique character in biblical dramas. Even though the narrator is a character in the drama, s/he alone has the capacity—indeed, the responsibility—to cross the performance plane, to wander in and out of the story, to mediate between the events being incarnated onstage and the gathered audience. Even God is "bound" within the dramatic frame of the performance. Everyone save the narrator alone functions within the world established by the drama. But the narrator, in order to tell the tale, must break the plane and speak directly to the audience, thus having one foot within the world of the story and one foot beyond it, stepping into the world inhabited by those gathered for the performance. In this capacity the narrator controls the pacing of the performance, when each character speaks and how quickly events unfold. This mediating function is an under-appreciated aspect

---

[30.]Again, this includes reference to the tradition of oral performers.

[31.]Some would argue that dramatic performance and the presence of a narrator are mutually exclusive realities. However, according to Jeff Barker, Professor of Theatre at Northwestern College in Orange City, IA, there are a number of examples in both modern and ancient theater traditions that include narration. The Greek "chorus" occasionally operated in a similar fashion; Shakespeare included various narrative devices in his plays (the character called "Prologue" in Henry V, and the "Chorus" in Romeo and Juliet, for example), and various twentieth century playwrights have incorporated different kinds of narrators as well, from Thornton Wilder's "Stage Manager" in Our Town to the character narrator Tom in Tennessee Williams' "The Glass Menagerie," to Barker's own play "When Scott Comes Home," written in a form called Chamber Theatre in which "the protagonist was played by two actors, one which would enact the play and one which would comment on the play." Barker, as part of his work directing the Ancient Hebrew Drama Project, has produced several biblical plays of varying lengths and complexity. One, called "And God Said," was a musical done in collaboration with Broadway composer Ron Melrose. He commented that "the narration serves to help the play live in the theatrical present." Jeff Barker, e-mail message to author, May 22, 2017.

of the narrator's role.[32] This is also part of the unique perspective on narration that biblical performance criticism offers the larger field of Old Testament/Hebrew Bible.

As I briefly mentioned in Chapter 2, the narrator's function was akin to that of a priest in ancient Israel. The priests traversed the space between the world of the worshiping community and the world of heaven, having one foot in each world during their ritual service. Through word (blessing, intercession) and deed (sacrifice) they would unleash the reality of heaven into the lives of those gathered on earth. "Perhaps the central concept of priesthood is mediation between the sphere of the divine and the ordinary world. A priest through his ritual actions and his words facilitates communication across the boundary separating the holy from the profane."[33]

The role of a shaman and a hungan[34] in contemporary animistic societies may shed further light on the mediating role of the biblical narrator. According to David Cole, the role of a shaman and a hungan is to make visible the invisible reality of the *illud tempus*, the "time of origins."[35] The *illud tempus* is a term for sacred time, the time of the ancestors, or the time before time. It is time infused with glory. It is the

---

[32.]Narrative critics such as Meir Sternberg and Adele Berlin have significantly deepened our understanding of the role of the biblical narrator, elucidating elements such as narrative omniscience and reliability. Cf. Sternberg, *Poetics of Biblical Narrative*, passim. See also Berlin, *Poetics and Interpretation*, 52. With respect to the mediating function of the narrator, Sternberg does refer to it frequently, but in a very different way than how I am describing it here. See, for example, Sternberg, *Poetics of Biblical Narrative*, 141, 321 (on the artful and reliable mediation of the story). A possible exception is found on p. 121 in reference to narrative clues that bridge the gap between "the time of action (the past in which Jacob struggled with the angel or a man of God was called a seer) to the time of the epic situation (the present in which the narrator faces his contemporaries)." Sternberg brushes up against what I am suggesting, but draws different conclusions from it based on his assumptions about the explicitly *literary* function of the narrator.

[33.]*NIDOTTE*, s.v. "כָּהַן."

[34.]*Hungan* is the Haitian term for the priest of a possession cult. Cole uses it as "a person of any nationality who seeks possession as a blessed state of nearness to the gods." Cole, *Theatrical Event*, 14.

[35.]Cole, *Theatrical Event*, 7.

time that is made accessible through ritual, and through performances
of ancestral stories. Biblically speaking, it is the "in the beginning" of
Genesis, the tower of Babel, the call of Abram, the parting of the Red
Sea; it is the sacred history in which the beloved ancestors lived and
experienced God's presence and power, captured in the ancestral stories
and incarnated through performance.

The shaman is the "cosmic voyager" whose responsibility is to lead
the community on an ascent from its own world to the *illud tempus*. The
hungan, on the other hand, enables the descent of *illud tempus*
personages into the midst of the gathered congregation. Both the
shaman's and the hungan's bodies and voices are the vehicles through
which the ascent or descent takes place, and each of them manifests the
sought after reality through traditionally dramatic means: speaking,
dancing, silence, clapping, movement, props, lighting, etc.[36] The
shaman and the hungan both exist in the world *between* the present and
the past and become the point of overlap between the two. Their
achievement, like the achievement of the narrator in biblical dramas, is
to facilitate *communion* between past and present, text and context, the
drama and the audience, the ancestors and their descendants, between
God and God's people. Every actor on stage participates in this process
of colliding the past with the present, of course, but the narrator is the
bridge—to switch from analogy to metaphor—allowing passage in both
directions. The narrator brings both "worlds"—the "real world" of the
story and the "real world" of the gathered congregation—closer and
closer together until they coalesce into a single reality through which
transformation is made possible.

Dialogue

The biblical dramas are suffused with speech. So much so that by
far the most frequent verb used in the Hebrew Bible is אמר, "to say."[37]
The most common action taken by anyone throughout the Bible, and

---

[36.]Cole, *Theatrical Event*, 12–57, esp. 12–14.

[37.]It appears 5,317 times. The next most common verb is היה, "to be, become,
happen," which appears 3,576 times.

particularly in the dramas, is the act of speaking. אמר is used by the narrator to introduce dialogue.[38] In performance, dialogue is not quoted speech; it is the speech itself. Characters are not quoted as saying such and such, but rather speak the words themselves, and they speak them to each other. The narrator does not tell us what Potiphar's wife said to Joseph in her bedroom. She says "Lie with me!" in our hearing, as we watch her take hold of his garment.[39] The characters in biblical dramas speak for themselves. Periodically the narrator will offer a summary of dialogue,[40] but the primary mechanism the composer chose to express each character's point of view was for them to articulate it themselves.

Characters speak to each other in the present tense; their speech is simultaneous with their actions and other events happening in the drama. The sailors in Jonah unload their ship *and* cry out to their gods *while the storm rages over and around them.*[41] A conclusion to be drawn from this is that present action was important to the biblical composer. The narrator continually steps out of the present moment of the action to speak to the audience in order to draw them further up and further in to the events unfolding on stage, establishing a complex experience of time. The dialogue, in establishing an immediate encounter, must be understood in relation to the work of the narrator who is constantly working to bring the presentness of the story and the presentness of the audience together, collapsing the difference between them, mediating their intimate and formational encounter.

Dialogue is a chief means by which the conflict in biblical dramas is developed. The narrator also plays a role in developing and

---

[38.]The two most common forms used by the narrator are the vav-consecutive וַיֹּאמֶר (this is the 3ms form), and the infinitive לֵאמֹר.

[39.]Gen 39:12.

[40.]For example, in 1 Sam 17:23, just after David arrives at the Israelite camp with supplies for his brothers, Goliath emerges once again from the Philistine camp and the narrator simply reports that "he spoke these [same] words, and David heard him." Another example may come from the exchange between Naaman and the king of Aram in 2 Kgs 5:5. It appears as though the narrator introduces Naaman's speech, but actually provides the words himself in summary: "Thus and so said the girl from the land of Israel."

[41.]Jon 1:4–5.

identifying the tension. The narrator's primary role, however, is to introduce and frame the dialogue.[42] Dialogue also indicates a scenic shift—along with shifts of location, whether temporal or geographic. In each scene a character (or perhaps a group speaking as one) engages another character (or group) in conversation. The ensuing dialogue expresses, in large part, the point of view each character embodies and reveals, and the ways these contrasting points of view intersect is an important way the dramas develop the conflict. The insertion of speech by a new character—almost always introduced by the narrator—generally indicates a new scene has begun.

Finally, the context of performance provides an explanation for a peculiar practice employed by the biblical composer that Robert Alter struggled to comprehend from a literary perspective. Namely, the verbal expression of inner thoughts by a single character. In Alter's words: "The biblical preference for direct discourse is so pronounced that thought is almost invariably rendered as actual speech, that is, as quoted monologue."[43] What Alter fails to consider is that monologue is a technique inherent to drama and is an efficient and effective way to develop a character, set up irony (which is predicated on exclusive knowledge the audience is in on), and is consonant with the preference in drama to show rather than tell. A preference for "telling" would involve the narrator didactically describing and defining the conflict, each character's relation to it, and what viewpoint is preferred. It would no longer be a story. A preference for "showing" places value not on explanation but engagement, it seeks to get and then keep the audience's interest. Therefore, it is more nuanced, less obvious; it requires attention on the part of the audience to make their own connections based on their assessment of each character's trustworthiness within the boundary of the story. Stories that emphasize "showing" over "telling" are not easily

---

[42.]Cf. Robert Alter, "the primacy of dialogue is so pronounced that many pieces of third-person narration prove on inspection to be dialogue-bound, verbally mirroring elements of dialogue which precede them or which they introduce." Alter, *Art of Biblical Narrative*, 65.

[43.]Alter, *Art of Biblical Narrative*, 67–68.

reduced to "morals" but rather are "fraught" with tension. They are complex and invite a lifetime of reflection and engagement.

Point of View

In literature, point of view refers to "the way in which the reader is presented with the materials of the story, or, viewed from another angle, the vantage point from which the author presents the actions of the story."[44] In biblical drama point of view is not limited to the narrator, for each character within the drama embodies a perspective which is expressed through dialogue, movement, gestures, tone of voice. The narrator can also influence the audience's interpretation of a particular character's point of view.

In biblical dramas the conflict is often introduced and/or developed by contrasting two or more points of view. The tension is intimately tied to the respective points of view presented through dialogue and narration. The drama's theological affirmation is likewise connected to the point of view that prevails when the conflict is eventually resolved. Point of view is akin to worldview in biblical drama; it represents the perspective a character takes on the world, their theology, their understanding of the source and structure of power, their faith and trust (or lack thereof) in God's presence and provision.

Sometimes the contrast between characters' respective points of view are explicitly clear. The king of Israel begs Elisha, who has delivered the Aramean army to his doorstep: "Can I strike them down? Can I strike them down, my father?!" To which Elisha vociferously responds: "You shall not strike them down!" He demands, instead: "Set bread and water before them so that they may eat and drink and return to their lord."[45] The narrator privileges Elisha's perspective, and when the king acquiesces and, in accordance with the conventions of Middle Eastern hospitality, sets "an elaborate feast" (not just bread and water)

[44.] Holman, *Handbook to Literature*, 343–44.
[45.] 2 Kgs 6:21–22.

before the Aramean army, they do indeed eat and drink and return to their lord, so that the drama, which began with war,[46] ends with peace.[47]

The contrast between the perspectives of Samuel and God in 1 Sam 16 is another good example. Samuel is at Jesse's house on a mission to anoint the next king of Israel. In verse 6 Samuel looks at Jesse's eldest son Eliab and declares: "Surely the Lord's anointed one stands before him!" Immediately, God intervenes, correcting Samuel: "Do not pay attention to his appearance, to his height or his stature, for I have rejected him. For the way humans see is not the way. Humans see with the eyes, but the Lord sees with the heart" (v. 7).[48] Clearly Samuel's point of view is incompatible with God's (this is true of the audience as

---

[46.]2 Kgs 6:8.

[47.]2 Kgs 6:23. Of course, "Sometime later," as the following drama begins (2 Kgs 6:24), Aram musters for war against Israel once again, indicating that the peace of friendship is a soft whisper in the face of the strong cultural headwinds of violence, perhaps not unlike the "sound of silence" Elijah experienced on Mt. Horeb in 1 Kgs 19:12.

[48.]I am aware that the translation I offer here ("humans see *with the eyes*, but the Lord sees *with the heart*") goes against the grain of traditional renderings of this verse. Most major translations render ראה as "look," (with the exception of JPS (1985)), and take the preposition ל to indicate the indirect object of "look," and so to name what is seen—the "outward appearance," and "the heart" respectively. My translation ("see with") follows that of Robert Alter ("For man sees with the eyes, and the Lord sees with the heart." Alter, *Art of Biblical Narrative*, 149.), and I believe it more accurately reflects the comparison being made in the Hebrew between two bodily organs: the eyes and the heart. The former is the organ of sight, but God tells Samuel (and the audience) that the ways they have been accustomed to seeing (and the meaning they associate with what they see) is making them blind; rather, they need to see in a new way, to see the way the heart sees, the way God sees. The two organs are not compared as the objects of sight, but the *vehicles* of sight. The heart is the vehicle of *true* seeing as it is unencumbered by the "outward appearance" of things. Further, the *HALOT* lexicon defines this specific phrase (with explicit reference to 1 Sam 16:7) as "literally to see according to the eyes." *HALOT*, s.v. "ראה." This, again, describes the processes of the seeing organ (either eyes or heart), not primarily *what* that organ sees ("outward appearance"). The rendering I am suggesting here perhaps allows me to have my proverbial cake—and eat it too, for although it prioritizes the vehicles of sight (eyes and heart), it nevertheless still implicitly contrasts the objects of sight as well (outward appearance/what can be seen, and what is on the inside/the heart of someone).

well, since it is filled with humans, who see the way humans see—"with the eyes"). The remainder of the drama continues on this theme, drawing it out as each remaining son (the process is abbreviated after the third) comes forward and receives the same report: "The Lord has also not chosen this one" (vv. 8, 9, 10). As Robert Alter adroitly observed, the whole interaction is infused by a play on the theme of *sight*. "The whole event is an exercise in seeing right, not only for Jesse and his sons and the implied audience of the story, but also for Samuel, who was earlier designated a seer."[49] What Alter fails to see, however, is that this is not just a *literary* play on the theme of sight, but a *literal play* on the theme of sight, so that the audience—literal and implied, ancient and modern—learns to see as God sees ("with the heart") *along with Samuel*.[50] The narrator guides the tale from the perspective of Samuel, inviting the audience to see as he does, in order to tighten the empathetic connection between them so that by the end when Samuel learns what it means to see rightly, the audience's perception is similarly affected: "Rise. Anoint him, for this is the one" (v. 13).[51]

[49.] Alter, *Art of Biblical Narrative*, 149.

[50.] My decision to render 1 Sam 16:7 as "see with the eyes" and "see with the heart" is particularly relevant here, since the objective of the drama is, in large part, to develop in the audience *not* just the capacity to look *at* the right things (at someone's appearance or at someone's heart), but to *see rightly*, to see "with the heart."

[51.] The narrator—appropriately, I think—is not content to make it easy for the audience to see as God sees, however. The capacity to see beyond the limits of appearance is not a skill instantly developed. It requires practice and commitment and trust. The description the narrator provides of David in verse twelve, in fact, focuses on his *outward appearance* ("He was ruddy-faced with beautiful eyes and a goodly appearance"), and is the only justification offered for his anointing outside of God's imperative to Samuel to "rise and anoint." Notwithstanding David's size and birth order, the narrator does not provide evidence of what God may see in David's heart that makes him worthy of the kingdom. Alter is undoubtedly correct in offering the justification that David's appearance "happens to be joined with an inner nature made to do great things" (Alter, *Art of Biblical narrative*, 150), but that is an assumption born out by the rest of the David cycle. At this point the narrator demands our trust in this regard. The Bible's dramas are more committed to showing than telling; they reject easy answers and resist oversimplification. The invitation to those who see this drama of divine seeing unfold on stage is to be aware of the ways they have been

The following chapter, 1 Sam 17, is another good example of how contrasting points of view enlarge the audience's capacity to feel the tension, engage the story, and in the end be changed by it.[52] Goliath is introduced first. His appearance is described in detail by the narrator from the perspective of the Israelite army (vv. 4–7), but as is typical in biblical drama, he presents his perspective on his own terms. He does not mince his words. His perspective, which we could call "the power of the sword," does not require nuance to grasp:

> Why have you come out as an army to fight? Am I not the Philistine, and are you not servants of Saul? Chose for yourselves a man that he might come down to me. If he prevails against me in battle and strikes me down, then we will be to you as servants. But if I prevail against him and strike him down, then you will be to us as servants; and you will serve us. . . . I defy the armies of Israel on this day! Give me a man that we may fight together![53]

Goliath is supremely confident that there is no man in Israel who could defeat him in hand-to-hand combat, and so battle by proxy is a certain way to secure victory. His assumptions are affirmed as all of Saul's army trembles at his speech. The impact of Goliath's words is enhanced by the narrator's introduction describing the size and heft of his armor (vv. 4–7). Later on when David rushes to meet Goliath in the valley as the "man"[54] Israel has chosen to fight with him, Goliath again mocks

---

formed to see value and power in size and birth order (appearance), and to go and practice seeing as God sees.

[52.]The following description will not engage the albeit interesting debate on the relationship between 1 Sam 16 and 1 Sam 17, which each contain contradictory versions of how David (first) meets Saul. For one scholar's take on it, with emphasis on how each chapter is necessary to develop an appropriately complex characterization of David see Alter, *Art of Biblical Narrative*, 147–153.

[53.]1 Sam 17.8–10.

[54.]The narrator (momentarily adopting Goliath's point of view) describes how Goliath sees David (v. 42) not only as a נַעַר (*na'ar*, "boy, youth"), but also as אַדְמֹנִי עִם־יְפֵה מַרְאֶה (*'admony 'im-y'pheh mar'eh*, "ruddy [faced], with beautiful

Israel—and now David as well—and doubles down on the same perspective: "Am I a dog that you are coming at me with sticks? . . . Come on then, and I will give your flesh to the birds of the air and the animals of the field" (vv. 43–44).

In stark contrast to Goliath is the point of view of David, who engages Goliath (and others) with his own perspective, which echoes and subverts a number of elements in Goliath's speeches. David's perspective could be called "the power of the Lord." He, too, does not mince his words: "You are coming at me with a sword and with a spear and with a javelin, but I am coming at you in the name of the Lord of Hosts, the God of the ranks of Israel whom you have defied. On this day the Lord will deliver you into my hand . . . [F]or neither with sword nor spear does the Lord save, for the battle is the Lord's and he will place [all of] you[55] into our hand" (vv. 45–47).[56]

Saul's unenviable position of being "caught in the middle" of these two radically opposed perspectives adds complexity to the story by presenting a character that most people watching (then and now) can relate to, even without ever having been a king. Saul's pragmatic view is seen in various ways. He creates incentives for someone to rise up and fight Goliath,[57] he initially rejects David's offer to fight Goliath on the grounds that he has no training and is too young.[58] His options extinguished, Saul finally sends David off to fight without armor or weapons. Surely his army's defeat is assured, and Israel's fate as servants of the Philistines is equally as certain. He has given up. Anyone with enough moxie to go and fight gets his stamp of approval—even an

---

appearance"). In other words, the opposite of everything Goliath demanded from Israel. Not only was David *not* a man, but he was a pretty boy to boot. Saul and his army "defied" Goliath and his taunts too, but in a way nobody expected!

[55.]The second person pronominal suffix is in the plural in the Hebrew (v. 47).

[56.]Cf. vv. 26, 34–37.

[57.]"The man who strikes him down the king will greatly enrich, he will give him his daughter, and will exempt his father's house from taxes in Israel" (v. 25).

[58.]"You are not able to go up against this Philistine in battle! Indeed, you are just a boy (נַעַר, *na'ar*), and he has been a warrior since he was a boy (נְעוּרִים, *n'urim*)" (v. 33).

unarmed shepherd boy, too young to join the army in the first place. Saul's blessing to David drips with irony, or, perhaps, sarcasm: "Go! And may the Lord be with you!" (v. 37). Nothing in the immediate context suggests Saul is inspired by David's passionate speeches invoking the power of the Lord (vv. 26, 34–37, 45–47) and is now sending him off confidently to victory. Thus, Saul's perspective could be summarized as: "Bless the Lord but take a sword."

The narrator also has a perspective, and sometimes chooses to use that position to influence how certain characters are received. The conclusion of the story of David, Goliath, and Saul is one such occasion. There is very little dialogue after the climax when David proclaims to Goliath that the Lord's victory is at hand (vv. 45–47) and slings his smooth stone at Goliath's head (v. 49). Throughout the dénouement, the narrator ties up the loose ends of the foregoing drama, but chooses, instead, to leave some unraveled, by contrasting the image David presented of himself throughout the drama (to the Israelite troops, Saul, and Goliath), with an image of David now in flux at the end. The descriptions of Goliath's death and the state of David's hands contrast between verse 50 and verse 51. In verse 50 David's hands are empty ("and a sword there was not in the hand of David"), and the cause of Goliath's death was the stone David lodged in his head. By contrast, in verse 51 David now holds Goliath's sword ("and he took his sword"), and uses it "to kill" Goliath and cut off his head.[59] Does the battle belong to the Lord or to the sword?

The narrator further complexifies the matter of David's evolving point of view in verse 54. Goliath went from feared warrior to naked and headless. Israel went from certain death to stunning victory. How has David changed? On the one hand, this experience has changed everything about David's life. Not only have his fortunes changed (he will receive the spoils promised by Saul), not only has he been

---

[59.]The contradiction is not resolved by making recourse to the fact that David had said he would cut off Goliath's head (v. 46).

catapulted onto the national stage as the savior of Israel,[60] but he has also now killed another human being. The narrator subtly implies what immediate impact this experience had on David as a character. David took the head of Goliath to Jerusalem (v. 54), ostensibly to proclaim Israel's victory to the country, and to make sure everyone knew he was the victor. But Goliath's armor David keeps for himself (v. 54). Previously he was uncomfortable wearing armor (v. 39) and preferred the feel of his staff over a sword in his hand (v. 40). Perhaps now his perspective is changing. There is blood on his hands now—and a sword *in* them—and he keeps Goliath's armor for himself. Is the narrator foreshadowing what will become of David as king of Israel, the warrior king, the one who could not build the Temple because of the blood (of Goliath, of Uriah, and many others) on his hands?[61] This conclusion by the narrator subtly adds complexity to the characterization of David, casting a sliver of doubt on the fullness with which he embodied his earlier perspective ("the power of the Lord"), and situating him for a life in politics in which he will be required, as Saul was, to navigate the exigencies of the kingship.

Notwithstanding the foregoing, the fact and the means of David's victory serve as the composer's affirmation of the perspective David articulated throughout the drama ("the power of the Lord"). The subtle shift I am suggesting does not cast doubt on the Bible's affirmation of the battle belonging to the Lord; it casts doubt on the character of David as one who perfectly embodied that perspective. It is a more human portrayal of David as someone who is equal parts courageous, passionate, and flawed.

Movement and Gesture

The English word "theater" comes from the Greek word θέατρον (*theatron*), which is derived from the verb θεάομαι (*theaomai*)

[60.]Like many war heroes before him, his feats in battle are put to song. In the following chapter the women sing his praises ("Saul has struck down his thousands, and David his ten thousands!" (18:7)), and by doing so they infuriate Saul (18:8).

[61.]Cf. 1 Chron 22:8.

meaning "to see, perceive," and by extension "to visit." According to
Boogaart, "The theater is the seeing place, and seeing as well as hearing
is one of the ways we define a theatrical experience and distinguish it
from other similar experiences such as storytelling. The biblical texts
demand seeing as well as hearing; they require enactment. Their full
range of meaning is found on the stage not the page."[62] What is implied
in Boogaart's claim is certainly that silent reading is not sufficient to
bring a biblical drama to its fullest expression, but even a voice is
insufficient. What is needed is the partnership of voice *and body*. The
purposeful presence and movement of bodies on a stage fundamentally
changes the delivery and reception of the script, and has the potential to
bring out the fullness of meaning contained within it, which is often
glossed over in silent readings, however carefully conducted.

This is due in no small part to the role the body plays in
communication in general, and the role it plays in performance in
particular.[63] Israelite dramas, like all dramas everywhere, draw on the
presence and utility of the actors' bodies to tell the story. Movement and
gesture is what I am using to refer to the broad spectrum of nonverbal
communication that are inseparable from the spoken word in any kind
of communication event, and which receive a heightened sense of
purpose and focus in performance. The types of nonverbal actions
referred to by the shorthand "movement and gesture" includes but is not
limited to: gestures; movements of the limbs, hands, head, feet, and legs;
facial expressions; eye behavior (length and/or direction of gaze);[64]
posture; tone of voice (*how* the words are spoken); touching (oneself or

---

[62.]Tom Boogaart, "Israelite Theatre," Paper Presentation, Calvin Symposium on
Worship, Calvin College, Grand Rapids, MI, January 28, 2010.

[63.]"A list of all the situations in which nonverbal communication plays a
significant role would be almost endless, and would include areas such as dance,
theater, music, film, and photography." Knapp, Hall, and Horgan, *Nonverbal
Communication*, 27.

[64.]Interestingly enough, in at least one biblical drama a staring contest of sorts (the
direction and length of two characters' gazes) takes center stage as the narrator
provides explicit (if ambiguous) stage directions describing the tense and emotional
interaction between Elisha and Haza'el. Cf. 2 Kgs 8:7–15, esp. v. 11.

others), etc.[65] Reference to movement and gesture—nonverbal communication—is another way of describing the end toward which blocking decisions are made in preparation for performance.[66]

An excellent example of the centrality of movement and gesture can be found by returning to the climax of the story of David and Goliath in 1 Sam 17. After David proclaims the certainty of divine victory at his hand, he slings his stone and flings it at Goliath's head. The narrator describes the ensuing action this way: "And the stone sank into his forehead, and he fell on his face upon the earth" (v. 49). This action brings about the resolution of the conflict. Earlier, Goliath had laid out his terms this way: "If he prevails against me in battle and strikes me down, then we will be to you as servants" (v. 9). The meaning of the moment is not captured simply by the fact that Goliath is dead; it is the *manner in which* he dies that embodies the resolution of the conflict. This must be seen to be grasped. One would expect Goliath to fall backwards if struck hard enough in the face to have a stone lodge itself in his forehead. But the narrator is careful to say he fell forward, with his face "toward the earth" (אַרְצָה, *'artsah* "earthward," v. 49). Goliath embodies in his death the fulfillment of his declaration in verse 9; he collapses into a posture of servitude to David (and Saul), and a posture of worship to the God of Israel whom he had defied (see vv. 10, 26).

Another example that likewise involves a would-be power ending up face-down then decapitated before the God of Israel is found in 1 Sam 5. When the Ark of the Covenant is captured by the Philistines, it is brought before their god Dagon to humiliate it in its defeat. But their joy turns sour the following morning when they discover, upon entering the House of Dagon: "Behold! Dagon was fallen with his face to the earth before the face of the Ark of the Lord" (v. 4). Dagon, like Goliath, is paying homage to the Lord.[67] The priests' misery is compounded as the narrator adds irony to insult: the priests proceed to pick Dagon up and restore him to his pedestal. Again, this must be seen to be fully

---

[65.] Knapp, Hall, and Horgan, *Nonverbal Communication*, 13–14.

[66.] See Chapter 2.

[67.] Boogaart, "Israelite Theatre."

appreciated. The priests of Dagon carry the god they think is carrying them.[68] This is the foolishness of idolatry demonstrated in movement and gesture. The composer chooses to show rather than tell, and the showing requires bodies in order to be seen and understood.

Given the fact that nonverbal (embodied) communication plays such a considerable role in communicating meaning, movement and gesture also help to clarify meaning in less dramatic ways than in the examples from 1 Samuel above. Sometimes they are explicitly stated by the narrator, such as the reference to the facial contortions of king Nebuccadnezar in response to the defiance of Shadrach, Meshach, and Abednego.[69] Or the visible change that comes over Gehazi's body as he transitions from hurriedly stashing the silver and clothing he stole from Naaman—perhaps pausing to wipe the dust and dirt from his clothes— before taking his first nonchalant stride into Elisha's house, presenting a forced air of normalcy that everyone—the audience along with Elisha—have no trouble seeing through.[70] Another example is Abraham's pathos-laden response to Isaac's penetrating question: "Where is the lamb for the burnt offering?"[71] Embodying this response in a compelling way requires much from an actor. Abraham is a complex character in Genesis, and he cannot be portrayed adequately as a faithful robot. He is a loving father *and* a faithful God-fearer.[72] Abraham's response discloses a profound ambiguity. So much hangs in the balance of his answer. He weighs the fear of the unknown with the terror of the known even as he attempts to keep Isaac in the dark about the task before him. The words in Abraham's response, devoid of context, appear to present Abraham as positively confident in hope. But words do not exist in a vacuum; Abraham's face, body, hands, posture, tone of voice, and eye contact (or lack thereof) provide the means whereby

---

[68.]Boogaart, "Israelite Theatre."

[69.]Dan 3:19

[70.]2 Kgs 5:24–25.

[71.]Gen 22:7–8.

[72.]Cf. Gen 22:12. For a contrasting view on a similarly complex portrayal of Abraham in Genesis see the insightful analysis by Dana Fewell and David Gunn. Fewell and Gunn, "Abraham and Sarah," 90–100.

Abraham's words take on meaning. His proximity to Isaac, not to mention Isaac's nonverbal response(s) to Abraham also contribute to the meaning exchanged between them.

The above examples demonstrate how movements and gestures are carriers of meaning, giving visible and physical expression to the conflict in the story and helping bring it to its resolution. The significance of the actor's body as a locus of meaning in performance cannot be overstated, particularly in light of the profoundly disembodied state of the academic study of theology and the Bible in the West today.[73] For too long Western scholarship has assumed the words on the

---

[73.]In her insightful essay titled "Walking in the Truth: On Knowing God," Ellen Charry describes three epistemological crises that have widened the chasm between Christian theology as it was conducted historically (what she calls "sapiential" theology or sapiential knowing, which is the kind of theology that "joined knowing God to living rightly." (144)), and as it is conducted today. The result of the third (postmodernity) is not yet knowable because we are still in it, but the result of the first two were devastating to more embodied ways of knowing. For example, she argues: "Theology turned from an interest in the good life, and the wisdom that forms persons into it, toward a narrower positivist vision of truth as either correspondence to events and facts or the logic of ideas without remainder. In short, the practical, pastoral bent of classical (normal) theology was defeated by the need to refute the diversity of religious belief in the Middle Ages and later by the need to sustain Christianity in the face of secular sensibilities. These powerful forces effectively separated knowledge from the knower and knowledge from goodness. In the face of these forces the sapiential knowledge of God perished." Charry, "Walking in the Truth," 146. Dwight Conquergood critiqued a similar reality from a different perspective as he advocated for the place of performance studies within the academy. "The visual/verbal bias of Western regimes of knowledge blinds researchers to meanings that are expressed forcefully through intonation, silence, body tension, arched eyebrows, blank stares," etc. Conquergood, "Performance Studies," 146. The embodied way of knowing in performance studies offers a corrective to the "hegemony of textualism" (147). He offers a nuanced perspective on what is needed, and performance studies' role in this process, however. "The performance studies project makes its most radical intervention, I believe, by embracing both written scholarship and creative work, papers and performances. We challenge the hegemony of the text Cbest by reconfiguring texts and performances in horizontal, metonymic tension, not by replacing one hierarchy with another, the romance of performance for the authority of the text" (151).

page represent the end of a long road of meaning, and that the only body parts required to operate the vehicle that grants access to meaning along that road are eyes and brains—whether the attempt is to decipher the poetics of the Bible's narrative art or "excavate"[74] the history and development of Israelite religion. Hands are important too, but primarily for writing what the eyes see and the brain thinks. The paradigm shift biblical performance criticism calls for,[75] which understands the scholar's body as not only an essential aspect of the exegetical process, but also a means of revelation itself in performance, offers the academy one potential avenue for recovering a more embodied epistemology.

Conclusion

Part 1—Chapters 1–3—attempted to establish the foundation on which performance criticism is built, when what we know of the history of the people of Israel is set alongside what we know of their culture and the character of the texts they left us. Chapter 1 traced the genealogy of orality throughout the last century or so of Old Testament scholarship to draw attention to how recent research into the interplay between orality and textuality in Israel orients scholarship of the narratives along a trajectory toward performance. Chapter 2 proceeded along that same trajectory toward performance in three ways. First, the context of performance invites a reconsideration of the genre of the narratives, which I determined were, in fact, dramas, the scripts of ancient plays. Second was the recognition of a deficit within biblical studies concerning how to engage the narratives as dramas, and so I drew on the work of performance theorists and scholars beginning to articulate the contours of biblical performance criticism to help address this deficit. Finally, I offered a methodology for biblical performance criticism of Old Testament narratives that takes seriously the oral and performance context in which they were developed, which provides a way to "re-oralize" the dramas and leads to deeper readings of the scripts. Chapter 3 identified five essential elements of Israel's dramatic

---

[74.]This term is used by Alter in Alter, *Art of Biblical Narrative*, 13–14.

[75.]See Chapter 2.

tradition and offered brief examples of how those elements contribute to communicating meaning, and how sensitivity to them gives the interpreter access to meaning otherwise difficult to find.

Part 2—Chapters 4–6—will attempt to build up from this foundation by offering extended performance-critical interpretations of three dramas in the Elisha cycle found in 2 Kings: The Widow's Oil in 2 Kgs 4:1–7, Naaman's Healing and Gehazi's Greed in 2 Kgs 5, and the Bands of Aram in 2 Kgs 6:8–23. If the proof of the pudding is in the tasting, then these chapters will offer a taste of what a performance-critical approach to the narratives can reveal. They are, indeed, just a taste, for the entire serving is accessible only in a live performance. They are, perhaps, more like freeze-dried powder awaiting the addition of the remaining ingredients of actors, audience, and stage to complete the pudding recipe. Although the metaphor is, perhaps, overly dramatic (forgive me), the point is that a written description of a performance is but a shadow of the performance itself. One potential benefit, however, is that the written medium does provide the space in which to draw out and nuance elements of the performance that could be missed while viewing. Part 2 is dedicated to such an effort.

PART 2

THE FRUIT OF BIBLICAL PERFORMANCE CRITICISM

CHAPTER 4
THE WIDOW'S OIL: 2 KINGS 4:1–7

Introduction

This brief drama tucked away in the opening chapters of the Elisha cycle may seem to be a rather straightforward story in which Elisha helps a woman trapped in poverty to survive and thrive by the power of YHVH. However, biblical performance criticism reveals some of the gaps in the story, related to various elements of the plot as it unfolds in narration. For example, does Elisha first come to the woman in verse 1, or does she go out seeking the prophet? What is a faithful human response to the in-breaking of heaven through the miraculous? In various cases some of the essential commands Elisha makes on the woman are not narrated, but clearly must have taken place for the story to work. Additionally, biblical performance criticism highlights a somewhat ambiguous but critical group of participants in the drama: the neighbors. There is also the question of "Who is on stage?" at various points in the drama. For example, we discovered that, although the debt collector is explicitly mentioned only in verse 1, and is referred to by implication in verse 7, his role and "presence" is felt throughout the drama.

This story deals not only with someone stricken by poverty caused by unfortunate widowhood, but penetrates even deeper into the fundamental themes of life and death, threat and redemption, fear and faith. A unique challenge this drama poses is how to give concrete expression to these potentially abstract notions in a performance. This chapter is dedicated to demonstrating how performance can help one to understand the role of these elements in the narrative, how they can be expressed in ways that bring the narrative to life, so to speak, and how performance raises unique questions that lead the interpreter(s) to discover new meaning latent in the script.

A Translation for Performance

CONFLICT

Scene 1
[1]A woman, the wife of a member of the sons of the prophets, cried out to Elisha:

> *Your servant, my husband, is dead. And you know that your servant was one who feared the Lord. Now the debt collector has come to take away my two children to be his slaves!*

DEVELOPMENT

[2]Elisha said to her:

> *What can I do for you? Tell me, what have you in the house?*

She said:

> *Your servant has nothing in the whole house, except a single jar of oil.*

[3]He said:

> *Go. Borrow vessels from the streets, from all your neighbors.*
> *Empty vessels.*
> *Not just a few!*
> [4]*Enter your house and close the door behind you and behind your children. Pour into each and every vessel. When each is full, set it aside.*

CLIMAX

Scene 2

[5]She left Elisha. And she closed the door behind her and behind her children. They were bringing the vessels to her, and she was pouring. [6]When the vessels had all been filled, she said to her son:

> *Bring me another vessel!*

He said:

> *There are no other vessels!*

And the oil stopped.

RESOLUTION

Scene 3

[7]The woman went and told the man of God. He said:

> *Go. Sell the oil. Pay off your debt. You and your children will live on what is left over.*

Setting / Conflict (v. 1)

Second Kings 4.1–7 is aptly named "The Widow's Oil." As such a name suggests, it is a drama about death and life, grief and gladness, emptiness and fullness. The opening equilibrium is one of devastating loss, the effects of which reverberate throughout every aspect of the woman's life and family. The unnamed widow and her jar of oil consume the mind of the narrator from beginning to end. And it is her oil that occasions the drama's climax and eventually saves the woman and her children from the clutches of death and its consequences thereby securing for her sufficient resources to continue living long into the future.

The narrator introduces the principal characters in verse 1, namely, the woman and Elisha. We know nothing about the woman outside of

how the narrator introduces her. Her name is not provided, though
Elisha is identified by name; all we are given is her indirect relationship
to Elisha via her late husband who was a member of the "sons of the
prophets" (בְּנֵי הַנְּבִיאִים, *benei hanevi'im*). What we know of this group
comes from the sundry references to them throughout the book of
Kings.[1] They are generally poor, they married and had children, and
lived in their own quarters.[2] There were groups variously located in
Gilgal, Bethel, and Jericho[3] and with the exception of 1 Kgs 20.35–43,
Elisha is presented as the leader of these prophetic schools; he regularly
teaches them[4] and helps them solve a variety of internal issues.[5] The
only objective information provided about the woman by the narrator in
verse 1, therefore, is that she is poor, the wife of a member of Elisha's
prophetic guild, and she has come to Elisha with some kind of issue.[6]
The tension in and severity of her issue is anticipated by the narrator's
use of "to shout, call out" (צעק), a word generally used to cry out for
help or deliverance.[7]

The conflict is introduced immediately. "Your servant, my husband,
is dead" (v. 1). The woman speaks these words to Elisha herself. This is
an "extremely pertinent"[8] decision made by the composer for the
purposes of enhancing the emotive effect of the tension. "The widow is
the asking party; she is best qualified to plead her cause. Having as a

---

[1] 1 Kgs 20:35; 2 Kgs 2:3, 5, 7, 15; 4:1, 38; 5:22; 6:1; 9:1; and a reference in the
singular (בֶּן־נָבִיא) in Amos 7:14.

[2] *NIDOTTE*, s.v. "Prophecy."

[3] See esp. 2 Kgs 2.1–15, 4:38.

[4] 2 Kgs 4:38.

[5] 2 Kgs 6:1–7, another story in which Elisha works a miracle the effects of which
have significant economic implications for the individual involved.

[6] Targum Jonathan and Josephus (*Antiquities*, 9:47–48) both identify the woman
as the widow of the prophet Obadiah who secretly hid and provided food for 100
prophets to protect them from Jezebel, which Josephus postulates was the source of
his debts (Cf. 1 Kgs 18:3, 13). The connection is likely due to the fact that both are
described as ones who "feared the Lord" (יְרֵא אֶת־יהוה), though this identification
"need not be taken too seriously," so Hobbs, *2 Kings*, 50.

[7] *HALOT*, s.v. צעק.

[8] Fokkelman, *Reading Biblical Narrative*, 12.

spokesperson someone in distress lends dramatic impact to the opening and invites the reader to follow her with sympathy."[9] These are the first words of dialogue spoken by any character, and they immediately reveal the emotional and circumstantial depth of the woman's crisis. This is to be a story about death and widowhood.

The drama does not linger on the personal grief associated with tragic loss of life, however. The woman continues her outcry to Elisha: "And the debt collector has come to take away my two children to be his slaves" (v. 1). Instead of focusing solely on the personal effects of a loved one's death, this drama penetrates the places where personal tragedy intersects with politics, economics, and society, and considers how Israel's God is present in those dire and volatile circumstances.

The debt collector is the dramatic representative of the power of death in 2 Kgs 4.1–7. Or, to borrow Brueggemann's phrase, the creditor is the one through whom the "politics of death" are manifested at the expense of and without regard for the powerless widow.[10] Though the creditor is not responsible for the man's untimely death, his presence and activity in the wake of the tragedy—regardless of the extent to which he was, perhaps, just "doing his job"[11]—is presented as the embodiment of the forces of death now competing with the woman and her childrens' lives and livelihood. That this is true is made clear through a series of contrasts between life and death. The first is rhetorical and the second is spatial, and therefore performative. The first contrast, contained in the script itself, is voiced by the woman (v. 1) and

---

[9.]Fokkelman, *Reading Biblical Narrative*, 12. Cf. "The more the author wishes to make the story dramatic, the more he reduces the narration and allows the personae to speak for themselves." Amit, *Reading Biblical Narratives*, 51.

[10.]Brueggemann, "Culture of Life," 16–21.

[11.]"The creditor, for all we know, is not mean or rapacious. He is simply committed to the laws of the market whereby debts must be paid, collateral must be held, and defaults must be faced honestly and unflinchingly. Likely he intends the widow no ill…" Brueggemann, "Culture of Life," 17. See also Liethart, *1 & 2 Kings*, 186. Liethart borrows a similar phrase from Pope John Paul II to make the same point: "During the time of the Omrides, Israel is living in a *culture of death*, a result of the Omride devotion to dead idols, and death permeates the daily lives of the people of Israel" (emphasis added).

Elisha (v. 7) respectively. The woman's opening speech (v. 1) links the
theme of death to the debt collector's devastating threat by a causative
association ("... my husband is dead ... *and* the debt collector has
come...."). The theme is returned to in the drama's final words, spoken
this time by the prophet Elisha (v. 7), which together with the woman's
opening line form an *inclusio*: "Sell the oil. Pay off your debts. You and
your children will *live*." Elisha can only speak of "living" *after* the debt
has been paid off (v. 7).

A second contrast is revealed through the blocking of the story. In
one performance of this drama we chose to set the stage, so to speak,
with a silent montage, to provide the back story to the conflict and to
introduce the character of the debt collector. In this opening scene, the
debt collector enters from down-stage left[12] and approaches the woman
at center stage to collect the debt from her. Upon finding her finances
wanting he threatens to seize the children before retreating to up-stage
left, where he lurks throughout the drama until its closing scene.
Fokkelman, reflecting on the narrative from a purely literary
perspective, nevertheless anticipated this dramatic blocking when he
noted, at the end of verse 1, "the shadow of the creditor looms"
throughout the narrative.[13] In our performance his shadow is literally
cast across the stage where the woman and her children dwell in the
fragile security of their home, behind closed doors.[14] Elisha, on the other
hand, stands opposite the creditor up-stage right throughout the majority
of the drama. These two characters, each representing the powers of
death (debt collector) and life (Elisha), establish a horizontal axis along
which the tension of the drama runs. Exactly between them, at center
stage, is the woman's home, where she and her children cower as the

---

[12.]Stage directions are from the perspective of the *actors* looking out at the
audience. So the direction "stage left," from the perspective of the *audience*, is the
right-hand side of the stage. "Down-stage" is the location on stage closest to the
audience, and "up-stage" is located at the back of the stage, furthest from the audience.

[13.]Fokkelman, *Reading Biblical Narrative*, 12.

[14.]Another performance of this drama interpreted Elisha's insistence that the
woman "close the door" of her home as an act of security to keep out the creditor (vv.
4–5).

drama begins. She is caught in the crosshairs of the struggle between death and life, both literally and metaphorically.

The woman's existential crisis, deepened by the debt collector's threat of indentured slavery, functions as the point of intersection for all of the drama's characters: the woman, her children, Elisha, the debt collector, *and the woman's neighbors*, who have largely been overlooked as characters in this drama. Caeserius of Arles, preaching in the late fifth and early sixth centuries, was sensitive to the presence of the neighbors in the narrative, though he allowed them only an allegorical and anticipatory function: "[T]hose neighbors from whom she borrowed vessels prefigured the Gentiles."[15] Apart from the allegorical reading, the neighbors play a critical role within the drama *as characters*. First, the woman's neighbors failed to live into their mosaic responsibilities to provide care and support to her and her children, which could have helped avert her crisis. Second, they provided the means whereby the miracle could take place by lending the widow empty vessels—whether they did so generously, begrudgingly, or inadvertently is unclear. Finally, and most importantly—and least noticeably—their willingness to purchase the miracle oil in the end provided the means for her to repay her debts and "live on what is left over" (v. 7).

Commentators are quick to point out the legitimacy of the creditor's logic—to take the widow's sons as compensation for the debt—according to Mosaic Law, thereby absolving the community of responsibility. For example, Marvin Sweeney, citing Exod 21:1–11 and Deut 15:12–18, observes, "When a person is unable to repay a debt in ancient Israel or Judah, that person is subject to a legal form of debt slavery."[16] John Gray, while citing different passages,[17] nevertheless comes to the same conclusion, albeit toward more historical and comparative ends: "In permitting the enslavement of the children of a

---

[15.]Oden, *Ancient Christian Commentary*, 157.

[16.]Sweeney, *I & II Kings*, 288.

[17.]In addition to Exod 21:7, he adds Isa 50:1 and Neh 5:5.

debtor, Hebrew law in the Book of the Covenant is at one with the Code of Hammurabi."[18]

These, however, are not the only applicable texts from Mosaic Law. In addition to making allowances for indentured slavery to compensate for debts, the law also stipulated the community's responsibility to care for widows and orphans, and not to exploit their vulnerability. God self-identifies throughout Exodus and Deuteronomy as the one "who executes justice for the orphan and widow."[19] For example, Exod 22:21–22—the chapter directly following the reference cited above absolving the creditor's guilt—holds Israel to a higher standard of justice for the most vulnerable elements of Israelite society: "You shall not ill-treat any widow or orphan. If you do mistreat them, I will heed their outcry (צְעָקָה, tse'aqah) as soon as they cry out (צָעֹק יִצְעַק, tsa'oq yits'aq) to me."[20] Not incidentally, the same word is used by the narrator to describe the widow's outcry in 2 Kgs 4:1–7 as is used here in Exod 22 (צעק "cry out"). God is indeed hearing the outcry (צְעָקָה, tse'aqah) of the widow, through the medium of his prophet, Elisha, the man of God. "Slavery is sometimes required in ancient Israel as a mechanism for making restitution for property crimes, and an Israelite might also enter slavery to pay off a debt," grants Liethart.[21] He continues, "Though the widow pursues a legitimate legal option, her creditors act unjustly. Yahweh himself protects orphans and widows, *and Israel is to follow his lead*."[22]

On the heels of God's command to Israel not to ill-treat any widow or orphan come stipulations regarding the practice of usury:

> If you lend money to my people, to the poor among you, you shall not deal with them as a creditor; you shall not exact interest

---

[18.]Gray, *I & II Kings*, 492. See also Hens-Piazza, *1–2 Kings*, 250; Cogan and Tadmor, *II Kings*, 56; Liethart, *1 & 2 Kings*, 186; Seow, "First and Second," 186; and Buttrick, *Interpreter's Bible Commentary*, 204.

[19.]Deut 10:18, cf. Deut 24:17–22, NRSV.

[20.]JPS (1985).

[21.]Liethart, *1 & 2 Kings*, 186.

[22.]Liethart, *1 & 2 Kings*, 186, emphasis added.

from them. If you take your neighbor's cloak in pawn, you shall restore it before the sun goes down; for it may be your neighbor's only clothing to use as cover; in what else shall that person sleep? And if your neighbor cries out to me, I will listen, for I am compassionate.[23]

Brevard Childs, commenting on this passage, connects it to the plight of the widow in 2 Kgs 4:1.

> The stranger (*ger*) was vulnerable to wrong-doing because he lacked the protection of his clan. The widow and the orphan were exposed to violence without the support of husband and father.... The style shifts to the first person as God places himself directly in the role of special protector. The vicious nature of money-lending is more than clear from other references to the practice (cf. Lev. 25.35–37; Ez 23.20–21; I Sam. 22.2; II Kings 4.1; Ps. 109.11).[24]

Beyond the explicit biblical evidence, Hannelis Schulte argues that there was a general breakdown of the fabric of Israelite society happening throughout the northern kingdom during the ministry of Elisha, due to the overtaxation and generally oppressive policies of the Omride dynasty, which contributed to the widow's plight and may have

---

[23.]Exod 22.25–27, NRSV.

[24.]Childs, *Book of Exodus*, 478–9. James K. Mead also sees the creditor's actions as excessive: "Thus, while some commentators point out that the creditor of 4: 1 may have been within his rights...the rhetoric of the whole passage gives the reader the feeling that the creditor's cause is unjust...and that his treatment was harsh." Mead, "Elisha Will Kill?," 168. Similarly, "[T]he claim of the creditor on the debtor's demise to make good his loss from the children is felt to be unjust." Eichrodt, *Theology of the Old Testament*, 2:241. For a larger discussion of the relevant texts and historical context of slavery in both the ANE and OT context, see the articles "Slavery (ANE)" and "Slavery (OT)" both by M. Dandamayev in *ABD*, 4:58–62 and 4:62–65 respectively.

hindered the community from coming effectively—or willingly—to her aid. Schulte articulates the problem thus:

> The story of the woman who was supposed to hand over her two sons to a creditor indicates that old tribal ties offered no more protection (2 Kgs 4:1-7). Otherwise she would have been able to turn to her or her husband's kinship group, rather than to the man of God. Without a doubt clans were being broken up into smaller units at that time, into family units with their own land and homes. Even so, relatives would have helped those in distress, had poverty not assumed the upper hand in the agricultural realm, overtaxing the clan's ability to redeem debts.[25]

Harold Bennet concurs, suggesting that "this breakdown in the major kinship subgrouping devastated any extant social welfare systems for the relief of widows, strangers, and orphans."[26] In the case of the widow in 2 Kgs 4:1–7, either her neighbors are incapable of coming to her aid, or they refused to do so and were therefore complicit in the oppressive policies of the creditor and the larger economic and political system of which he is a representative. Either way, the community is not without some measure of culpability.

Nor is Elisha himself absolved of all responsibility. As Rentería has said, the widow "confronts Elisha and challenges him, reminding him that her husband feared Yahweh, undoubtedly a reference to the fact that he was a member of Elisha's close followers, and therefore his widow is entitled to the prophet's care."[27] Beyond the woman's expression of entitlement and beneath her implicit challenge to Elisha to resolve the issue is her appeal to YHVH: "And you know that your servant was one who feared the Lord" (v. 1). The woman approaches Elisha as YHVH's earthly representative and the leader of her and her husband's community, but her reference to her husband's "fear of the Lord" (יָרֵא, אֶת־יְהוָה *yare' 'et-YHVH*) also functions as an appeal to the highest

---

[25.] Schulte, "End of the Omride Dynasty," 140.

[26.] Bennett, *Injustice Made Legal*, 152.

[27.] Rentería, "The Elijah/Elisha Stories," 108.

power, and serves to frame the entire drama in an explicitly theological framework. This adds a layer of complexity to the horizontal axis established on stage through the positions of Elisha and the debt collector by introducing a vertical axis along which another, more fundamental tension runs. The woman is, in effect, asking the representative of YHVH if YHVH will live up to the promises that her religious community undoubtedly celebrates:

> Father of orphans and protector of widows
>   is God in his holy habitation. (Psalm 68:5)

> The Lord watches over the strangers;
>   he upholds the orphan and the widow,
>   but the way of the wicked he brings to ruin.
>   (Psalm 146:9)

The woman wants to know if YHVH will live up to the character their tradition teaches and puts the issue to Elisha with emotive force couched in respectful deference for his position.

It is no wonder the woman does this, for her situation is dire in the extreme. She has already lost much of what is dear to her, and now all that remains of her life and hope is hanging in the balance with the possibility of the debt collector returning at any moment to make good on his threat, which would complete the process that death began of emptying her life of all that makes it meaningful and rich. The tension between death and life is therefore worked out dramatically in the woman's life through the motif of emptiness and fullness. At this point in the drama death has left everything empty: her home, her kitchen, her cupboards, her bed, her bank account. And with the looming inevitability of her children entering indentured slavery, her future is also being poured out.

In order to establish the narrative context that compelled the woman to cry out to Elisha, and to honor the drama's tension as fully as possible, one performance group chose to begin with a series of tableaus, which also introduced the characters and their various circumstances and relationships. This silent introduction also served to engage the audience's interest and deepen their empathy for the widow and her children.

I have already described the initial blocking of the primary actors on the stage, save one important group: the neighbors. Standing around the edges of the stage, establishing its boundaries, are the woman's neighbors. In one of our performances, for purposes of symmetry and consistency, we had three neighbors: one at center stage left, one at center stage right, and one up-stage center. This arrangement establishes a geographic context in which to understand Elisha's use of "the streets" (חוץ, *chuts*, "outside," v. 3).

The series of silent tableaus that began our performance unfolded in the following way. The neighbors are in place around the perimeter, and the woman and her children are alone at center stage inside their home. Elisha and the creditor are in opposing corners down-stage (nearest the audience), creating an initial horizontal axis that will be recreated in opposing corners up-stage partway through the drama. The children, likely quite young,[28] rummage through the various storage containers in the house searching for food. Their search is unsuccessful. Meanwhile the widow attempts to comfort them and quiet their collective anxiety. Just then there is a loud knock at the door. When the woman opens the door she is confronted by the debt collector. He motions to the woman that he needs his money. In desperation she gestures that she has none and begs for mercy, falling to her knees. The debt collector moves past her, enters her home, briefly searches for anything of value, then motions to her children as the arranged price. She responds again by pleading for mercy, then pushes him toward the door. He leaves willingly, but it is clear he intends to return to take them; this is

---

[28.]Their age is uncertain. Nuances of the word *yeladim* (יְלָדִים) range from newborns, to weaned children, to teenagers, to youths, to young men old enough to serve in foreign courts, to descendants. *NIDOTTE*, s.v. יֶלֶד. Marvin Sweeney assumes a young age when he says "The woman is not to be taken by the creditor as a debt slave, but her two sons would be considered economically more viable *as they mature* over the coming six years." Sweeney, *I & II Kings*, 289, emphasis added. See also Eng, *Days of Our Years*, 74–87.

expressed by the simple gesture of pointing back at them as he walks away to assume his position up-stage left. The woman, knowing her time is now very short, locks her door and runs to Elisha.[29]

Development (vv. 2–4)

In biblical drama, conflict is developed primarily through dialogue, movement, and gesture. This story presents a complex and interesting combination of these elements that simultaneously develops the conflict, commands the audience's full attention, and subtly reveals the theological affirmations embedded in the drama's unfolding plot.

Of the 121 individual words in these seven verses, two-thirds of them (80) are direct speech, suggesting that this drama is dialogue driven; the composer gave control of (most of) the storytelling to the characters instead of the narrator. With the notable exception of verse 5, which is entirely devoted to narration—and is the climax of the drama[30]—the characters carry the plot and develop the conflict from its

---

[29.]This is, of course, only one possibility for how to block the scene. Here the accent falls on the desperate situation the woman is in, her inability to provide for the material needs of her children, and how the debt collector's arrival is the catalyst that sparks her pursuit of Elisha's help. Another possibility we have explored is to focus instead on the relationship between the woman and her neighbors. In this scenario the woman approaches each neighbor asking for help, and all turn their backs on her, unable or unwilling to provide the support she needs. After this, the debt collector comes, and it proceeds similarly. This blocking establishes a context for the woman's relationship with her neighbors that adds depth to her future interactions with them regarding the collection and eventual sale of the oil. The blocking described here could certainly be combined with the blocking described above, though timing and pacing are important, and the introductory tableaus should not be too long. The important element is that the tension is more fully introduced in ways that anticipate the specific details of dialogue and narration, and that the audience is prepared for and more fully drawn into the details of the plot than if the performance began with the opening words of the narrator in v. 1.

[30.]Although I would parse out the relationship between composition and narration differently than what Fokkelman assumes (see Chapter 3 on the Role of the narrator), he has nevertheless made an insightful point by remarking that the narrator, who "allocated for himself so few lines, has kept the core of the plot for himself after all." Fokkelman, *Reading Biblical Narrative*, 14.

introduction through to its resolution. Much of the narration in verses
1–4, 6–7 are merely cues to the actors of when it is time to speak, or
descriptions of actions the characters do. These descriptions are not
presented without intention, however.

Apart from a seven-word exchange between the widow and her
children in verse 6, which sets up a critical declaration by the narrator
("and the oil stopped immediately"), all of the dialogue is between Elisha
and the woman. Elisha's initial response to the woman (v. 2) is charged
with theatrical ambiguity. The lexical definition of each individual word
is clear, but *meaning* is contextual, and performance reveals the
ambiguity inherent in Elisha's question: "What can I do for you?" (מָה
אֶעֱשֶׂה־לָּךְ, *mah 'e'eseh lakh*). The meaning of his question is dependent
upon how the line is delivered and where the emphasis is placed. Is
Elisha testing the woman's resolve by asking "What can I do for *you*?"
Or, is he unsure of her plight and what his response should be and is
therefore buying time? ("*What* can I do for you?")[31] Is he, instead,
attempting to ferret out the full extent of her faith, asking her why she
has come to him, the man of God, and not to some other source of power
that could solve her problems? ("What can *I* do for you?") Perhaps in
reality it is a combination of several of these, and other possibilities
besides. In performance, the person embodying Elisha must interpret the
question, and communicate their conclusion through vocal and
nonverbal means. Elisha's question, however, is not met with a response.

The open-endedness of Elisha's question combined with the absence
of a response by the woman suggests there is a dramatic pause between
Elisha's first and second questions, further evidence of the dramatic
nature of these stories. The pause is charged with ambiguity and creates
space for character development. What fills the pregnant silence of that
moment? Does the woman throw up her hands in desperation,
communicating that she is at a loss, and had hoped *he* would know what
to do for her? Does she remain prostrate before him, hoping her silence

---

[31]Cf. 2 Kgs 4:27. When the Shunammite woman arrives at his home, seeking his
help for her dead child, Elisha reveals to Gehazi "[T]he Lord has hidden it from me,
and has not told me."

will force him to come up with something on his own? Our conclusion was to have Elisha's question embody compassionate presence on the one hand, and to push her toward deeper ownership of her crisis on the other. Her response was to remain silent, kneeling, face downward, waiting for Elisha to clarify his expectations. Receiving no reply, Elisha proceeds, though it remains unclear what he knows about the extent of her situation and if he yet has a plan for how to answer his own question.

Perhaps still buying time or searching for something to go on, Elisha poses a second question to the widow: "What have you in the house?" (‎[32]‏ מַה־יֶּשׁ לָךְ בַּבָּיִת, *mah yesh lakh babbayit*). The woman does not remain silent this time, but answers the question: "Your servant has nothing in the whole house, except a single jar of oil" (שֶׁמֶן אָסוּךְ, *'asukh shamen*). The woman's response is remarkable. It is succinct, straight to the point, honest, comprehensive, and displays appropriate deference for a woman in her position. Revell notes that the woman "uses the most self-effacing form in which request can be made. It thus expresses the greatest humility and by implication the greatest respect for the addressee."[33] We are led to believe she is being honest; nothing suggests we should conclude otherwise, and Elisha certainly believes her story of abject poverty and hopelessness.[34]

It is impossible to know precisely what kind of container is being referred to with the *hapax legomenon* אָסוּךְ (*'asukh*, "jar"). Further, it is

---

[32.]I will use the *qere* versions throughout. In this case, as Joüon and Muraoka have noted, throughout this passage the *ketiv* shows evidence of "some influence of the northern dialect," a process of "Aramaising" in the 2fs suffix: כִי- (vv. 2, 3, 7). Joüon and Muraoka, *Grammar of Biblical Hebrew*, 290. For the debate about the alleged Northern Dialect as reflected in the Elijah and Elisha stories, see, e.g., Schniedewind and Sivan, "The Elijah-Elisha Narratives," 303–37.

[33.]Revell, *Designation of the Individual*, 301.

[34.]This widow does not express her hopelessness quite as explicitly or emphatically as the widow of Zeraphath does to Elijah in 1 Kgs 17:12, but one can nevertheless feel her hopelessness leak out of her speech. Indeed, her first word is אֵין (the particle of negation, "there is not"), which seems to be where her focus is. Her last two words, "jar of oil" (שֶׁמֶן אָסוּךְ), name her only possession, apparently an afterthought, barely worth mentioning—not unlike a small collection of loaves and fish—since the "whole house" is empty.

impossible to know what precise type of oil filled it, and what function it served in the life of the woman and her family, and eventually in the larger community. Any conclusion is tentative and conjectural. The following description details the two primary options.

The first option is based on etymology. The *Hebrew and Aramaic Lexicon of the Old Testament* (HALOT) identifies the root of אָסוּךְ (*'asukh*) as the verb סוּךְ "to grease oneself with oil only for the cosmetic treatment of the body" or "to anoint someone."[35] In each case[36] the verb (סוּךְ) has cosmetic connotations in which the face or body is anointed with oil to make one more presentable, often as part of a beautification process. This oil would have been scented with spices and was ubiquitous in the ancient world, used by rich and poor alike.[37]

Two brief examples will illustrate the function of this oil. The Lord, speaking through the prophet Ezekiel to Jerusalem, likens Jerusalem's unfaithfulness to a hypothetical birth narrative in which Jerusalem was a child left for dead by Amorite and Hittite parents. The Lord approached the infant, cleaned it up, and empowered it to live. The baby grew into a woman "at the age for love"[38] at which time the Lord came and found her again, covered her nakedness, committed himself to her, washed her, anointed her (סוּךְ), and then clothed her with fine fabrics, adorned her with ornaments, jewelry, piercings, and a crown. The anointing functions as part of this larger process of the woman moving from shameful nakedness to adorned beauty.[39]

In Ruth 3, Naomi hatches her plot for Ruth to receive the favor of Boaz at the threshing floor, instructing her daughter-in-law to wash,

---

[35.]*HALOT*, s.v. סוּךְ.

[36.]Cf. Deut 28:40; Ruth 3:3; 2 Sam 12:20 (this is a conjectural reading, it appears in BHS as the only instance of the Hifil, and means "to anoint oneself"), 2 Sam 14:2; 2 Kgs 4:2; 2 Chr 28:15; Ezek 16:9; Dan 10:3; Mic 6:15 (these examples all in the Qal); Exod 30:32, the Hofal "be anointed."

[37.]"Perfumes and cosmetics were worn by both men and women, rich and poor, in ancient Israel. Practically everyone used scented oils to mask offensive odors and to protect the skin from the dry heat and the bright sun." King and Stager, *Life in Biblical Israel*, 280.

[38.]Heb. עִתֵּךְ עֵת דֹּדִים, "your time [was] the time of lovers," Ezek 16:8.

[39.]Heb. וַתִּיפִי בִּמְאֹד מְאֹד, "And you were very, very beautiful," Ezek 16:13.

anoint (סוּךְ) herself, and put on clothing, which many translations contextually interpret as Ruth's "good" or "best" clothes.[40] Again, anointing is here used as part of a process of making oneself socially presentable. "To be able to put on oil was apparently considered an integral part of looking and being at one's best."[41] The derivative nominal אָסוּךְ ('*asukh*), then, could have been a bottle that contained the oil used for such cosmetic purposes.

The multiplication of this oil by the prophet would lend an air of superficiality to the miracle that I find difficult to sustain, even though it was a value-added product that would sell at a good price, and may have shared some of the liturgical significance of holy oil.[42] Further, it is unlikely the woman would have kept a valuable jar of oil in the home given the circumstances; this interpretation would cast unnecessary doubt on the genuineness and urgency of her plight.

A second option is to consider the jar a small container of pure olive oil, which was likewise ubiquitous throughout ancient Israel and was used for a wide variety of purposes, both domestic and sacred. Olive oil (שֶׁמֶן) had an array of essential life-sustaining functions, and was "a staple of life and an important crop"[43] throughout the biblical period. It was used as "a dietary staple, medicine, and fuel for ceramic lamps; as a base for cosmetics, perfumes, and oils; and in ritual contexts, such as the anointing of kings at their coronation, as libation offerings, and as fuel for sanctuary lamps."[44] It was a desirable commodity throughout the Ancient Near East since it was an everyday product, and could therefore be sold on the international market (Ezek 27:17), included as part of a nation's tribute (Hos 12:1 [2 Heb]), or used as payment for another nation's services (1 Kgs 5:11 [25 Heb]). It was even applied to

---

[40.]Cf. NRSV, TNIV, and NASB "best"; CJB "good"; JPS "dress up" (v. 3).

[41.]*NIDOTTE*, s.v. סוּךְ.

[42.]Johs. Pederson makes a loose connection between the mixture of oil "used in everyday life for beautification by anointment" to both the holy incense with which it shared a "similar refinement," and also the "holy oil for anointment" which also "came to be made from a certain recipe." Pedersen, *Israel*, IV: 357.

[43.]*NIDOTTE*, s.v. שֶׁמֶן.

[44.]King and Stager, *Life in Biblical Israel*, 97.

leather to keep it from drying and cracking (2 Sam 1:21).[45] Israel and its neighbors had an oil economy just like many countries throughout the modern world do.[46]

This great diversity of potential uses of olive oil creates interesting interpretive possibilities that I believe favor it as the oil that filled the אָסוּךְ ('asukh), rather than a mixed blend intended for cosmetic purposes. That the oil could have multiplied from a small jar that was little more than an afterthought to the woman into vessels that spread throughout the woman's entire community, silently sustaining their lives by lighting lamps, healing wounds, and filling bellies lends the miracle both practical and theological significance. Further, in this story's counterpart in the Elijah cycle (1 Kgs 17:8–16) the widow of Zarephath has pure olive oil, which she used for cooking (v. 12). This correspondence does not demand an interpretation of pure olive oil in 2 Kgs 4:1–7 but does make it the more likely possibility.

Elisha's response to the woman's acknowledgment that she had some oil is as unexpected as it is full of gaps. It moves the plot in unforeseen directions and poses particular challenges to the interpreter. Many of Elisha's commands to the woman in verses 3–4 receive no narrative fulfillment. The most glaring occurrence of this happens in the break between the end of verse 4 and the beginning of verse 5. Verses 3–4 contain Elisha's list of seven commands to the woman: "go" (לְכִי, lekhi), "ask for vessels" (שַׁאֲלִי־לָךְ כֵּלִים, sha'ali-lakh kelim), "not just a few" (אַל־תַּמְעִיטִי, 'al-tam'iti), "enter" (וּבָאת, uvat), "shut" (וְסָגַרְתְּ, vesagart), "pour" (וְיָצַקְתְּ, veyatsaqt), and "set aside" (תַּסִּיעִי, tassi'i). In verse 5 the narrator reports only that the woman fulfilled three of those commands ("and she went" (וַתֵּלֶךְ, vattelekh), "and she shut" (וַתִּסְגֹּר, vattisgor), "[she was] pouring" (מוֹצֶקֶת, motsaqet)). The most essential

---

[45.]*NIDOTTE*, s.v. שֶׁמֶן. Apparently this use became so common that to "oil the shield" became an idiom for "to make war" (Cf. Is. 21.5). *Jewish Virtual Library*, s.v. "Oils,"
http://www.jewishvirtuallibrary.org/jsource/judaica/ejud_0002_0015_0_15052.html (accessed October 2, 2013).

[46.]As a colleague of mine once reflected, "They had olive oil; we have crude oil, but oil means the same thing to both of us." Boogaart, "Vessels."

command for the success of the miracle is not reported: collecting the vessels.[47] However, since the narrator later describes how she pours the oil (מוֹצֶקֶת, *motsaqet*), and then asks her son to fetch "another vessel" (עוֹד כֶּלִי, *'od keli*, v. 6), the clear implication is that she does, in fact, collect the vessels.[48]

The interplay between prophetic command and unnarrated obedience in this critical scene sets up an expectation that the woman obeys Elisha not only with respect to collecting vessels, but she obeys Elisha in everything, whether or not her obedience is reported: "Her obedience to the man of God is constant," observes Hobbs.[49] A performance of this passage must portray the fulness of the woman's obedience. The woman cannot simply leave Elisha's presence and walk immediately into her house, her arms magically filled with empty vessels. Were she able to do so she would undoubtedly not have needed the prophet's assistance! Performance is a necessary means for bringing out the latent dimensions of the plot not recorded in the final script.

Enacting the fullness of the woman's obedience does not compromise the integrity of the narrative selection. By reporting on only three of Elisha's seven commands to the woman, the narrator focuses the audience's attention on what will become a central motif of the drama, and a critical theological affirmation. This affirmation is embedded in the interplay between the miracle conducted behind closed doors, and the ultimate distribution of the oil throughout the community. I will return to this theme in detail below.

[47.]Fokkelman is certainly right to suggest that the narrator is selective about what actions to narrate, but is uncharacteristically uncreative in his conclusion as to why only the specifically chosen actions are reported: "The writer can then decide dutifully to report the execution of all seven instructions in v. 5, but that would be rather boring . . . ." Fokkelman, *Reading Biblical Narrative*, 13.

[48.]As Cogan and Tadmor point out, the ancient interpreters of the Hebrew Bible into Greek struggled with this apparent oversight; the Lucianic recensions of the LXX contain the addition "and she did so" following "And she went" in v. 5. The addition is unnecessary, however, since "the ellipsis in MT is not unusual and can be maintained." Cogan and Tadmor, *II Kings*, 56.

[49.]Hobbs, *2 Kings*, 46.

The actor is presented with a range of possibilities as to how to fulfill Elisha's command to collect the vessels, each with slightly different accents. One particularly effective option is to insert dramatic pauses into Elisha's speech to the woman in verses 3–4 in which she fulfills each series of commands immediately upon hearing them. Elisha says "Go. Borrow vessels from the streets, from all your neighbors. Empty vessels." and the woman promptly responds by walking directly to the closest neighbor, standing center-stage right, and proceeds to begin collecting the vessels from each of them in turn. An implication of this interpretation is that Elisha travels throughout the "streets" (חוּץ, *chuts*) with her, accompanying her to her neighbors' homes, his presence serving as an incentive to the community to oblige the widow's request if, say, a neighbor is hesitant or initially unwilling to be compassionate or generous toward the woman. Elisha's word takes on added meaning in this context, telling the woman in the earshot of her neighbor to collect "not just a few" (אַל־תַּמְעִיטִי, *'al tam'iti*) empty vessels. After the collection process is complete Elisha gives his final instructions (v. 4).

There is, perhaps, a small grammatical indication that the above interpretation—in which the woman collects the vessels in real-time as Elisha elaborates his instructions to her—is the intended one. In Elisha's final set of instructions he refers to the vessels the woman is to pour the oil into (lit. "over" עַל וְיָצַקְתְּ, *veyatsaqt 'al*), followed by the demonstrative adjective, "all of *these* vessels" (כָּל־הַכֵּלִים הָאֵלֶּה, *kol-hakkelim ha'eleh*), possibly indicating that the vessels have already been collected and are in Elisha's vicinity for him to refer to with the demonstrative "these."[50] In this scenario the widow collects the vessels without knowledge of Elisha's plan. The emphasis would therefore fall on her blind obedience. It also puts the narrator's report of her entering

---

[50] The demonstrative could also take the initial use of "vessels" as its referent in v. 3 (שַׁאֲלִי־לָךְ כֵּלִים "borrow vessels"). When זֶה (or the plural אֵלֶּה) is used, "what it refers to can be pointed to, whether actually or mentally" (Joüon and Muraoka, *Grammar of Biblical Hebrew*, 531). They cite 2 Kgs 4:3 in the section on the demonstrative, but do not clarify if the referent was being pointed to "actually" or "mentally" (534).

her home and shutting the door in sharper relief as it does not compete with the widow collecting the vessels. This was our interpretation.

Another option is to have Elisha speak his entire set of instructions (all of vv. 3–4), then the woman leaves his presence with full knowledge of what she is collecting the vessels for as she moves from home to home making her repeated requests. The emphasis in this scenario would be on the woman's *faithful* obedience, having already been told the extraordinary plan in its entirety.[51]

Either way the scene is played, one thing becomes visible as the woman (likely with her children in tow, to keep them close by) wanders the streets, carrying an ever-increasing collection of empty vessels from home to home. Elisha is making a living parable out of the woman's life; as the burden of empty vessels increases, the irony deepens simultaneously. The death of her husband and threat of slavery for her children has left the woman as empty as her house, as empty as one of the vessels she carries. The woman and the vessel are one and the same. In the end it is unclear which is the greater miracle, filling the vessels with oil or filling the woman with life and vitality again. This symbolism is latent in the script, the full impact of it can only be drawn out through performance.

Once the vessels are gathered, their destination is the woman's home. Once inside, the narrator's emphasis falls on the privacy Elisha instructed the woman to create, symbolized in the shutting of the door "behind her and behind her children" (בַּעֲדָהּ וּבְעַד בָּנֶיהָ, *ba'adah uv'ad baneiha*, v. 5). Several commentators note the peculiarity of the narrator's repetition of the closed doors, but offer little to no comment on what it may mean.[52] The interpretive key to unlocking the meaning

---

[51.]Hobbs would likely favor this interpretation as he comments on the presence of miracles throughout 2 Kgs 4, and the interpretive challenge they present the historian, saying "properly seen, such miracles are the results of faith, not the inspiration of faith." Hobbs, *2 Kings*, 54.

[52.]Cf. Hobbs, *2 Kings*, 50; Fretheim, *First and Second Kings*, 147; Hens-Piazza, *1–2 Kings*, 251. Sweeney, *I & II Kings*, 287, 289. Sweeney understands the motif to function on two levels. First, it functions to connect 2 Kgs 4:1–7 with the following narrative, 2 Kgs 4:8–37 as the motif occurs in both dramas (vv. 4, 5, 21, 33). Secondly,

of the narrator's emphasis is, I believe, the interplay between action and
gesture brought out in performance, particularly between the woman
and her neighbors in the concluding scene in the drama, which provides
the context in which the private-public dialectic plays itself out. I will
return to this theme at the end.

Climax (vv. 5–6)

The woman and her children are now cramped in their home, which is
full of "not just a few" empty vessels. Imagine the scene. The woman
and her children on one side, the empty vessels piled up on the other,
filling the space with their emptiness and assailing her and her אָסוּךְ
(*'asukh*) with mocking silence. As the night is darkest just before the
dawn, so too the tension peaks just before the climax when the outcome
is in doubt and the fate of the woman and her children hangs in the
balance between the oil and the vessels. But the woman, again, obeys
the word of Elisha and begins to pour the oil into the first vessel.

The miracle is described with the "remarkable suggestiveness of the
Bible's artistic economy."[53] No elaboration is given as to the mechanics
of the miracle. No account is rendered as to how long it took to fill all of
the vessels from just a small jar. No description of the woman or her
children's response is offered. The narrator's use of the participles
"bringing" (מַגִּשִׁים, *maggishim*) and "pouring" (מוֹצֶקֶת, *motsaqet*),
however, does point to two distinct realities, both of which are made
manifest in performance. First, as Joüon and Muraoka have noted, the
sequence of two participles signals "two durative actions" happening
simultaneously and continuing over time.[54] Performance is uniquely

---

and almost as an afterthought, he adds "The closed door suggests the miraculous nature
of the event" (289). Similarly, Rofé identifies the shutting of the doors, along with
several other motifs throughout the Elisha cycle, as "instances of magic practices of
different kinds." Rofé, "Classification," 427–440. Cohn offers a helpful insight,
contrasting the "public prophecy" Elisha delivered in 2 Kgs 3 with the miracle in 2
Kgs 4:1–7 which, as Elisha has designed it, is "shrouded in secrecy," so that the
"neighbors, who have lent the woman their vessels, cannot see" it. Cohn, *2 Kings*, 25.

[53.]Alter, *Art of Biblical Narrative*, 122.

[54.]Joüon and Muraoka, *Grammar of Biblical Hebrew*, 623.

suited to simultaneous action. For example, in verse 5 the children bring their mother empty vessels and store the filled ones (הֵם מַגִּשִׁים אֵלֶיהָ, *hem maggishim 'eleha,* "they were bringing to her") while she is busy pouring (וְהִיא מוֹצֶקֶת, *vehi' motsaqet,* "and she was pouring"). Other media could perhaps intimate and suggest simultaneous action, but only drama can manifest such activity in the service of plot, characterization, and the development and resolution of conflict.

In the second place, the use of the participle signals a dramatic slowing of the pacing of the scene. Pacing is an essential element of effective theatre, and the narrator is here controlling the pacing by bringing all of the focus on to the action as it is in the process of happening. "[T]he direct objects of both the 'bringing' and the 'pouring' have been left out. This double ellipsis of vessels and oil is significant: in this way, our undivided attention is directed toward the action itself, its long duration, and the cooperation between the widow and her boys."[55] Similarly, Richard Nelson suggests the woman's "act of borrowing jars is not reported, as the plot has been stripped down to its core, but a contrasting interest in the details of their filling throws the emphasis on the miraculous process itself."[56]

The role of the narrator, as described in Chapter 3, was to facilitate the connection between the story and the gathered congregation. Like a shaman, the narrator straddled two worlds—the past and the present— and it was the narrator's responsibility to ensure that these two worlds collided in such a way that facilitated the congregation's communion with the story being made present through performance. This unique role sets the narrator apart from the other characters in the drama who are confined to its boundaries and speak only to each other. The narrator, however, never speaks directly to the other characters, but tells the story to the audience or congregation. Further, this relationship between narrator and congregation, when coupled with the narrator's

---

[55] Fokkelman, *Reading Biblical Narrative,* 14.
[56] Nelson, *First and Second Kings,* 171.

omniscience,[57] creates the possibility of the narrator intimating or representing the role played by God which is implied in the script.

This climactic scene is one such possibility. The word of Elisha anticipates the miracle by articulating to the woman what she is to do with the vessels she collects. The prophet does not, however, imagine that his word is the power that animates the miracle. Rather, in the mind of the prophet, the miracle is made possible by the grace and power of the God in who's service he stands continually.[58] This perspective is assumed by the storyteller, though not explicitly articulated (for instance, by inserting the phrase "according to the word of the Lord"). In our performance the narrator began the scene by ushering the congregation beyond the walls and closed doors into the home of the widow at the moment the miracle is manifested. This happens through a simple movement. The narrator begins by entering the space on stage defined loosely as the woman's home just after saying "And she closed the door behind her and behind her children." By the time the woman and her children are situated in the house, preparing to begin pouring, the narrator is standing directly above the kneeling widow. From this position on stage the narrator can both describe the scene from the point-of-view of the woman and also embody the divine source of the multiplication. At the same moment the words "And she was pouring" (וְהִיא מוֹצֶקֶת, vehi' motsaqet) are spoken, the narrator—standing directly above the woman who begins miming the action of pouring oil into a vessel—opens both hands—fingers down, palms out, one hand higher than the other—suggesting a vertical flow descending from above the woman, through the narrator's outstretched hands, through the אָסוּךְ ('asukh) she is holding, and into the vessel over which she is pouring.

[57.]Cf. Sternberg, *Poetics of Biblical Narrative*, 85. "[T]he narrator speaks with the authority of omniscience." Though there is some debate on the precise nature of the narrator's omniscience, no one claims the narrator is ignorant of the details of the story being told, even when those details include intimate knowledge of God's thoughts and intentions.

[58.]Cf. 2 Kgs 3:14, 5:16.

Elisha's earlier instructions to the woman (v. 4) add further evidence of a divine presence in this moment. Here Elisha creates an "unusual"[59] pairing by using the preposition "upon" with the verb "pour" (וְיָצַקְתְּ עַל, *veyatsaqt 'al*) with respect to filling the empty vessels. Hobbs observes that this "combination is used for the practice of anointing"[60] and is unexpected in this context. In addition to a context of anointing, the pairing is employed to describe the act of pouring "over" an object that cannot be filled. For example, in 1 Kgs 18:34, while confronting the priests of Baal, Elijah instructs the people to fill four jugs (כַּדִּים, *kadim*) with water and pour (יצק) them over (עַל, *'al*) the altar wantonly, to soak it thoroughly. In Isa 44:3 YHVH promises to pour (יצק) water out upon (עַל) the thirsty land. The only use of יצק עַל that comes close to the present instance is Lev 14:15, part of the description of the purification rite for those healed of leprosy. During the ritual the priest pours oil *into* (עַל) his left hand, filling it like a bowl to hold the oil for use throughout the rite. Each of these examples testify to divine presence and symbolize divine activity. Elisha does not tell the woman to pour the oil wantonly over the array of collected vessels, but frames her act of pouring in a theological context by drawing on the language of anointing in his instructions for this deeply significant act.

The narrator does not reveal the woman's or her children's reaction to the miracle in words, though a performance cannot avoid presenting their interpretation of the gravity of the event nonverbally. As I suggested above, the first vessel is fraught with the greatest degree of tension. The mother kneels, holding the אָסוּךְ (*'asukh*), and one child brings the initial vessel. Does she pour immediately? Does she pause briefly, allowing the silence of the moment to speak of the paradox of her profound emptiness being met by an equally profound faith? Does she look at both of her children for strength, drawing life from their faith? Does she shrug her shoulders before she begins with a sort of

---

[59.]Hobbs, *2 Kings*, 50.

[60.]Hobbs, *2 Kings*, 50. Hobbs identifies Lev 2:1, 6 and 2 Kgs 9:3, though examples abound of יצק על being used in the context of anointing (Cf. Gen 28:18, 35:14; Exod 29:7; Lev 21:10; Num 5:15; 1 Sam 10:1).

"Well, let's see if this works" attitude? As she begins to pour, all of the tension she held in her body, multiplied by the tension held by the audience, is released in joy and amazement. The joy and exultation of the scene confirms to the woman and her children that YHVH does, in fact, fulfill YHVH's promises, which seemed to hang in the balance at the beginning of the drama.[61]

The climactic scene concludes with a masterful bit of storytelling. The widow, fully absorbed by the task of pouring and filling has not noticed that their stock of empty vessels has disappeared. "Bring me another vessel" she demands, the urgency in her voice rising in concert with the oil level in the final vessel as it approaches the lip of the container; she does not want any time or oil to go to waste. The first word of the child's response "there is not" (אֵין, 'ein) echoes the widow's pathetic response to Elisha in verse 2, only now with the opposite effect: it is not that the house is empty because "there is nothing" in it, but rather there is nothing *empty* left in the house save the אָסוּךְ ('asukh) itself, now drained to the bottom of its miraculous contents. The oil from the אָסוּךְ has not only filled all of the vessels, which themselves likely fill her "whole house," but the woman's heart and hope has been (re)filled as well. The child's straightforward honesty breaks any tension that may remain, or may have been introduced by the woman's urgency: "there is no other vessel" (אֵין עוֹד כֶּלִי, 'ein 'od keli, v. 6). Moreover, it acts as a dramatic segue for the narrator to report the end of the miraculous flow, "And the oil stopped" (וַיַּעֲמֹד הַשֶּׁמֶן, vayya'amod hashamen, v. 6).[62] The אָסוּךְ has fulfilled its divine purpose and now sits empty on the floor in dramatic contrast to the rows of filled vessels,

---

[61] Cf. Pss 68:5, 146:9.

[62] This instance of "oil" (שֶׁמֶן) as subject of the verb "stand still" (עָמַד) is unique to this verse. There are two other instances of liquid ("water" מַיִם) "standing still," in Jonah 1:15 and Josh 3:13, 16. The basic meaning appears to be that of an object in motion coming to rest. One wonders if its unusual use here in 2 Kgs 4 is intended to, however fleetingly, call to mind two other miracles in which people are saved from impossibly desperate situations: the crossing of the Jordan (Josh 3) and the sailors' deliverance from the storm (Jonah 1).

indicating that abundance does not necessarily mean excess. There is no miracle oil remaining in her jar to save for future use.

Resolution (v. 7)

Now that the miracle is complete the woman wastes no time; she returns immediately and directly to Elisha to report on what transpired, and (likely) to solicit advice for how to move forward since the threat on her children has not yet been assuaged. The narrator, more interested in pressing forward to tie up the drama's loose ends, does not supply the woman with any dialogue to summarize her experiences inside the house. Instead, the narrator breezes by her report in two words: "And she went" (וַתֵּלֶךְ, *vattelekh*), "and she told" (וַתַּגֵּד, *vattagged*). Here the narrator refers to Elisha not by his proper name, as he did in verse 1, but by "his primary quality of 'man of God.'"[63]

Elisha's response to the woman concludes the drama's script. It is an interesting choice on the part of the narrator to give Elisha the last word.[64] This conclusion creates a beautiful symmetry—an *inclusio*—ending on the same theme with which it began, this time as with the first, voiced by the principal character uniquely situated to speak it.[65]

The expectation of implied obedience on the part of the woman to Elisha's commands, established in verses 3–6 above, suggests the prophet's final commands (v. 7) are likewise obeyed promptly, and in full. Elisha begins by instructing the woman to "go" (לְכִי, *lekhi*), just as he did the first time she came to him (v. 3). Elisha wants the woman to be clear that though the God her late husband feared (v. 1) acts in power to transform circumstances, she is not absolved of responsibility to

---

[63.]Fokkelman, *Reading Biblical Narrative*, 16. Cf. "Symmetrically, the scene ends as it began with the woman presenting herself before Elisha, now called a 'man of God.'" Cohn, *2 Kings*, 26.

[64.]Fokkelman, *Reading Biblical Narrative*, 12.

[65.]"[Elisha's] speeches in vv. 3–4 and 7 offer the solution to the pressing problem, so it is appropriate to grant him the last word. In this way, alternating the speakers creates a balance between the opening and the ending: the woman opens; the prophet closes." In Fokkelman, *Reading Biblical Narrative*, 12.

participate in the unfolding of the transformation. This is a theme of Elisha's throughout the dramas contained in 2 Kgs 4.[66]

Elisha's second command is to "sell the oil" (מְכְרִי אֶת־הַשֶּׁמֶן, *mikhri 'et-hashamen*, v. 7). The practical application of the miracle for the woman's crisis is now made clear: the miracle oil will generate the necessary capital to pay off her debts. But whether she gathered enough vessels to secure her future remains to be seen. The most logical and likely option for the widow is to return to the very neighbors from whom she borrowed the empty vessels in order to return them, now filled with miracle oil, for a profit. This is the interpretive key performance provides to unlock the mystery of the closed (and locked) doors: the oil, multiplied in private, now goes public, spreading throughout the community, infiltrating their homes, their lives, and their bodies with the anonymous grace of God.

In performance the woman responds immediately to Elisha's command to "sell" by returning—her arms now full of full vessels—to each of her neighbors to sell the oil. After the initial confusion registers on the face of each subsequent neighbor, they all receive the oil and dutifully pay her for it. They will likely never purchase better oil again.[67]

Once the woman finishes selling the oil there is just one command remaining for Elisha to give. He tells her: "pay off your debts" (וְשַׁלְּמִי אֶת־נִשְׁיֵךְ, *veshallemi 'et-nishyekh*, v. 7). Occasionally biblical narrators will infuse a closing moment with a final bit of tension which puts the resolution achieved in the climax in doubt. This is the case in this moment.[68] After Elisha's words fade into silence, the woman slowly

---

[66.]Cf. v. 41 "Serve the people and let them eat," and v. 42, 43 "Give it to the people and let them eat" (NRSV).

[67.]There are distant echoes of Jesus' first miracle reported in John's gospel here in which Jesus turns water into wine (John 2:1–12) in which the steward remarks to the groom, "Everyone serves the good wine first, and then the inferior wine after the guests have become drunk. But you have kept the good wine until now" (v. 10). Interestingly enough, as Hobbs reports, "Some of the Peshitta MSS regard this as a miracle of turning water to oil." In Hobbs, *2 Kings*, 50.

[68.]Another example of this from the Elisha cycle is 2 Kgs 2:13–14. When this scene is performed it becomes clear that Elisha must strike the Jordan twice and cry out to "the Lord God of Elijah" between the two strikes, casting a brief shadow of

turns and faces the creditor, who's shadow has "loomed" across the stage since the opening scene. She approaches him and holds out the money to pay the debt and restore balance and security to her life. The creditor is stunned; this is a very unexpected turn of events. Whence came this money? He takes the money, makes sure it is sufficient, and—this is the critical moment—turns and walks off the stage and out of the woman's life. Different stages offer different possibilities here, but one effective choice is to have the creditor walk up the center aisle of the gathered community (audience) and out the back of the building. By leaving the stage and the vision of the audience, the tension created along the horizontal axis between the creditor on the one side and Elisha on the other with the woman and her children in the middle is broken; life has conquered death.

The dramatic exit of the creditor anticipates Elisha's concluding declaration in which he reveals the ultimate victory of life over death. He speaks no longer in the imperative but the imperfect, describing "a verbal action for which, in the mind of the speaker . . . the conclusion is not in view."[69] The situation Elisha envisions will continue, like the oil did, until the need no longer remains. He describes the extent of the miracle in the most practical of terms: "You and your children will[70] live on what is leftover." In Hebrew, "will live" (תִחְיִי, *ticheyi*) is the second to last word in the drama, almost perfectly mirroring "is dead" (מֵת, *met*), the third word spoken by the woman in verse 1. The *inclusio* indicates the establishment of a new equilibrium that pulses now with vitality, as

---

doubt as to whether he has received the "double portion" from Elijah and will in fact be his successor. His second strike both confirms him as the successor and may playfully imply, as an astute colleague pointed out to me, that "to receive the double portion requires double the work." Tom Boogaart, personal communication, February 13, 2012.

[69] Pratico and Van Pelt, *Basics of Biblical Hebrew*, 130.

[70] A modal translation of the verb is also possible: "You and your children *may* live" or "*can* live." The subjunctive would not diminish the potency of the promise, but rather would introduce a level of contingency, suggesting the woman must be responsible in her stewardship of this gift, which, if squandered, could be lost.

opposed to the pathos that characterized the drama's opening scene. Death has given way to life.

Yet another dramatic *inclusio* concludes the drama. Not only does death give way to life, but deficit is displaced by sufficiency. The final word is, appropriately, "leftover" (נוֹתָר, *notar*). As there was just enough oil to fill each of the collected vessels, there will likewise be enough resources leftover to last as long as the woman's and her children's need remains. Further, the woman, now filled with the grace of God incarnated in the multiplied oil is transformed into a source of grace from which her neighbors' lives are filled. And the miracle oil itself, multiplied in secret, anonymously sustains the woman's community, lighting their lamps, filling their bellies, and healing their wounds.

CHAPTER 5
THE HEALING OF NAAMAN AND THE DOWNFALL OF GEHAZI: 2 KINGS 5:1-27

Introduction

In contrast with the simplicity and seemingly straightforward drama of the Widow's Oil, the Healing of Naaman is a rather complex drama; it is much longer, has several more characters, and includes scenes in many different locations spanning two countries, including: the throne rooms of two kings, inside Naaman's house, at the Jordan River, outside and inside (then outside again, and then again inside) Elisha's house, a dream sequence in the house of the Aramean god Rimmon, a capture sequence by an Aramean raiding party on a little girl's home, and much more. Thematically, the drama deals with the source, structure, and distribution of power, comparing the violence of military or monarchic ways of dominating their neighbors with the subtle, life-affirming, merciful power of God. It further touches on matters of pride and humility, disease and healing, greed and generosity.

A number of performative challenges face the would-be interpreter of 2 Kgs 5. Among them are: how to understand and then represent the nature of Naaman's (and later Gehazi's) "affliction"; how to represent a raid on a village in which a child is taken captive; how clearly to represent many different locations onstage, and how to transition between them smoothly and comprehensibly, especially when the various locations include multiple countries and palaces, riverbanks, a prophet's home, a house of worship, or a path out in the open; and how to visually show the connection between the "affliction" of Naaman at the beginning, and the "affliction" of Gehazi at the end, which Elisha clearly describes as "the affliction of Naaman." Biblical performance criticism also identifies gaps in the narration, while simultaneously supplying a means to "fill in" the gaps. One gap occurs between verses 3–4. In verse 3 the little girl reveals to her mistress—Naaman's wife—

that Naaman could be healed at the hand of "the prophet in Samaria." In verse 4 Naaman discusses this revelation with the king of Aram. However, there is no explanation for how Naaman learned of what the little girl said to her mistress! These and other challenges are described and discussed below.

A Translation for Performance

SETTING / CONFLICT

[1]Naaman was the general of the army of the King of Aram. He was a great man in the service of his lord. His face was lifted high because through him YHVH had given victory to Aram. The man was a mighty hero, who was afflicted.

[2]The Arameans went out in raiding parties, and they took captive a little girl from the land of Israel. The girl served the wife of Naaman.

RISING ACTION

Scene 1
[3]She said to her mistress:

> *If only my lord could be in the service of the prophet in Samaria—he could cure him of his affliction!*

Scene 2
[4]He entered the palace and told his lord:

> *Thus and so said the girl from the land of Israel.*

[5]The King of Aram said,

> *Go! Enter the land of Israel! I will send a letter to the King of Israel.*

So he went, and he took in his hand ten talents of silver, six thousand pieces of gold, and ten outfits of expensive clothing.

Scene 3

[6]He brought the letter to the King of Israel. It said:

> ... *And now, as this letter has come to you, see that I have sent to you Naaman, my servant. You must cure him of his affliction.*

[7]When the King of Israel read the letter, he tore his clothes, and he said:

> *Am I a god that I have power over a person's living and dying? This one demands that I heal a man of his affliction! Be on the alert! He sets a trap for me!*

Scene 4

[8]When Elisha, the man of God, heard that the King of Israel had torn his clothes, he sent a messenger to the king, saying:

> *Why have you torn your clothes? Let the man come to me; let him know that there is a prophet in Israel.*

[9]So Naaman came—with his horses and his chariot—and he stood at the door of the house belonging to Elisha. [10]Elisha sent a messenger to him, saying:

> *Be on your way! Wash seven times in the Jordan! Your flesh shall return to you. Now be clean!*

[11]Naaman became enraged. He went away and he said:

> *Behold, did I not say to myself: The prophet will come out respectfully; he will place himself in my service; he will call on the name of the Lord, his God; he will wave his hand over the*

infected place; he will cure the afflicted one. [12]*How much purer*
are the Amana and Pharpar, the rivers of Damascus, than all
the waters of Israel? Could I not wash in them and be clean?

Naaman turned homeward and went away in a bullish rage. [13]But his
servants approached him; they talked with him, and they said:

> *My father, if the prophet had asked of you some great deed,*
> *would you not have done it? He simply asked you to wash and*
> *be clean.*

CLIMAX

Scene 1

[14]Naaman went down, and he dipped in the Jordan seven times,
according to the word of the man of God. His flesh returned to him like
the flesh of a little boy. Naaman was clean.

Scene 2

[15]He returned to the man of God—he and all his camp. He entered
Elisha's house, placed himself in his service, and said:

> *Indeed, I now know that there are no gods in all the earth except*
> *in Israel. Now please take something as a gift from your servant!*

[16]He said,

> *As surely as the Lord lives, the Lord in whose service I stand, I*
> *will take nothing.*

He pressed him to take something, but he refused. [17]Finally, Naaman
said:

> *If not, then could something be given to your servant: two mule-*
> *loads of earth? For your servant will never again offer burnt*
> *offerings or sacrifices to others gods, but only to the Lord.*

[18]Except—in this one case, would the Lord pardon your servant? When my lord enters the house of Rimmon to worship there; when he leans on my arm so that I worship in the house of Rimmon; when I worship in the house of Rimmon, would the Lord pardon your servant in this one case?

[19]And he said to him,

Go in peace.

Naaman went from him a short distance.

FALLING ACTION

Scene 1

[20]Gehazi, the servant of the man of God, said to himself:

Behold, my lord has refused Naaman, this Aramean, and has not taken from his hand any of the gifts he brought. As surely as the Lord lives, I will run after him, and I will take from him something!

[21]Gehazi pursued Naaman, and Naaman saw someone running towards him. He scrambled out of the chariot to meet him, and said:

Is all well?

[22]And he said,

All is well. My lord has sent me with this message: Behold, two young men have just come to me from the hill country of Ephraim, from the sons of prophets. Could you give—to them— a talent of silver and two outfits of clothing?

[23]Naaman said,

Agreed! Take two talents of silver!

He pressed him to take them. He tied the talents of silver into two bags along with the two outfits of clothing. He gave them to his two young men, who lifted and carried them while in Gehazi's service.

Scene 2
[24]When Gehazi came to the citadel he took the goods from their hands. He stowed them in the house and sent the men on their way. [25]Gehazi slipped into the house, but stood at a distance from his lord. Elisha said to him,

> *Where have you been, Gehazi?*

He said,

> *Your servant has gone neither here nor there.*

[26]He said to him,

> *No? Was not my heart present as a man turned away from his chariot to meet...you! Is there a time to take silver, to take clothing, olive orchards and vineyards, sheep and cattle, male and female servants? [27]The affliction of Naaman shall cling to you and to your descendants forever.*

DÉNOUEMENT
Gehazi went forth from him as one afflicted, as white as snow.

Setting / Conflict (vv. 1–2)

The first word in 2 Kgs 5 introduces the audience to the drama's main character by name: Naaman. This is accomplished through an inversion of the Hebrew word order, placing the subject before the verb, a typical

syntactic device used to introduce a shift in scene or to mark the beginning of a self-contained narrative.[1] The rest of verse one overwhelms
the audience with a long and detailed list of Naaman's
accomplishments. This Naaman is the general of the King of Aram's
armies (שַׂר צָבָא, *sar tsava'*); he is "a great man" (אִישׁ גָּדוֹל, *'ish gadol*)
with the esteem of his king; his "face is lifted up" (וּנְשֻׂא פָנִים,[2] *unsu'
phanim*) on account of his victories (תְּשׁוּעָה, *teshu'ah*). Not only so, but
as if it were an afterthought, the narrator continues to declare Naaman a
"mighty warrior," or "charismatic hero" (גִּבּוֹר חַיִל, *gibbor chayil*). Like
the well-delivered introduction to a famous speaker that lists
accomplishment after accomplishment, the narrator waxes eloquent
about Naaman like an adoring fan. However, by the end of verse one it
becomes clear that the extended introduction serves a dramatic purpose
as the final word forces the audience to reconsider everything that came
before it. The introduction builds to a climax that is as devastating as it
is unexpected. This Aramean hero—who even has the favor of the gods
of Aram's enemies[3]—is afflicted (מְצֹרָע, *metsora'*).

In order to understand properly the meaning of this news we must
first understand what is meant by the Pu'al participle מְצֹרָע (*metsora'*),
traditionally translated "leper." The interpreter is greatly aided in this
pursuit by the tools of historical and linguistic analysis. The fact that
Naaman plays a critical and highly physical role in the life of the
Aramean nation makes it clear that the illness being referred to by the
corresponding noun form צָרַעַת (*tsara'at*) is not the disease that is

---

[1.]Long, *2 Kings*, 67. Cf. Joüon-Muraoka, "The statistically dominant and
unmarked **word-order** in the verbal clause is: Verb—Subject. . . . At the very
beginning of a statement, we usually find the order S—V." Joüon and Muraoka,
Grammar of Biblical Hebrew, 581; emphasis original.

[2.]The phrase implies respect and favor. The only other instance in the Hebrew
Bible of the words נשׂא and פָנִים connected as they are here comes in Job 34.19: אֲשֶׁר
לֹא־נָשָׂא פְּנֵי שָׂרִים *'asher lo-nasa' pnei sarim*, "who does not lift the face of princes,"
or, "who shows no partiality to nobles" (NRSV). Cf. Joüon and Muraoka, *Grammar
of Biblical Hebrew*, 417.

[3.]The narrator is clear that Naaman's victories—and therefore the favor of the king
of Aram—were the gift of Israel's God ("because through [Naaman] YHVH had given
victory to Aram" כִּי־בוֹ נָתַן־יְהוָה תְּשׁוּעָה לַאֲרָם).

referred to today as Hansen's Disease (leprosy).[4] Indeed, Philip King
and Lawrence Stager argue צָרַעַת "has no connection with leprosy as it
is diagnosed today."[5] The other uses of צָרַעַת throughout the Hebrew
Bible—particularly in Leviticus—confirm this. In Lev 13–14 צָרַעַת is
used to describe the infected state of both clothing and houses.[6] The
flexibility of the term to describe an infected person, house, or item of
clothing suggests that it perhaps describes the presence of mold or fungi
of some sort, as Cogan and Tadmor argue,[7] and prioritizes the visual
impact of the "infection." Therefore, it is likely that צָרַעַת, in essence,
describes the marked discoloration of a surface, whether cloth, stone, or
skin. Naaman's disease was likely more akin to the blotchy skin
pigmentation condition known as vitiligo[8] than to Hansen's Disease.
However, the social, cultural, and theological meaning made about that
skin discoloration in the ancient world was neither simple nor subtle.

The interpreter further is aided in the pursuit of understanding the
nature and significance of צָרַעַת by the visual imagination elicited by
performance. For example, performance prompts questions about
representation. With respect to Naaman's disease, what elements were
problematic? What threatened his position, his office, his power, or his
identity? Very likely it was not physical, or he would not have been able
to remain in his position as general of Aram's armies, a position which
would require robust physical health and strength. It is also unlikely that
they feared it was contagious, for he met face-to-face with the king to
discuss what the little girl had said (v. 4). Perhaps the text itself gives us
an indication of the dilemma. When Gehazi is struck with Naaman's

---

[4.]Cogan and Tadmor, *II Kings*, 63.

[5.]King and Stager, *Life in Biblical Israel*, 78.

[6.]Cf. Lev 13:47–59 concerning clothing; Lev 14:34–54 concerning houses.

[7.]Cogan and Tadmor, *II Kings*, 63.

[8.]Vitiligo is a purely visual condition, and the effects are primarily social.
According to the Mayo Clinic website, "Vitiligo affects people of all skin types, but it
may be more noticeable in people with darker skin. The condition is not life-
threatening or contagious. It can be stressful or make you feel bad about yourself."
"Vitiligo   Overview,"   Mayo   Clinic,   accessed   May   19,   2017,
http://www.mayoclinic.org/diseases-conditions/
   /home/ovc-20319041.

affliction, he is described as turning "like snow" (כַּשֶּׁלֶג, *kashaleg*, v. 27).[9] The narrator seems to suggest that the problem for Naaman as well as for Gehazi was related to skin color. But, interestingly, the impact on Naaman and Gehazi was the opposite of what it generally has been in modern times. Gehazi's curse—and Naaman's disability—was whiteness. Cheryl Townsend Gilkes has drawn attention to this reading of 2 Kgs 5. "Not only does Gehazi become white, but it is a whiteness that his descendants are cursed to inherit – 'unto thy seed forever'."[10] Whiteness is not uniformly negative in the Hebrew Bible, of course—consider Isaiah's use of כַּשֶּׁלֶג (*kashaleg*, "like snow") in 1:18: "if your sins are like scarlet, like snow will they be made white." But when whiteness is applied to skin color, the effect does seem to be negative, and associated with disease.[11]

Naaman's disease very likely had something to do with a skin discoloration that led to a stigmatism among Aramean (and Israelite) society that had profound social and theological consequences—for Naaman (and later Gehazi), but also for his king. The lengths to which Naaman and the king of Aram go to find healing is testimony to this fact. It should at least be clear by now that Naaman's disease was not the disease associated with the term "leprosy" as it is understood in the modern world. Because of this, I have chosen to render the noun צָרַעַת (*tsara'at*) as "affliction" and the Pu'al participle מְצֹרָע (*metsora'*) as "afflicted one." These terms are ambiguous enough to suggest, on the one hand, a serious disease with visible expression (such as blotches of white on the body, or even albinism), and on the other hand to imply an effect beyond the physical appearance of Naaman's skin. Naaman's

---

[9.] 2 Kgs 5:27. Cf. "as white as snow" in NRSV, TNIV, NASB, KVJ, ASV, NET.

[10.] Townsend Gilkes, "Jesus Must Needs Go Through Samaria," 72. Powery makes a similar point while coming from a slightly different angle in Powery, "Origins of Whiteness," 83–88.

[11.] Cf. Num 12:10 when Miriam, like Naaman and Gehazi, was מְצֹרַעַת כַּשֶּׁלֶג, "afflicted, as white as snow." In communities where the normative skin color is darker, whiteness is often stigmatized as an aberration, in the same way that dark skin is stigmatized as an aberration in white normative societies.

affliction is more than skin deep.[12] It follows, then, that if he desires
complete healing, the healing will also need to be more than skin deep.

The צָרַעַת of Naaman is the unifying thread woven through the entire
tapestry of 2 Kgs 5. Indeed, מְצֹרָע is the final word in verse 1; צָרַעַת is
the first word in verse 27. Naaman is dramatically revealed as מְצֹרָע at
the outset of the story and, after being miraculously healed (v. 14) his
צָרַעַת clings to Gehazi and his family "forever" (לְעוֹלָם, le'olam), which
brings the drama to a close (v. 27). The need to represent the צָרַעַת
visually in performance has generated a number of creative ideas among
my students over the years. Several performances have incorporated a
variation of a similar idea: representing the צָרַעַת with a white cloth tied
onto Naaman, and later Gehazi. Using the same cloth to represent
Naaman's and Gehazi's affliction demonstrates the continuity of צָרַעַת
throughout the drama, for Naaman and Gehazi are afflicted with the
same disease.[13] The motif is introduced in verse 1, at the conclusion of
the narrator's list of Naaman's accolades when, at last, Naaman is
humbled as the narrator approaches him to tie the cloth on his arm, while
simultaneously speaking the final word of the verse: מְצֹרָע. All is not
well in the kingdom of Aram.

The next character introduced by the narrator, the little girl, contrasts
with Naaman in every conceivable way. Naaman is called by name, she
is nameless;[14] Naaman is a big man (אִישׁ גָּדוֹל, 'ish gadol), she is a little

---

[12.]"Although the psychosomatic aspects of illness sometimes have been forgotten
by modern medicine, and spiritual aspects rejected, the OT perspective on sickness
and disease is multifaceted and holistic. This understanding must be kept in mind when
we examine specific instances of sickness and disease in the Historical Books of the
OT." O'Mathúna, "Sickness and Disease," 896. The drama of 2 Kings 5 makes an
explicit connection between the internal "diseases" of greed, deceit, and violence, and
the external condition called צָרַעַת, which manifests as some form of whiteness.

[13.]Cf. 2 Kgs 5:27: "The *affliction of Naaman* shall cling to you and to your
descendants forever." Emphasis added.

[14.]De Regt suggests that "unnamed characters, which are only defined in terms of
nouns indicating kinship, title, social category, or their occupation or role, e.g., 'the
waiter', typically have no significance either beyond the scene in which they are
introduced or in some other context, and come at the bottom of the hierarchy of main
characters in a text." De Regt, *Participants in Old Testament Texts*, 4. This common

girl (נַעֲרָה קְטַנָּה, *na'arah qetannah*); Naaman is a great warrior (גִּבּוֹר חַיִל *gibbor chayil*), she is a servant (לִפְנֵי, *liphnei*), "in the service of" Naaman's wife; Naaman is the commander of the Aramean armies (שַׂר צָבָא, *sar tsava'*), she is a captive from one of Naaman's raids; Naaman is an Aramean (אֲרַמִּי, *'arami*), she is from the land of Israel (מֵאֶרֶץ יִשְׂרָאֵל, *me'erets yisra'el*).[15] At a deeper level, the two characters represent fundamentally opposed ways of being in the world: Naaman the way of power and "might makes right," the little girl the way of vulnerability, wisdom, and love. The personal and national conflict symbolized by Naaman's צָרַעַת is channeled and developed through the little girl's prophetic revelation regarding the prophet in Israel. As Naaman and the king of Aram blunder in their attempt to interpret the little girl's message according to their worldview, their actions threaten to undermine the little girl's wisdom, and almost start a war. As Hobbs observed, "[t]he literary problem"[16] is figuring out how to bring Naaman and Elisha together in a way that is consonant with the little girl's insight. I suggest that the "literary problem" has a dramatic solution.

Performance renders the multi-layered contrasts between Naaman and the little girl both visible and tangible. Naaman, the powerful and famous leader of Aram's armies, enters Israel with his raiding party (גְּדוּדִים, *gedudim*) and returns to Aram with the spoils, including but not limited to the little girl.[17] The narrator's report isolates the little girl

---

pattern is broken in one significant way in 2 Kgs 5, namely, that the significance of the little girl—only one of the story's several unnamed characters—reaches far beyond the specific scene she appears in. Indeed, her brief words to her mistress are nothing less than the most important bit of dialogue in the entire drama, without which the entire story collapses. For more on the roles of unnamed participants in OT dramas, see van Peursen, "Participant Reference in Genesis 37," 89–90.

[15.]Cf. Cohn, "Form and Perspective," 174. For comment on further contrasts between these and other characters in light of the surrounding stories about Elisha see Leeb, *Away From the Father's House*, 50.

[16.]Hobbs, *2 Kings*, 59.

[17.]It is highly unlikely that the only result of the raid was the capture of a single slave girl. It is much more likely that Naaman's men confiscated *everything* mentioned in Elisha's list to Gehazi in v. 26. As Hobbs remarks in a comment on v. 26, "Such comprehensive catalogs of wealth and prosperity are a common feature of the Former

because she is the salient element of Naaman's spoils (for the story), though Naaman could hardly imagine the role she will soon play in determining the course of his life. At the moment of capture, she is nothing more than a slave girl, a commodity, an afterthought.

The dramatic enactment of the raid and kidnapping accomplishes a number of important functions. First, it establishes the various locations of the narrative on the stage, orienting the audience to the whereabouts of Israel, Aram, and Naaman's house. Second, the audience watches the raiding party seize a number of items, which will resurface again later on among the "gifts" Naaman brings to the king of Israel and Elisha.[18] Finally, the audience witnesses the realities of war as not only the stealing of property, but stealing human beings as well.

This is the moment that brings the characters of Naaman and the little girl into sharp relief. Imagine the scene unfolding in performance. Naaman, under the king's command, sends his men into Israel. As they move stealthily across the stage, the little girl sits on the ground playing. Or perhaps she sits among the audience members (who do not know she is an actor in the performance), which would bring the action and tension intimately close to those surrounding her when she is captured. As the soldiers notice her and move toward her with purpose, it becomes clear what is going to happen. As they approach, perhaps she stiffens, paralyzed by fear; or perhaps she screams, knowing the danger these men represent. As they get close she tries to flee, but has nowhere to go. They each take an arm and drag her as she screams across the stage toward Aram. Perhaps she looks frantically at those sitting around her

---

Prophets." As such, Naaman and his men would have targeted each item on the list to increase their own wealth, and disempower their weaker neighbor. Hobbs, *2 Kings*, 68.

[18.]There is no direct evidence in the text for this interpretation, and it is admittedly superfluous and playful. However, it would contribute to the ambiguity of the king of Israel's (mis?)interpretation of the king of Aram's letter in v. 7 if part of the gifts presented were goods stolen by Aram from Israel. Further, this would add another layer of irony to Gehazi's wolfish deed: he would unwittingly steal back what had been taken by different means that nevertheless lead to similar ends, thus perpetuating the destructive cycle of greed and weaving its web ever tighter.

for help.[19] They forcefully throw her to her knees at center stage—where Naaman will soon kneel in the same position to wash himself in the Jordan, and where Gehazi will eventually fall to his knees, weighted down by the burden of the consequences of his greed. The stage clears as the men fade into the background. Now the little girl is alone at center stage. The wife of Naaman sits center stage right, Naaman stands behind her with a hand on her shoulder, his affliction-cloth flowing visibly down his arm. The girl crawls tentatively toward her new mistress, stopping to look back in the direction of her lost home, and eventually arrives and assumes her position in the service of (לִפְנֵי, *liphnei*) Naaman's wife. The little girl is completely vulnerable and powerless; she is at the whim of her new master and mistress. One has to wonder whether the little girl's parents were left alive, and what she witnessed as she was being dragged from her home. Performance creates the opportunity for the emotional force of that raid to be made real in the space, creating an uncomfortable and remarkable juxtaposition as soon as the little girl opens her mouth in verse 3.

Having introduced the two principal characters of the opening verses of the drama we are now able to articulate the conflict, a necessary initial step in dramatic analysis. The conflict, as was briefly mentioned previously, centers on Naaman's "affliction." But, just as a rock is cast into a pool of water, disturbing the pool's surface in ever-widening circles, so too ripples of conflict emanate out from that center in multiple directions. In the first place, within Naaman's own person, his affliction perhaps casts doubts on the longevity of his status as general of Aram's armies. Moreover, even though he is well-respected by his lord, his appearance sets him apart from the crowd in ways he is

---

[19.]During one performance this exact scenario happened, un-rehearsed. During the discussion afterwards a couple of members of the audience remarked at how powerful and painful the experience was for them to have been seated next to the little girl, and how helpless they felt when she was taken away from them, leading to an entirely different experience of the story than they had previously had—they *felt* the little girl's experience instead of thinking about it, which led them truly to hear her remarkable words to her Aramean mistress (v. 3) in the immediate context of her capture (v. 2) for the first time.

clearly eager to resolve. This affliction casts a lengthening shadow over his legitimacy, his status, and ultimately his pride. At the national level Naaman's affliction is the Achilles' heel of the kingdom of Aram, standing as testimony that the power it wields over its neighbors and over life itself was far from total.[20] Naaman's illness demonstrates the limits of his power and the power of the king and his counselors over the most basic and fundamental aspect of life: health and well-being, which is captured well in the Hebrew word שָׁלוֹם (shalom), which figures prominently (and ironically) throughout the final pericope (especially vv. 19–22). At the international level Naaman's affliction almost sparks a war between Aram and Israel as the king of Aram's attempt to secure Naaman's healing is misinterpreted by his counterpart in Israel as a thinly veiled provocation (v. 7).

Finally—and ultimately—Naaman's affliction occasions the conflict between competing theologies about the source, structure, and distribution of power. This conflict pits the alluring power of kings and kingdoms (represented chiefly by Naaman and Gehazi, but also the two kings) against the counterintuitive power of the kingdom of God (represented by Elisha and the little girl). Both theologies understand power to be structured hierarchically. The structure and one's relative position within the hierarchy is described through the repeated use of the prepositional phrase לִפְנֵי (liphnei, "in the service of," lit. "to the face of"). The fundamental difference between the two competing theologies is that for kings and their kingdoms power is a limited good and is inherently reductionistic and oppressive (it is expressed through warfare and the capture of humans and land as property[21]). For YHVH and his prophet power is unlimited and humanizing[22]—but there are

---

[20.]"The king was a source of power. His wisdom, his knowledge, his judgments, and his campaigns went forth from the throne room like electricity from a power plant. Everyone was wired to him…. A king in Israel and Aram verified his authority and justified his position by being the provider." Boogaart, "Drama and the Sacred," 46.

[21.]Cf. vv. 1–2, 26.

[22.]Cf. vv. 3, 14.

consequences for forsaking it.[23] In the end, the narrator's tale leaves little doubt about which theology is affirmed and which is rejected.

Rising Action (vv. 3–13)

The rising action unfolds over the course of four scenes. Each scene is set in a different location and all are dominated by the character of Naaman as we follow him on his seemingly straightforward quest into the land of Israel to secure healing at the hands of Israel's prophet. However, the quest hits snag after snag and on more than one occasion seems all but doomed to failure—or all out war.

Scene 1 - Naaman's house (v. 3)

This first scene is very short, but contains the dialogue on which the entire plot hinges. Although Naaman is not given any lines, and it is unclear whether or not he is physically present in the scene, his condition drives the dialogue and motivates the little girl to speak. The little girl's speech seems to transition the story from prolegomena into "narrative time."[24] Though she is only physically present in verses 2–3, the effect of her presence and her words permeates the entire drama. Her words set the story in motion. All of the gears of the kingdom begin whirring as soon as she speaks.

And her speech is remarkable: "If only my lord could be in the service of the prophet in Samaria—he could cure him of his affliction." Not only does she, a young, foreign, unnamed slave girl articulate knowledge and wisdom that has eluded general, king, and (one would assume) the king's most trusted counselors,[25] but she expresses this advice as genuine concern[26] for the very man responsible for her forced

---

[23.]Cf. v. 27.

[24.]Long, *2 Kings*, 70.

[25.]Not to mention "all of the king's horses and all of the king's men."

[26.]The exclamation אַחֲלֵי is attested only twice in the Hebrew Bible, here in 2 Kgs 5.3, and in Ps 119.5: "Oh that my ways would be steadfast in keeping your laws!" In both cases it expresses the desire of the speaker for reality to be different. Joüon and Muraoka, *Grammar of Biblical Hebrew*, 350.

capture and removal from her family—and possibly even the death of her family and the destruction of her village.[27] There is no indication of how much time passes between her capture and her confession, but as the story is told it has been mere moments, which further sharpens the contrast between captor and captive, and makes her altruistic act all the more audacious. The selfless wisdom of the little girl is later brought to mind in verses 11–12 as Naaman, the "great man," is offended by Elisha's slight and devolves into a childish rant.

It is clear from the fallout of the little girl's words that they are accepted by all who heard them, whether directly or indirectly. No one questions her integrity or motivation, and the veracity of her word is vindicated when Naaman is successfully healed in accordance with the word of "the prophet in Samaria" in verse 14. The question posed by scene 2, however, is the extent to which her words are *comprehended* by those who heard them. The circuitous route Naaman and his entourage take to arrive at the Jordan River suggests that something essential in the little girl's dialogue was "lost in translation."

Scene 2 - The Palace in Aram (vv. 4–5)

The scene in the palace is dominated by two interrelated realities. First, the narrator creates suspense in the telling of the story through the effective use of ambiguity, generated by two carefully placed gaps in the telling of the story. Second, the effects of the ambiguities are magnified by the gross misinterpretation of the little girl's message on the part of Naaman and the king of Aram, which sabotages the purity of her vision and deepens the suspense, gripping the audience into a fuller engagement with the plot and its eventual resolution.

The first gap in this scene is located between verses 3 and 4. In verse 3 the little girl speaks her line directly to her mistress. Verse 4 begins with "And *he* entered, and *he* told his lord" (וַיָּבֹא וַיַּגֵּד לַאדֹנָיו, *vayyavo' vayyagged ladonav*). The antecedent of the pronominal subject is initially unclear; who is the "he" referring to? Is "he" even the

---

[27]"The goal of these groups was usually not conquest . . . but pillaging and robbery." *NIDOTTE*, s.v. "גָּדַד."

appropriate pronoun here? Different manuscript traditions represent different attempts to reconcile the ambiguities of this textual gap. Marvin Sweeney summarizes the discrepancies:

> The pronouns present problems because the context suggests that the Israelite maidservant or her mistress goes in to speak to 'her' master, viz., "and she went in and told her lord" (LXX) or "and they went in and told her lord" (Peshitta). The MT presupposes that Naaman went in to tell his master the king after hearing about the matter from his wife. Targum Jonathan agrees with MT."[28]

These differences point to the underlying challenge of how to make sense of this gap. Ultimately, the plot requires the pronoun to refer to Naaman, for if the pronoun is changed to "she" or "they," following the LXX and Peshitta respectively, another more complicated problem is created: how and when does Naaman get into the king's presence to receive his charge and letter to go to the king of Israel? Naaman must be the one "entering" and "telling" in verse 3, and "his lord" must refer to the king of Aram. Further, as De Regt has shown, Naaman is the "major participant" in 2 Kgs 5. As such, he can "be referred to by means of a pronoun or inflectional affix"[29] even when he is not the nearest antecedent to the pronoun or affix. However, the question remains: How did Naaman hear or receive the little girl's message?

Performance provides a space in which new interpretations become possible. Drama's ability to present simultaneous action could allow Naaman to be on stage in a different part of the house and overhear the little girl's wish for his healing. Or, perhaps Naaman is present with his

---

[28.]Sweeney, *I & II Kings*, 294–95.

[29.]De Regt, *Participants in Old Testament Texts*, 26. Although De Regt suggests that such references back to the major participant are typical and therefore it is unnecessary to speak of "ambiguity," I would argue that, in this case, at least some ambiguity exists. This ambiguity is demonstrated in part by the textual discrepancies cited above, and in the dramatic gap discussed in the paragraphs following this footnote citation.

wife and the little girl as she expresses her desire to her mistress, and Naaman simply leaves and goes to the king. Perhaps Naaman neither overhears nor is present in the room, but his wife brings the message to him in a flurry of animated excitement, prodding him to take this new information to the king straight away. One strength of this final possibility is what could be called the telephone effect. The little girl expresses the particulars of her wish to her mistress; her mistress takes the message and shares it with Naaman; in her excitement she may not have gotten all of the facts straight; Naaman then takes the message and presents it to the king of Aram. By the time the message has been repeated the third time, the likelihood of the message staying intact decreases considerably.

Herein lies the second gap. The composer has replaced the little girl's message, on the lips of Naaman, with the intentionally ambiguous phrase "thus and so" (כָּזֹאת וְכָזֹאת, *kazot vekhazot*).[30] Cogan and Tadmor miss the function of the composer's device and incorrectly translate this phrase as "word for word."[31] The device is intended to communicate the exact opposite message, however. It is intended to create ambiguity and therefore tension around the faithful transmission of the little girl's message from character to character, and from palace to palace. This interchange creates a nuanced web of knowledge and ignorance among characters and audience that is exploited by the narrator as the audience's knowledge is played against the characters' ignorance[32] and vice versa.[33] Dramatic irony and the development of tension through suspense are powerful forces in dramatic performance because they deepen the audience's investment in the unfolding plot.

[30.]*HALOT*, s.v. "זֶה"; *BDB*, s.v. "זֶה."

[31.]"[Naaman] came and told his master *word for word*. . ." Cogan and Tadmor, *II Kings*, 61.

[32.]For example, the king of Israel is ignorant of the true purpose of the king of Aram's letter and interprets it as a pretense for war in v. 7.

[33.]In the present example, only the characters directly involved know what message was delivered. For more on dramatic irony see Bar-Efrat, *Narrative Art*, 125–128; and David, *From Balaam to Jonah*, 13–18.

The king of Aram's response to Naaman's summary of the little girl's message suggests that the message has been distorted along the way. As soon as the king of Aram responds with "I will send a letter *to the king of Israel*," the audience is aware that something is amiss; Naaman entering into "the service of the prophet in Samaria" (v. 3) has been overlooked or ignored, and the probability of Naaman's healing is placed in jeopardy. Naaman's posture of humility has been replaced with a great show of strength as the king of Aram sends his general to the king of Israel with wildly extravagant "gifts" (v. 5, 15), no doubt intended to demonstrate the power and wealth of Aram, and to compensate the Israelite monarch for curing Naaman, something he is clearly incapable of doing.

Scene 3 - The Palace in Israel (vv. 6–7)

The response of the king of Israel to the king of Aram's letter demonstrates at least two realities. First, the king of Israel is anxious because there is an imbalance of power in the region; Aram has enjoyed military victories over Israel, and likely her neighbors as well (vv. 1–2). He interprets this letter as a (thinly) veiled threat of war, a trap that the king of Aram is setting for him (v. 7). The conclusion of the king of Israel's speech is delivered in the second person plural imperative; it is delivered directly to the audience, which is thus drawn into the unfolding drama now as a character. Perhaps the audience becomes the king's attendants and counselors, or perhaps the nobility who were present in the king's throne room on that particular day.

Second, the two kings represent opposite ends of the same point-of-view. Namely, they are helpless in the face of illness, and conflicts are best resolved by a demonstration of power, particularly military power. The king of Aram and his general Naaman are in the position of power vis-à-vis Israel (v. 1); the king of Israel is in the position of weakness. Both kings (mis)interpret the little girl's message through their particular power paradigm. As Walter Brueggemann has observed, "Men of power are accustomed to dealing only with other men of power.... As the Syrians have misunderstood, so the Israelite king misconstrues, and perceives the military mission of the Syrian general to be provocation."[34]

In several performances we have spatially demonstrated the correspondence between Aram and Israel's assumptions about power, as well as the power dynamic between the two crowns. In one such performance, each palace was represented symbolically by a chair/throne (represented by an "X" on the figure below), which were set at opposite ends of the stage, forming a horizontal axis that spans the entire space, saturating it with their particular perspective of power. The focal point of the tension between the two nations became the center of the stage, where the Jordan River symbolically divided the two nations. This is the precise location where, later in verse 14, Naaman's healing will undo the power structure assumed by kings and kingdoms and will reveal the true power which flourishes in the kingdom of God. This horizontal axis of power also allowed us to make a spatial distinction between the kingdoms of Aram and Israel on the one hand, and Elisha and the little girl on the other, who together represent the theology of power the story ultimately affirms. This alternative power structure is represented by a diagonal line intersecting the vertical and horizontal axes at the center of the stage. Instead of locating Elisha's house somewhere along the horizontal axis between Israel and Aram, his house was located upstage and toward Israel. The two kings never wander beyond the boundary of the horizontal axis, thus reinforcing spatially what is inherent in the script: both kings miss the point of the little girl's message about the one who can direct Naaman to the true source of healing and power: the prophet in Samaria.

Scene 4 - At the Door to Elisha's House (vv. 8–13)

At this point in the drama Naaman's healing quest seems all but lost. The king of Israel responded not with compliance to the king of Aram's letter, but by tearing his clothes and crying out to all in earshot that Naaman and his lord are setting a trap for him. Naaman is likely

---

[34.]Brueggemann, *1 & 2 Kings*, 332.

preparing to pack up the silver, gold, and clothing (v. 5), and return to his lord unhealed and enraged.

Into the plot's dead end[35] comes Elisha, who "hears" the king of Israel has torn his clothes, but also seems to be aware of Naaman's quest, and perhaps even the little girl's speech. Elisha sends his own message to the king of Israel: "Let the man come to me; let him know that *there is a prophet* in Israel" (v. 8). Elisha's intentions clearly go beyond healing Naaman and relieving the Israelite king of an embarrassing situation. The repetition of the word "prophet" (נָבִיא, *navi'*), now on the lips of the prophet himself, validates the little girl's prophetic insight (v. 3). His message serves as a source of hope to Naaman, and critique to the king. Through Elisha's intervention the composer "mocks the impotence of royal authority."[36] Indeed, "the king, too, must be taught 'that there is a prophet in Israel'."[37]

In one of our performances, intentional blocking deepened the impact of this critique. First, Elisha stands in his house upstage left with his back to the space occupied by the kings. Throughout the entire opening half of the narrative Elisha stands with his back to everyone, whether on stage or in the audience, embodying his critique of palace power politics and its reductionistic paradigm.[38] Second, the characters of Elisha and his messenger speak Elisha's message simultaneously (v. 8), demonstrating the correspondence between command and fulfillment, and the efficacy of Elisha's word. The success of this delivery contrasts with the breakdown of the little girl's message within the Aramean bureaucracy and appears to put the quest back on track; Naaman is finally en route to "the prophet" (vv. 3, 8).

[35.]Cohn, "Form and Perspective," 175.

[36.]Cohn, "Form and Perspective," 174.

[37.]Cogan and Tadmor, *II Kings*, 67.

[38.]Brueggemann comments on the critique this and other stories in the Elijah-Elisha cycle make of palace policies this way: "The stories, unlike the royal list, open to the listeners in daring imagination the claim that the world does not need to be perceived or engaged according to dominant shapings of power, to privileged notions of authority, to conventional distributions of goods, or to standard definitions of what is possible." Brueggemann, *Testimony to Otherwise*, 35.

When Naaman and his entourage arrive at Elisha's house, Naaman stands at "the opening of the house" (פֶּתַח־הַבָּיִת, *petach-habbayit*). There is some debate about whether Naaman waits for Elisha to come out to him, or whether he is prevented from entering the house by Elisha's messenger.[39] A careful analysis of the script, particularly Naaman's monologue in verse 11, makes clear that he purposefully waited outside the door or gate, expecting Elisha to come to him. As Naaman waits with growing impatience for the prophet "to come out respectfully" (יֵצֵא יָצוֹא, *yetsei' yatso'*, "he would surely come out") and present himself before the Aramean general, the audience becomes aware of a striking irony which recalls the little girl's words in verse 3 ("if only my lord could be *in the service of the prophet*") and invites them to consider yet again the ways power and entitlement cloud and confuse communication. Elisha does not come out to greet Naaman; he sends a messenger. Elisha and the messenger again speak in unison while Elisha remains with his back to the entire performance space. "Go. Wash seven times in the Jordan" (v. 10).

[39.]Sweeney argues for Elisha preventing Naaman's access as a demonstration of his, and YHWH's power: "The portrayal of Naaman's arrival emphasizes his power, but the prophet keeps him waiting at the door. In this manner, the narrative highlights the prophet's (and YHWH's) greater power and importance." Sweeney, *I & II Kings*, 99. According to Hobbs, Naaman waits as "a sign of his respect for the prophet." He views it as a mirror of the Shunemite (cf. 2 Kgs 4:15). Hobbs, *2 Kings*, 64. Berrigan perceives a battle of the egos, suggesting Naaman waits to force Elisha to come to him, but "Elisha will not deign to rise and step to the portal of his house. He sends a messenger . . . ." Berrigan, *Kings and Their Gods*, 141. Cogan and Tadmor claim "The present verse is misconstrued in all modern translations" and argue that the text reads that Naaman "*waited . . . for Elisha.*" Cogan and Tadmor, *II Kings*, 64; italics original. However, they come to this conclusion by incorrectly associating the function of the preposition לְ in 1 Kgs 20:38 with its function here in v. 9. In 1 Kgs 20:38, לְ directly follows the verb עמד and modifies it: (וַיַּעֲמֹד לַמֶּלֶךְ, "he stood (waiting) before the king"). In 2 Kgs 5:9, לְ does not modify the verb עמד, but expresses a genitive relationship between Elisha and the house (וַיַּעֲמֹד פֶּתַח־הַבָּיִת לֶאֱלִישָׁע "and he stood (at) the opening of the house of Elisha," or, in other words, "the house *belonging to* Elisha"). Nevertheless, their conclusion that Naaman chose to stand there to make Elisha come out to him most accurately reflects the interaction between the two as the script presents it.

Naaman's response to Elisha's message and its delivery is abrupt and explosive. Indeed, his response is almost utterly unique in biblical narrative. Rarely does a character reveal the contours of their inner world with such clarity and thoroughness.[40] And his speech makes very clear that he never had any intention of fulfilling the little girl's word as it was spoken. Naaman did not plan to enter into the prophet's service, but the opposite. Healing would not come by means of humility and submission, but by magic: "and he would wave his hand" (וְהֵנִיף יָדוֹ, *veheiniph yado*, v. 11) and a demonstration of divine power: "and he would call on the name of the Lord his god" (וְקָרָא בְשֵׁם־יהוה אֱלֹהָיו, *veqara' beshem YHVH 'elohav*, v. 11). Not only is Naaman offended by Elisha's acute lack of propriety, but the means of healing Elisha offered do not compute in Naaman's worldview in which true power is visible on the surface of things: mighty rivers (v. 11), feats of strength (v. 13), military victories (vv. 1–2). To simply wash in a humble river would have been humiliating, a sign of weakness, not strength.

Exasperated by his entire experience in Israel, Naaman turns toward home and begins to walk. The narrator's description of his action (וַיֵּלֶךְ בְּחֵמָה, *vayyelekh bechemah*, "and he went away in a rage") calls to mind a bull, as בְּחֵמָה (*bechemah*) sounds like בְּהֵמָה (*behemah*) "cattle." Naaman storms off "in a bullish rage" (v. 12). But his servants draw up their courage, approach him, and speak to him. Their posture and gestures echo those of the little girl in verse 3 as they do as she did previously, offering a critical word of wisdom when it was most needed. "Once again, the information or exhortation necessary for successful restoration is mediated to the powerful through low-status persons."[41] Further, "[t]he servants of Naaman and the young girl have similar roles in the story. The girl begins the process of healing and the servants help to complete it."[42] This theme will reach its fullest expression in the

---

[40.]Surprisingly, there is another example of a biblical character articulating their inner monologue later on in this very drama when Gehazi does the same thing (v. 20). Neither monologue depicts the respective character in a positive light.

[41.]Leeb, *Away From the Father's House*, 51, n. 27.

[42.]Hobbs, *2 Kings*, 60.

following verse as the power paradigm Naaman lives in will be undone between the banks of the Jordan River.

Climax (vv. 14–19)

The drama's conflict, which emanates from Naaman's affliction and is perpetuated by the clash of different points-of-view representing different power structures is resolved over the course of two scenes. The first scene, at the Jordan River, contains the critical healing that leads to Naaman's confession of Israel's God as the only God "in all the earth," and awakens him to the power of the kingdom of God manifested in Elisha, the "man of God." The second scene contains the fulfillment of the little girl's word from verse 3, and provides the space in which Naaman's healing can move beyond being merely "skin deep."

Scene 1 - At the Jordan River (v. 14)

Naaman, apparently convinced by his servants' wisdom (v. 13), makes his way to the Jordan. But how easily did Naaman make this decision? Was he merely convinced by the logic of his servant's argument and he proceeded dispassionately to the water's edge? In order to get to the Jordan, the narrator tells us, Naaman had to *descend* (וַיֵּרֶד, *vayyered*, "and he went down"). His descent is geographic, moving from the elevated riverbank down into the water. But his descent is also personal, signaling a change in his posture toward the prophet's message. According to Hobbs, "[a] double meaning might be intended. Naaman descended to the Jordan and also demonstrated his humility."[43] Esther Menn concurs: "Once Naaman does acquiesce to being treated as a person of no special conse-quence, as a child might be treated summarily ... he is healed immediately."[44]

The book of Jonah provides another example of the verb ירד assuming a double meaning, both geographic and emotional. Throughout the book Jonah is commanded to "arise" (קוּם, *qum*) three

---

[43.]Hobbs, *2 Kings*, 69.
[44.]Menn, "A Little Child Shall Lead," 345.

times, twice by God (1:2, 3:2) and once by a pagan sailor in whose speech God's commands are echoed (1:6). Jonah responds to the three-fold command to rise by "descending" (ירד) three times (1:3, 5). Throughout the book of Jonah, to "arise" is to move toward God and God's call; to "descend" is to reject God and God's call. Jonah's descent is also, then, both geographic and personal. In chapter one he descends as far down as he can safely go: down to the bowels of the boat. But he is also as far down as he can go internally, in a "deep sleep."[45] In this state he is completely passive and unresponsive to the sailors' cries and fears. His descent continues in chapter two when he cries out "from the belly of She'ol."[46]

Naaman finds himself not in the belly of She'ol, but wading into the Jordan River, the very river he just disparaged as worthless compared with the Amana and Pharpar of Damascus (v. 12). A performer must present the change in Naaman's posture and composure as believable and authentic. Naaman must *choose* to humble himself and submit to the prophet's word. If he does not, the critical healing scene loses much of its emotive power. This can be accomplished through simple blocking and nonverbal communication. After the servants offer their wisdom, they back away to give their angry master space. Naaman turns his back to servants and audience alike, creating privacy to consider what is better: persisting in his bullishness or acknowledging the higher wisdom of his underlings. After a dramatic pause, Naaman releases the tension in his body: his shoulders relax, he exhales, he turns around to face the audience and the Jordan, and begins to walk, slowly and perhaps tentatively. Slowing down the pacing of this scene through blocking creates space for an emotional connection between Naaman and the audience. This connection will be exploited at the conclusion of this scene when Naaman is transformed, and the audience with him.

Having already begun to slow the pacing down between verses 13–14, once Naaman actually "enters" the river, the pace comes almost to a halt. The narrator chooses to let the gestures do most of the talking,

[45.] *HALOT*, s.v. "רדם."
[46.] Jonah 2:1 [Heb 2:3].

and so describes the climactic scene with an economy of words typical
of Hebrew narrative, "He dipped in the Jordan seven times, according
to the word of the man of God. His flesh returned to him like the flesh
of a little boy. Naaman was clean" (v. 14). In order to be faithful to the
script, a performance must demonstrate each "dip" in the Jordan, the
entirety of the washing ceremony. This all happens in silence. Naaman
is the only character on stage who is moving. The eyes of all are
transfixed on him as he kneels on the floor, repeatedly gesturing with
his hands toward the floor to bring up water, and bending down so his
head or arm or chest meet his hands and can be washed.

An important question raised by performance is: By what process is
Naaman's healing accomplished? In other words, is Naaman healed
one-seventh of the way with each "dip," or does it come like a flood on
the seventh plunge? There are two distinct advantages to the latter
option, one dramatic and the other theological. With respect to drama,
the tension deepens with each successive dip as Naaman and audience
alike must grapple with the apparent futility of this counter-intuitive
task. One must remember that initially Naaman had no interest in
obeying the prophet's word, and coming down to the Jordan was a risk
for him socially and emotionally. His willingness to take the risk opens
the audience to connect with him. If, as he washes unsuccessfully, he
pauses at times, looks around, is perhaps embarrassed, the audience's
investment in him is deepened as his humanity and humility are
affirmed through a display of genuine vulnerability. The investment of
the audience can be seen in the inevitability that they will count each of
Naaman's seven "dips" into the water. This investment enables the
healing, when it comes, to achieve a greater impact on the audience as
well as Naaman. Theologically, Naaman's persistence through six
unsuccessful washes demonstrates a commitment to obedience and a
growing faith in the man of God's word. These repeated gestures in this
emotionally charged context reveal a God who partners with humanity
to fulfill divine purposes; Naaman's faith combined with God's action
through Elisha's word accomplishes the miracle.

What is accomplished in the climax is more than just the removal of
Naaman's skin affliction. The narrator does not simply say "Naaman

was healed" (וַיִּטְהָר, *vayyiṭhar*). By describing Naaman's flesh returning to him like the flesh of a "little boy" (נַעַר קָטֹן, *na'ar qaṭon*, v. 14) the narrator evokes the little girl (נַעֲרָה קְטַנָּה, *na'arah qeṭannah*) from verse 2. נַעֲרָה קְטַנָּה and נַעַר קָטֹן are the same words in Hebrew, expressed in the feminine and masculine forms respectively.[47] Their connection in the original Hebrew is much tighter than their English counterparts.

Through this repetition the narrator has just expanded the scope of Naaman's healing from his flesh to the very structures of power that "lifted Naaman's face" (v. 1) and kept the little girl in servitude. The hierarchical structure of power that imbued Naaman's life with purpose and privilege has been undone. Now Naaman and the little girl are one.[48] Naaman himself will signal this transformation with his body and voice throughout verses 15–19 as he stands לִפְנֵי ("in the service of") the prophet, and refers to himself as "your servant" (עַבְדְּךָ, *'avdekha*) no less than five times in as many verses. Interpreting this scene as a Christian, one cannot help but hear an echo in the mouth of Jesus in Matt 18. When asked by his disciples who would be the greatest in the kingdom of heaven—a question that assumes a similarly earthly hierarchical arrangement of power as witnessed in 2 Kgs 5—Jesus responded by placing a child in their midst. After this symbolic gesture he said, "Truly I tell you, unless you *change and become like children*, you will never enter the kingdom of heaven."[49] Naaman embodies his childlike transformation first by raising his hands in the air to symbolically gesture gratitude to the God he will confess before Elisha in the next verse, and second by returning to his servants with joy and rushing them back to Elisha's house. It is important to note, however, that even though Naaman has been healed and the narrator has signaled the trajectory of his

---

[47.]"The terms glossed 'lad' and 'lass' are morphologically masculine and feminine forms derived from the same base." Revell, *Designation of the Individual*, 33.

[48.]The narrator's comment here comparing Naaman and the little girl is all the more remarkable in light of Milton Eng's conclusion that נַעַר קָטֹן describes "a young person below puberty but above the age of an infant or weaned child." Eng, *Days of Our Years*, 76. No longer is Naaman the thick-skinned man, he is a soft-skinned kid; no longer the war-hardened general, now he is a wide-eyed child.

[49.]Matt 18:3, NRSV; emphasis added.

transformation beyond his flesh to the very structure of power, Naaman's transformation has only just begun; it is still only "skin deep."[50]

Scene 2 - Inside Elisha's House (vv. 15–19)

Everything about Naaman's second visit to Elisha's house contrasts with the first. Earlier Naaman waited outside Elisha's house (וַיַּעֲמֹד פֶּתַח־הַבַּיִת, *vayya'amod petach-habbatyit*, v. 9); now he enters the house (וַיָּבֹא, *vayyavo'*, v. 15). Earlier Naaman expected Elisha to come out and stand before him (יֵצֵא יָצוֹא וְעָמַד, *yetse' yatso' ve'amad*, v. 11); now he fulfills the little girl's word (v. 3) and presents himself in the service of Elisha (וַיַּעֲמֹד לְפָנָיו, *vayya'amod lephanav*, v. 15). Earlier Naaman spoke from his perceived status as one in authority over Elisha (v. 11–12), now he refers to himself as Elisha's "servant" (עַבְדֶּךָ, *'avdekha*) five times in four verses (vv. 15–18). Earlier Elisha's God was a means to an end (v. 11[51]); now Naaman affirms the sovereignty of YHVH in all the earth (v. 15[52]). Perhaps Naaman's response here "sheds further light on why Elisha sent a messenger when Naaman arrived at his door, and was absent when the miracle occurred. His appearance could have led Naaman to conclude that the miracle was by his power alone. In Elisha's absence the miraculous power was credited to its true source."[53]

Over the next four verses (vv. 16–19) Elisha facilitates the completion of Naaman's transformation, moving his healing from his skin to his heart and mind. This transformation is signaled by the narrator through the repetition of the drama's "key thematic word"[54] לקח, "to take," which Brueggemann affirms "warrants considerable study."[55] The word can mean "take, accept, receive," as well as other

---

[50.]Menn, "A Little Child Shall Lead," 345.

[51.]". . . he will call on the name of the Lord, his God . . . he will cure the afflicted one."

[52.]"Indeed, I now know that there is no God in all the earth except in Israel."

[53.]Wray Beal, *1 & 2 Kings*, 335.

[54.]Long, *2 Kings*, 75.

[55.]Brueggemann, *1 & 2 Kings*, 339.

variations.[56] Indeed, most English translations[57] vacillate between these three English words to render the ten instances of the verb לקח in 2 Kgs 5.[58] I contend that its consistent use at critical moments in the drama, particularly during the climax, falling action, and Elisha's methodical repetition of it in verse 26 suggests that 2 Kgs 5 is something of a dramatic commentary on the practice and theology of "taking," which is to say a dramatic commentary on power. Therefore, לקח should be consistently translated as "take" throughout 2 Kgs 5, as I have done in the translation above.

Within the boundaries of the drama, the act of "taking" is understood as a demonstration of power within the framework of kings and kingdoms; it is an expression of greed and it is inherently reductionistic. In addition to the ten instances of לקח throughout the drama, which are mostly bunched in the final half, שבה ("to take captive") functions as a thematic synonym to open the drama (v. 2). Elisha's jeremiad to Gehazi in verse 26 connects Gehazi's "taking" (לקח) with Naaman "taking captive" (שבה) the little girl (v. 2).[59] In the end, Gehazi taking silver and clothing is no different than Naaman taking a child from her home and homeland to be a slave in his house.

Throughout the remainder of the climax (vv.16–19) Elisha models for Naaman an appropriate posture toward לקח: total rejection. In response to Naaman's imperative "*take* a gift from your servant" (v. 15), Elisha offers an emphatic reply: "As surely as the Lord lives, the Lord in whose service I stand (עָמַדְתִּי לְפָנָיו, 'amadti lephanav), I will take nothing" (v. 16). Elisha's posture before (לְפָנֵי) YVHV justifies his complete rejection of Naaman's urging to "take" something in compensation for his healing. Elisha is concerned to teach Naaman that

---

[56] *HALOT*, s.v. "לקח."

[57] NRSV, JPS (1985), NASB, ESV, TNIV, NKJV, ASV, to name a few.

[58] Once each in v. 5, 15, twice each in v. 16, 20, 23, 26.

[59] "Verse 2 does not name Naaman as the leader of the raiding bands (גדודים) which captured the Israelite girl, but the placement of this verse after the narrator's statement that Yahweh had given Aram victory by Naaman implies as much, as does the fact that Naaman comes into possession of the Israelite child." Lasine, "Go in peace," 16.

God's gracious healing cannot be paid for but only received. As Daniel
Berrigan lyrically put it: "What was freely received is freely given.
Reward would clog the flow of the Jordan within, the pure, healing
current of his soul."[60] But Elisha is equally, if not more concerned to
teach Naaman that because Elisha stands לִפְנֵי YVHV he does not stand
לִפְנֵי any king or kingdom; he does not participate in their destructive
system of power, expressed primarily through the act of לקח. It is not
until Elisha rejects Naaman's "gift"[61] that Naaman's healing moves
beneath the surface and takes root in his entire person.

This inner transformation is expressed semantically in the opening
of Naaman's final speech to Elisha (v. 17). Naaman's first word in
response to Elisha's refusal to take payment is וְלֹא (valo', "if not"),
"which has conditional force."[62] His second and third words are יֻתַּן־נָא
(yuttan-na', "let be given, please"). Naaman is not simply changing
tactics here; his entire posture in verse 17 contrasts with verse 15 in
several ways. First, his "if not" is a negation of לקח in favor of its
semantic opposite: נתן, "to give." Second, he moves from speaking in
the imperative (קַח qach, "take!") in verse 15 to a jussive form of the

---

[60.] Berrigan, *Kings and Their Gods*, 141.

[61.] In his 2010 monograph *The Lexical Field of the Substantives of "Gift" in
Ancient Hebrew*, Francesco Zanella identifies the use of בְּרָכָה (*berakhah*, "gift") in 2
Kgs 5:15 as an instance of בְּרָכָה as a "gift of goodwill," which is given "to gain favour
with a powerful and hostile recipient," but "can also be given outside of a specifically
violent and threatening situation, while still reflecting a situation of favour between
sender and recipient." He goes on to say that, in the case of Naaman, the Aramean
general "gives Elisha, who has cured him of leprosy, a rich בְּרָכָה-gift to thank him."
Zanella, *Lexical Field*, 76–77. However, since Elisha refuses the "gift" it would seem
"offers" or "attempts to give" would be a more accurate description of Naaman's
action. Beyond this semantic foible, the context seems to point more toward Naaman
offering Elisha the בְּרָכָה as compensation as opposed to simply gratitude, which calls
into question its placement in the category "gift of goodwill." Elisha by no means
rejects Naaman's goodwill; Elisha rejects Naaman's assumption that grace has a
monetary value and must be paid for, and that Elisha is responsible for the healing and
can therefore be compensated for it.

[62.] Sweeney, *I & II Kings*, 295

passive imperfect, which is further softened by the particle of entreaty[63] (יֻתַּן־נָא, *yuttan-na'*, "let be given, please"). Naaman chooses receiving over taking.

The actual content of Naaman's request is somewhat peculiar: "two mule-loads of earth" (v. 17). Naaman connects his request to the act of sacrifice, implying that he would use the soil to build an altar, which suggests the earth from Israel would function as a connection of sorts between Naaman's worship in Aram and the location of the object of his worship: the God *of Israel*. Naaman appears to assume that YHVH, like other gods of other nations, was bound by the political boundaries of the nation of Israel, and even though Naaman's miraculous healing revealed to him the futility and non-existence of those other gods (אֵין אֱלֹהִים, *'ein 'elohim*, v. 15), he seems to assume that YHVH's presence does not extend beyond Israel ("there are no gods in all the earth except in Israel," v. 15). The Israelite dirt—and the ensuing altar—would become a tangible reminder of his experience and a means of sustaining his connection to the God who healed him.

The "confusing"[64] structure and articulation of Naaman's request for prevenient grace in verse 18 makes perfect sense in the context of dramatic performance. The "grammatically clumsy and repetitive" elements are intentional and ought not be corrected through "emendations."[65] The artistry and intentionality of verse 18 is made

---

[63.]There is not widespread agreement of the syntactic function of the particle נָא־, which generally combines with jussive, imperative, and cohortative verbs, according to Arnold and Choi, *Guide to Biblical Hebrew Syntax*, 65. Lambdin argues that its primary function is "logical" in that it is used to describe a "logical consequence, either of an immediately preceding statement or of the general situation in which it is uttered." Lambdin, *Introduction to Biblical Hebrew*, 170. Joüon and Muraoka see it used mostly "for the purpose of adding a usually weak entreating nuance, which is roughly equivalent to a stressed and lengthened *Please* in English." Joüon and Muraoka, *Grammar of Biblical Hebrew*, 350.

[64.]Hobbs, *2 Kings*, 66.

[65.]Hobbs, *2 Kings*, 66. The emendations Hobbs suggests are 1. the addition of a conjunctive ו on לִדְבָר, the first word in v. 18, to strengthen the contrast between v. 17 and v. 18 "*But* in this matter...." And 2. changing the pronominal suffix on בְּהִשְׁתַּחֲוָיָתִי from a 1cs suffix ("when I bow down") to a 3ms suffix ("when he comes to worship").

clear through its chiastic structure. Robert Cohn laid out this structure in his article "Form and Perspective in 2 Kings V." Cohn isolated the phrase "he leans on my hand" as the center of the chiasmus. This decision creates an unnecessary imbalance, however, since it unevenly distributes the three-fold repetition of the word הִשְׁתַּחֲוָה in its various forms throughout the chiasmus—placing one instance before the line "he leans on my arm" and two after.[66] It makes more sense to spread the three instances out evenly through the chiasmus, as seen in the following arrangement:

A   in this one case,
B   would the Lord pardon your servant:
C   When my lord enters the house of Rimmon to worship there;
X   when he enters leaning on my arm so that I worship
             in the house of Rimmon;
C'   when I worship in the house of Rimmon,
B'   would the Lord pardon your servant
A'   in this one case?

The artfulness of Naaman's speech displayed in this structure suggests the grammatical awkwardness of the speech is likewise intentional. "[T]he wordiness of Naaman's statement reflects his halting speech, as he apologizes for his continued worship of the god Rimmon, a custom which he perceives to be offensive to Israel's God."[67] The clumsiness of the request is natural to its context.

"The change need not reflect an original reading. It is more likely to be a tendentious reading, since Naaman has already foresworn the worship of a foreign god." Hobbs, *2 Kings*, 57. The change need not be made at all, however. In fact, the emended version Hobbs suggests is less clear than the MT's "when I bow down," because Naaman is not asking for forgiveness for his lord the king bowing down, but for his own act of bowing, which he promises here to do only ceremoniously, only in body, not in heart. Apart from the contextual appropriateness of the awkwardness of Naaman's speech, the grammatical awkwardness could be seen as further indication of the oral nature of the drama. Cf. Miller, *Oral Tradition*, 72.

   [66.]Cf. Cohn, "Form and Perspective," 179.
   [67.]Cogan and Tadmor, *II Kings*, 65.

Drama creates unique interpretive possibilities for this moment, namely, simultaneous action, freeze frames, and flash back (or flash forward) sequences. For example, as Naaman bows before Elisha and begins his halting request for forgiveness, everyone on stage but Naaman freezes. Each phrase of the chiasmus matches a movement on the stage. During lines A and B Naaman remains prostrate before Elisha. During line C Naaman rises and moves toward the opposite side of the stage, where the king of Aram sits on his throne. As Naaman rises and approaches, the king of Aram also rises, and they meet in the middle to enact the bowing ritual Naaman is describing to Elisha. At line X—the mid-point of the chiasmus—Naaman puts out his hand and the king places his upon it, and they take a step forward, then bow down together.[68] Naaman speaks line C' while bowing with his lord in "the

---

[68.] I am persuaded by Cohn and Hobbs who take the phrase "he leans on my hand" to be "an idiom denoting not that Naaman was his physical support, but, rather, his 'right-hand man' (cf. 2 Kings vii 2, 17)." Cohn, "Form and Perspective," 179. "Naaman clearly asks for forgiveness for the resumption of his duties as the king's 'right hand man'." Hobbs, *2 Kings*, 66. The only other instance of שָׁאַן with עַל יָד in the Hebrew Bible is found in 2 Kgs 7:2, 17. In these instances it is likewise probable that the phrase identifies the relationship between the king and his aide, rather than describing the king's physical condition. Confirmation of this interpretation is found in 2 Kgs 6:30 in the same drama, when the king clearly walks through the town without aid, dressed in sackcloth and ashes. Perhaps the idiom points to a ceremonial responsibility in which Naaman, as the king's right-hand man, would process with the king into the House of Rimmon, while the king placed his outstretched arm upon Naaman's, to indicate both Naaman's elevated position within the kingdom, but his subservient position to the king. If something like this is in mind, it could add an element of pathos to Naaman's request, particularly if Naaman has been unable to fulfill this duty due to his skin disease/affliction. A former student who played the role of Naaman made this very discovery as she studied and prepared for the role. She reflected on this moment, with reference to the line "And he leans upon my arm" in v. 18, in the following way: "This line seems to be the central line of this section. What is so important about it? It speaks of intimate contact, support, and possibly about something that may not have happened before due to Naaman's skin condition. There is something about this leaning on his arm that Naaman doesn't want to miss out on and you can hear the hope in his heart as he lays this struggle out before the prophet who is before the face of God." Amy Klanderman, "Dramatic Analysis of 2 Kings 5," unpublished paper (Holland, MI: Western Theological Seminary, 2016).

house of Rimmon," and as he nears the end, he rises and moves back toward Elisha; the king of Aram simply fades back to his throne in Aram. The final two lines, B' and A' are delivered in the same position as A and B, with Naaman prostrate before Elisha. Thus the literary chiasmus achieves dramatic and physical expression.

The process of blocking this scene also raises another, deeper question of motivation: why does Naaman ask the prophet for prevenient grace? What is Naaman's intention or desire? Does his question express his intention to simply "go through the motions" of worship in the House of Rimmon with his body, but that his heart will remain in Israel? Or might it mean, rather, that he hopes his wholehearted devotion to his king and his god could be "credited to him as righteousness,"[69] as it were, in that the God of Israel would consider his worship of Rimmon as worship of YHVH? Is he motivated by some other purpose or desire?

Either way, the prophet grants Naaman's request with just two words in Hebrew: לְשָׁלוֹם לֵךְ (*lekh leshalom*), "Go in peace" (v. 19). Elisha does not ask Naaman to clarify his question; he simply sends him on his way in(to) שָׁלוֹם (*shalom*, "peace, wholeness, health, prosperity"[70]). His response, though brief, implies that Elisha has granted Naaman's request for forgiveness.[71] The presence of the word שָׁלוֹם (*shalom*) foreshadows Naaman's future question to Gehazi in verse 21, and Gehazi's false reply (v. 22). Naaman and his entourage depart joyfully from Elisha's house. They take several steps (כִּבְרַת אֶרֶץ, *kivrat 'arets*, "a short distance") across the stage toward Aram and freeze in motion, suggesting that the resolution just accomplished is not final.

---

[69] Cf Rom 4:3; Gal 3:6; Jas 2:23.

[70] *HALOT*, s.v., "שָׁלוֹם."

[71] This interpretation is not universal. Stuart Lasine has carefully laid out the various positions across the entire spectrum of interpretation, nicely captured in the title of his article "'Go in peace' or 'Go to hell'?" However, after surveying the biblical, linguistic, narrative, and historical data, he does not suggest a preferred interpretation. Lasine, "Go in peace," 3–25. I agree with Wray Beal who concludes: "The request is a bold assertion of trust in YHWH's gracious forgiveness and, while Elisha does not give explicit consent, it must be implied in his command that Naaman 'Go in peace.'" Wray Beal, *1 & 2 Kings*, 335.

Falling Action (vv. 20–26)

The final eight verses of 2 Kgs 5 complicate the symmetry of the almost storybook ending witnessed in the first nineteen verses. As was mentioned in Chapter 3, the ending of the drama may be prolonged through complicating elements in the falling action that include moments of suspense in which the outcome of the climactic resolution is thrown into doubt. Such is the case with this story. The resolution of the conflict—which functioned on a personal, national, international, and theological plane—created by Naaman's "affliction," which was achieved in the climax is unceremoniously thrown into doubt by none other than the prophet's servant. The one empowered to carry out the will and word of the prophet is the very one who undermines both his will and his word. In 2 Kgs 5:20–26, the action "falls" over three scenes. The first and third take place in and around Elisha's house, and the middle scene occurs at an unspecified location not far from Elisha's house along the route Naaman was taking back to Aram.

Scene 1 - Gehazi hatches a plan (v. 20)

The complicating factor in the drama's conclusion is Gehazi, the servant (נַעַר, na'ar) of Elisha, the man of God. He is introduced by name in verse 20. Gehazi is the only נַעַר in 2 Kgs 5 whose name is given. It is unclear if Gehazi is also the character referred to in verse 8 and again in verse 10 as Elisha's messenger. Though Leeb sees "no reason to believe"[72] the messenger and Gehazi are one and the same, in our performances we have generally chosen to make them the same character, which establishes a relationship between Gehazi and Naaman early on that is, in fact, grounded in the script. Indeed, a level of familiarity between Naaman and Gehazi is clearly assumed in their interaction in verses 21–23.[73]

---

[72] Leeb, *Away From the Father's House*, 51.

[73] E.g. Gehazi does not introduce himself to Naaman. Further, he does not refer to Elisha by name or title, simply אֲדֹנִי *'adoni*, "my lord" and Naaman is not in the least confused. It is possible that they were introduced at some point when Naaman entered Elisha's house in v. 15. Gehazi was certainly present for Naaman and Elisha's

Cohn has identified a number of ways the character of Gehazi contrasts with three of the most influential characters in the drama. These
contrasts draw attention to his deceitfulness, and their integrity. First,
Gehazi, who is identified as the נַעַר of Elisha, contrasts with the נַעֲרָה,
the little girl. Though they are both Israelites, she "was concerned to
help, not exploit, Naaman."[74] The contrast extends cross-culturally as
well. Gehazi, the "ignoble Israelite," functions as a foil to Naaman, who
becomes the "God-fearing foreigner."[75] Gehazi actually references his
foreignness pejoratively by calling him "this Aramean" (הָאֲרַמִּי הַזֶּה,
ha'arami hazzeh, v. 20). Their respective relationships with their
"lords" is also markedly different. "Naaman had asked for pardon in
advance for showing loyalty to his lord, while Gehazi criticizes his lord
for sparing Naaman and excuses himself in advance for his treachery."[76]
Naaman stood לִפְנֵי the king of Aram (v. 1) and also Elisha (v. 15), but
upon returning from his duplicitous quest Gehazi stands אֶל ('el, "opposite") Elisha (v. 25). The final juxtaposition is between Gehazi and "his
lord," Elisha (v. 25), which is primarily drawn out through Gehazi's
monologue (v. 20). Whereas Elisha vowed on the life of YHVH to take
nothing from Naaman, Gehazi vows to do the opposite, to take something—anything—from him. Gehazi's oath repeats much of the phras-
ing of Elisha's oath (v. 16), implying that it was a purposeful undermin-
ing of Elisha's word. The contrast is deepened when Gehazi eagerly
takes even more than what he asked for from Naaman (v. 23). "Notably,
although Gehazi invokes [YHVH's] name, unlike Elisha, he does not

---

exchange, which is where he learned of the "gifts" Naaman brought, and witnessed his
master "refuse" Naaman and not "take" anything from his hand (v. 21). The
assumptions made by the script itself with respect to Naaman and Gehazi's mutual
knowledge of each other suggests Gehazi was the messenger who interacted with
Naaman in the palace in Samaria (v. 8), and at the gate of Elisha's house (v. 10).
Perhaps Naaman feels some guilt over his response to Gehazi's message in v. 10,
which compels him to eagerly give Gehazi whatever he desires to take and more (vv.
22–23).

[74] Cohn, "Form and Perspective," 180.
[75] Cohn, "Form and Perspective," 180.
[76] Cohn, "Form and Perspective," 180.

call him 'the God before whom I stand'. Clearly, he does not 'stand before' [YHVH]; instead he 'runs after' Naaman."[77]

Each of these contrasts can be drawn out through spacing, blocking, and gestures in performance. For example, the little girl, Naaman, and Gehazi each take a kneeling position in the same spot on stage at different points in the drama. The intersection of character, context, blocking, and location creates a visual link between them and sharpens the contrast latent in the script. In verse 2 Naaman's raiding party captures the girl and throws her down to the ground at center stage. She is alone and vulnerable, a victim of Naaman and Aram's greed, power, and violence. Naaman soon finds himself kneeling in the same place, which has now become the Jordan River, where he becomes like the little girl and finds the healing she foretold (v. 14). These two moments form the backdrop for the drama's final scene in which Gehazi falls to his knees, directly over the spot where Naaman's "affliction" was dropped.[78] As Elisha's words "cover Gehazi's face"[79] he discovers he now has Naaman's affliction and flees from Elisha's presence (וַיֵּצֵא מִלְּפָנָיו, *vayyetsei milphanav*). This final movement forms a visual *inclusio* with the opening scene in which Naaman is before his lord (לִפְנֵי אֲדֹנָיו, *liphnei 'adonav*).

Scene 2 - Gehazi enacts his plan (vv. 21–24)

The interaction between Naaman and Gehazi along the path toward Aram presents a number of dramatic interpretive possibilities. First, the delivery of Gehazi's deceitful story and request brings to light a darkly humorous irony latent in the text. It has to do with the placement of the prepositional phrase לָהֶם (*lahem*, "to them") in verse 22. After convincing Naaman with his story of two youths (נְעָרִים, *ne'arim*) who are in

---

[77.]Cohn, "Form and Perspective," 180.

[78.]In v. 14 Naaman's healing is symbolized by the removal of the white fabric representing his affliction. In some performances the narrator, who originally put the fabric on Naaman in v. 1, also removes it in v. 14, acting as a representative of YHVH. The fabric then remains in this spot on the stage until v. 27 when the narrator again picks it up and puts it on Gehazi, just like with Naaman in v. 1.

[79.]Cf. Esth 7:8.

need[80] coming to Elisha he requests two outfits of clothing and a talent
of silver. If Gehazi's character pauses for a brief moment between תְּנָה־
נָא (tnah-na', "give, please") and לָהֶם (lahem, "to them"), the audience
leans forward in their seats wondering if Gehazi is going to accidentally
betray his chicanery to Naaman by saying "give, please, *to me.*" But,
after the brief pause Gehazi regains his internal footing and, while gesturing back toward home where the "two youths" await Naaman's
generosity, correctly says לָהֶם, "to them." The audience and Gehazi both
know that Gehazi narrowly escaped a mishap which would have seriously
undermined Naaman's reception of his lie.

This subtle yet not insignificant interpretation of Gehazi's delivery is
reinforced by research done into the function of the "lengthened
imperative" form, which Gehazi uses here. The regular form of the
imperative of נתן is תֵּן (ten, "give"); the lengthened form is made by
adding a ה to the end to make תְּנָה (tnah).[81] This form is further
qualified by the particle of entreaty נָא (na') resulting in תְּנָה־נָא (tnah-
na', roughly "give, please"). In his article "The Lengthened Imperative
קְטְלָה in Biblical Hebrew,"[82] Steven Fassberg demonstrates that in
"almost all of the examples of קְטְלָה the lengthened imperative is used
when the action of the verb is directed to the speaker (usually motion
towards the speaker); the regular imperative, on the other hand, is used
when the action of the verb is directed elsewhere."[83] In most cases the
direction *toward* the speaker is rendered explicit by a first person
pronominal suffix ("me") directly following the imperative form.

This conclusion was independently corroborated in a Ph.D. dissertation
by Ahouva Shulman who summarized her findings this way: "The long
imperative form is used where the speaker requests an action directed to himself, an action done for him/to him/towards him/with him

---

[80.]Gehazi tells Naaman they are from the "sons of the prophets" (בְּנֵי הַנְּבִיאִים *bnei
hannevi'im*). This was one of a number of generally poor (see 2 Kgs 4:1, 6:1–7)
prophetic communities that were under Elisha's tutelage (see 2 Kgs 6:1). A modern
equivalent to this could be "two missionary kids."

[81.]This is called a paragogic ה.

[82.]Fassberg, "Lengthened Imperative," 7–13.

[83.]Fassberg, "Lengthened Imperative," 10; emphasis added.

etc. In most cases the long form of imperative is used to suggest an action as a personal favour to the speaker as well as action towards the speaker."[84] If this is so, those listening to this story performed in Israel would likely have anticipated a first common singular suffix לִי (*li*, "to me") to follow the long imperative תְּנָה־נָא ("give, please").[85] This grammatical expectation, combined with a subtle delivery,[86] adds a layer of tragic comedy to a moment already saturated with irony as the audience helplessly watches Naaman get duped by Elisha's cunning servant.

The emotive effect of the irony in the scene is enhanced further by the time it takes Naaman to carefully pack the "gifts" into the two bags. By slowing the scene down considerably, Naaman's innocent joy—itself an expression of the transformation he has just received at the hand of Gehazi's master—is contrasted with Gehazi's wolfish delight as he oversees the perfect execution of his plan. Indeed, it worked out even better than he planned; Naaman gave him *two* talents of silver!

Not only does Gehazi get what he asked for and more, he also experiences an elevation in status—if only temporarily. Naaman gives the

---

[84.]Shulman, "Use of Modal Verb Forms," 66, quoted in Eickmann, "Long Imperative," 127.

[85.]Fassberg uses נתן with the preposition ל in his concluding summary to his article, stating his findings clearly: "The lengthened imperative קָטְלָה is used in Biblical Hebrew when the action of the verb is directed toward the speaker (תְּנָה לִי), whereas the regular imperative קְטֹל usually occurs when the action of the verb is directed elsewhere (תֵּן לָהֶם)." Fassberg, "Lengthened Imperative," 13.

[86.]A particularly effective rendering of this line that takes the above argument into account and would be immediately accessible to an audience of native Hebrew speakers could go as follows: Gehazi speaks most of his line looking off in the distance, as any untrained liar would do. When he gets to this line (תְּנָה־נָא לָהֶם, "give, please, to them") he pauses briefly after the ל ("to . . . ") and looks right at Naaman (very briefly, and totally accidentally), wondering if, in fact, he slipped and said לִי ("to me") without thinking (which, of course, is the actual truth). Seeing Naaman is none the wiser, he continues in earnest, almost over-speaking the לָהֶם ("to *them*") with attendant gesticulations (motioning vaguely toward Elisha), and perhaps raising his eyebrows in relief at the completion of his line—all of which the audience would easily interpret as delicious irony. Indeed, in performances of this drama in Hebrew to audiences that know no Hebrew, when this line is delivered in the way just described, it is clearly apparent what Gehazi has (almost) done and everyone laughs.

two bags of silver and the two changes of clothing to "his two men"[87]
who "lifted them up before" (וַיִּשְׂאוּ לְפָנָיו, *vayyiss'u lephanav*) Gehazi.
Not only does the pairing of נשׂא with לִפְנֵי call to mind the description
of Naaman whose face "was lifted high" (וּנְשֻׂא פָנִים, *unsu' phanim*) before his lord (v. 1), but it also suggests that, for a fleeting moment at
least, Gehazi has risen in social stature and power. Two performative
insights follow. First, Naaman's men lead the way back to Elisha's
house because a) the way is familiar to them since they only traveled "a
short distance" before Gehazi stopped them, and b) the men carry the
gifts "before" (לְפָנֵי) Gehazi, both literally and figuratively. As they
move across the stage and close in on Elisha's house, Gehazi realizes
that they are simply retracing their steps, and to return the gifts directly
to Elisha's front door would blow his cover. It seems logical, then, that
Gehazi would jump out in front of the men to stop them and then divert
them to another more strategic location to unload the booty. This moment of dramatic irony again plays the audience's knowledge against
the ignorance of Naaman's servants who, though confused, agree to veer
off course to the destination Gehazi chooses.

Second, after Gehazi "takes" (לקח) the goods from their hands he
"sends" (שלח) them on their way. The use of the intensive Pi'el form of
שלח here (v. 24) contrasts with every other instance of שלח in 2 Kgs 5,
which all appear in the Qal (vv. 5, 6, 7, 8, 10, 22). Though the Qal and
Pi'el forms of שלח are often indistinguishable in terms of meaning or
syntax, the Pi'el can have "more of a nuance of 'send away, dismiss'."[88]
In our performance, at each previous instance of שלח, the one sending
(whether the king of Aram or Elisha) simply held up a hand, motioning
toward the direction the messenger ought to go. In this case Gehazi
sends the men away with some urgency—out of fear of being caught,
and out of his newfound position of power. Perhaps Gehazi nudges or

---

[87.]The pronominal suffix "his" most certainly refers to Naaman and not Gehazi.
As a נַעַר ("lad, servant"), it is highly unlikely Gehazi would have אֲנָשִׁים ("men")
underneath him. And even if he somehow did, he would never have risked other people
connected to Elisha knowing about his devious dealings with Naaman. Further,
Naaman only saw one man running to meet him, not three (v. 21).

[88.]*NIDOTTE*, s.v. "שלח."

pushes them physically to speed their exit. In response to his sending, the men hurry across the stage and disappear into Aram.

Scene 3 - Gehazi's plan backfires (vv. 25–26)

After carefully depositing the materials in a location on the stage some distance from where Elisha stands inside the area representing his house,[89] Gehazi enters the house quietly and, instead of standing "before Elisha" (לִפְנֵי אֲדֹנָיו, *liphnei 'adonav*) as might be expected, he stands off to the side, or "opposite" Elisha (אֶל־אֲדֹנָיו, *'el 'adonav*). Gehazi's physical location on stage vis-à-vis Elisha is a direct contrast to Naaman's posture in verses 15–18, and calls to mind Naaman's childishly obstinate posture from verses 9–12. Unlike Naaman, Elisha is not fooled by Gehazi's trickery. He turns to face Gehazi and asks him plainly: "Where have you been, Gehazi?"[90] Despite Gehazi's attempt to deny culpability, Elisha is undeterred.

Elisha's response (v. 26) to Gehazi's lie (v. 25) constitutes the theological conclusion of the drama, achieved through the expert use of dramatic *inclusio*, drawing the hearer back to the themes introduced in verses 1–2 and initially resolved in verse 14. In one performance, Elisha and Gehazi move slowly out toward center stage as they talk. They stop at the very spot where Naaman was healed (v. 14) and the little girl was thrown down by her Aramean captors (v. 2). As Gehazi listens to Elisha's devastating dialogue he falls to his knees and assumes the same

---

[89.]It is unclear precisely what is meant by הָעֹפֶל (*ha'ophel*). It is translated variously as "hill" (NASB, ESV, TNIV, ASV, NET, CJB), "citadel" (NRSV, JPS (1985)), and "tower" (KJV). The LXX tried to make sense of the confusion through an emendation to the text: "The change in [LXX] from עפל 'hill' to אפל 'darkness' is most effective, and perhaps deliberate. It exploits the homonyms to the full, and draws out the theme of the 'dark deed' of Gehazi. However, it serves no purpose as an attempt to identify precisely where this 'ophel' was located." Hobbs, *2 Kings*, 67. Apparently it was a location other than the house of Elisha, but not where Gehazi stowed the stolen goods. He stored them "in the house," which was likely Elisha's house, perhaps in a temporary secret spot from which he would move them later.

[90.]The Hebrew is even more to the point: מֵאַיִן גֵּחֲזִי *me'ayin gechazi* "from where Gehazi?"

posture each of the previous characters took in that spot, visually representing the thematic thread that unites them to each other.[91] Through
some kind of prophetic insight Elisha was privy to the encounter between Gehazi and Naaman, even to the point of knowing the generosity
of Naaman's interaction with Gehazi.[92] Elisha also knows precisely
what Gehazi "took" (לקח) from Naaman, but his vision stretches beyond
Gehazi's traitorous taking to its treacherous end. Elisha's words pulse
with pathos. He rhetorically asks Gehazi if there is ever a time[93] to take
anything. The implied answer is clearly negative.

Elisha's list of "things to take" is arranged as four pairings; each pair
is made up of relatively equal items, and there is an ascending quality

---

[91.]This thread of connected gestures provides internal evidence against Jones (who
follows Schmitt, who follows Gunkel), who sees 2 Kgs 5 as a patchwork quilt of three
distinct and independent traditions, which are connected by only a "superficial" unity.
Differences between distinct traditions are manifest in either differences in "theme"
and "aim" (412, with direct reference to Gunkel and Schmitt), or the choice to say the
prophet's name or include the title "man of God." The three traditions Jones identifies,
then, are the "Elisha" tradition in vv. 1–14, the "Gehazi" tradition in v15b–16, 20–27,
and the "original proselyte tradition" in vv. 17–19a. Jones, *1 and 2 Kings*, 412–414.
My contention is that the unity of the chapter is much more than skin deep. Hobbs also
is convinced of the drama's essential unity. In fact, though he does not assume this
story was performed, he nevertheless offers a theatrical analogy: "In dramatic terms,
the three episodes are like three acts of a drama, each with their individual scene
changes and entrances and exits of the subsidiary characters upon the stage" (Hobbs,
2 Kings, 59). He is more right than he realizes. For a summary of various positions on
the internal (dis)unity of 2 Kings 5 see Long, *2 Kings*, 68.

[92.]"... a man stepped down from his chariot to meet you."

[93.]Many commentators and translations render הָעֵת as either "Is this a time"
(Cogan and Tadmor, *II Kings*, 62; Fretheim, *First and Second Kings*, 151; so also
NRSV, JPS (1985), TNIV, CJB) or "Is it a time" (Sweeney, *I & II Kings*, 294; also
NASB, ESV ("Was it a time"), KVJ, ASV, Young's Literal). These renderings imply
there could be a time to take in the way that Gehazi has done, but this is or was not
one of those times. Elisha's emphatic refusal to "take" anything from Naaman (v. 16),
justified by his posture standing לִפְנֵי יהוה suggests, however, that Elisha does not
believe there is ever a time to take silver or clothing or olive orchards or vineyards or
flocks or cattle or manservants or maidservants. In the economy of grace in the
kingdom of God it is never appropriate to take what is not yours. The translation I have
offered, "Is there a time" implies a negative answer.

to the list with respect to animate life and consciousness. It begins with objects made of raw materials, moves to plants, then animals, and concludes with human beings. The first pairing is punctuated with the infinitive לָקַחַת, "to take" (*laqachat*, "לָקַחַת silver and לָקַחַת clothing"), which identifies the only two items on the list Gehazi actually took from Naaman. However, the repetition establishes a pattern that is implied throughout the rest of the list. Though Gehazi took only the first two of the eight items, Elisha articulates the inevitable end to the trajectory established by his greedy lust "to take . . . something—anything" (v. 20). Blinded by his greed, Gehazi is concerned only that he takes; the *object* of his taking is of little concern to him.[94]

The final item on Elisha's list, שְׁפָחוֹת (*shphachot*, "female servants"), is an echo of the נַעֲרָה קְטַנָּה (*na'arah qetannah*), the little girl who was taken captive by Naaman's men and will one day grow up to be a שִׁפְחָה (*shiphchah*, "maidservant") in Naaman's household. In Elisha's mind, taking silver and clothing for no other reason than to exercise the power to take is the same as taking a human being to be one's slave. By framing this list as he does, Elisha calls to mind the Torah's ultimate list against greed: the tenth commandment.[95] Walter Brueggemann, following Marvin Cheney, argues that the tenth commandment has to do with the faithful appropriation of social power, particularly with respect to land, against the backdrop of the exploitation of the weak at the hands of the powerful.[96] This interpretation is compelling in the context of 2 Kgs 5 and the juxtaposition between Naaman and Gehazi. Elisha admonishes Gehazi for submitting to the seductive allure of earthly power in such a way as to make his heart indistinguishable from Naaman's prior to his healing at the Jordan. One recalls the narrator's elaborate description of Naaman's accomplishments, and the extent of his social and material power which opens the drama (vv. 1–

[94.]He vows to take not specific objects, but to take מְאוּמָה (*me'umah*), "(something) or other." *HALOT*, s.v. "מְאוּמָה."

[95.]Exod 20:17 and Deut 5:21.

[96.]Brueggemann, *Finally Comes the Poet,* 99–110. Bruggemann's interpretation of the tenth commandment follows Marvin Cheney's interpretation in Cheney, "You Shall Not Covet," 3–13.

2). Here in verse 26 Elisha, in effect, tells Gehazi that if he desires to share in Naaman's power through the exploitative seizure of property he must likewise share in Naaman's fate: צָרַעַת (*tsara'at* "affliction").

Dénouement (v. 27)

The drama is drawing to a close. The narrator is carefully guiding the story to its final scene and is laying the foundation of a new equilibrium. This drama ends, as so many biblical dramas do, in the same place it began, only now everything has changed. At the beginning Naaman was a man absorbed by power and broken by an affliction, he is now a humble servant of the man of God who recognizes the singular rule of Israel's God on account of the healing he has received in both body and heart. Gehazi, the previously faithful servant to the man of God now apparently leaves Elisha's service[97] having contracted Naaman's lust for power and its attendant affliction. And the character who binds them all together is the little girl, who, after being caught in the web of international politics and forced into slavery speaks a prophetic word that changes the course of nations, validates the ministry of Elisha, testifies to Israel's God as the true source of power, and serves as the standard by which Naaman and Gehazi's conduct is implicitly measured.

The curtain opened at verse 1 to a stage on which Naaman stood boldly and proudly "before his lord" as a long list of accolades celebrated his manifold greatness. As the curtain is drawn on the final scene, Gehazi is alone on stage, standing in the same place where Naaman previously stood, now burdened by Naaman's affliction. The devastating consequences of Naaman's greed, initially hidden by the narrator's

---

[97] וַיֵּצֵא מִלְּפָנָיו *vayyetsei millphanav* "and he went forth from his presence" or, perhaps, "and he left serving him" (v. 27). This interpretation is complicated by the fact that another story in the Elisha cycle, which perhaps takes place after Elisha's death, involves Gehazi reporting to the unnamed king of Israel all of the deeds of Elisha. The story is placed chronologically before Elisha's death is told (2 Kgs 13:14–21), so it is unclear if he is alive or not, but Gehazi seems to be acting as his representative to the king, whether at his behest or after his death. Cf. 2 Kgs 8:1–6.

praise in the opening scene, are now fully revealed to Gehazi, his descendants, and the audience. In one performance, after Elisha completes his pathos-filled line (v. 27a), he turns around and returns to his house with his back to the audience. Gehazi, who knelt down over the white מְצֹרָע fabric Naaman left when he washed in the Jordan[98] throughout Elisha's speech, now gathers it up, places it on himself the same way it sat on Naaman in verse 1, and slowly turns and walks across the stage as the narrator describes his exit: "Gehazi went forth from him as one afflicted, as white as snow" (v. 27b).[99] The silence of the moment combined with the visual of the white cloth bespeak the double-edged sword of Gehazi's affliction. Not only does he now carry in his body the external markers of his greed, but his successive generations will likewise bear the mark of his treachery, and endure the social isolation that goes along with it.

It is a sobering end to a rich and sophisticated story concerned with the character of power and the nature of greed. Along the way the mighty were brought down and the lowly lifted up. One man's ascent from sickness to health prompted another's descent from health to sickness. Kings and their palaces gave way to YHVH and his prophet. The gifts of the empire were forgotten and abandoned in favor of a wagonload of earth. The small and muddy Jordan does what the great and mighty rivers of Damascus could not. And the faith of the prophet's servant is out-shined by that of a pagan general and a little girl.

[98.] See note 9 above.

[99.] Another possibility we have explored, which I mentioned above, is to have the narrator either pick up the cloth that was previously removed from Naaman by the narrator in the same spot and now place it on Gehazi. In another performance the narrator held the cloth whenever it was not on a character. In this version the narrator placed it on Naaman while speaking the final word of v. 1, removed it from Naaman on the seventh washing in the Jordan (v. 14), and again placed it on Gehazi at the end of v. 27. The narrator often indicates or suggests the presence of God in a drama, and so this interpretation leaves room for God's role in both the healing and consequences of Naaman and Gehazi's actions respectively.

CHAPTER 6
THE BANDS OF ARAM: 2 KINGS 6:8–23

Introduction

This final story takes an altogether different approach to engaging the audience than the first two dramas discussed above. Whereas they employed tension to get the audience involved in the unfolding drama, this story primarily uses humor to accomplish the same thing. This poses a particular challenge for the actor(s) presenting the drama. In the first place, the challenge is how to express the humor that is clearly in the script without playing it up too far and reducing the story to slapstick. But a second challenge is closely tied to it, which is to employ the humor for the purpose for which it is intended, namely, to open up the audience and connect them to the characters so that they will be prepared to be transformed with the characters at the drama's climax.

In addition to handling the delicate matter of the appropriate amount of humor, this story presents several further challenges that performance illumines. The spectacular scene in which the horses and chariots of fire reveal themselves to Elisha's servant presents a peculiar challenge for faithful (and non-distracting) representation. A further challenge, which is more common in Old Testament dramas, is how to represent large armies with just a few actors, and how to demonstrate their movements across large geographical areas (from Aram to Dothan to Samaria). This drama's themes, like the drama in the previous chapter, revolve around the nature of power, but are worked out in very different ways. Instead of greed and disease, this story reflects on power through the lens of blindness and sight, rage and compassion, fear and faith, war and peace, the power of violence and the power of a shared meal.

A Translation for Performance

CONFLICT

[8]The king of Aram was waging war with Israel. And he consulted with his counselors, saying:

> *At place such and such you shall set an ambush.*[1]

[9]And the man of God sent word to the king of Israel saying:

> *Be on your guard that you do not pass by this place, for Aram has set an ambush.*

[10]And the king of Israel sent word to the place about which the man of God had spoken. And he warned it. And they were on their guard there—not once . . . not twice . . . .

DEVELOPMENT

Scene 1

[11]And a storm erupted in the heart of the king of Aram concerning this matter. And he called his servants and said to them:

> *Will you not tell me who among us is for the king of Israel?*

[12]And one of his servants said:

> *No, my lord the king. Indeed Elisha—the prophet in Israel—tells the king of Israel even the words you speak in your bedchamber.*

---

[1]Long's argument for amending this word from תַּחֲנֹתִי to תְּנִחתוּ is compelling: "For simplicity of solution and adherence to literary convention, it seems best to read *tinḥătŭ* in v. 8 and *nōḥătîm* in v. 9 from root *nḥt*, meaning 'to go down' in a military sense of 'falling upon to commit hostile action,' or, simply, 'attack'." Long, *2 Kings*, 81–82, and references. See also LaBarbera, "The Man of War and the Man of God," 639, n. 6.

¹³And he said:

> *Go! Find out where he is! Then I will send for him and capture*
> *him!*

And he was told:

> *Behold! In Dothan!*

Scene 2

¹⁴And he sent there horses and chariots and a great army. They came by night and surrounded the city.

¹⁵The servant of the man of God rose early. And he went out. And behold, an army was surrounding the city! Plus horses and chariots! And his servant said to him:

> *Ah! My lord! What can we do?*

¹⁶And he said:

> *Do no be afraid, for many more are there with us than there are*
> *with them.*

¹⁷And Elisha prayed, and said:

> *O Lord, open his eyes that he might see!*

And the Lord opened the servant's eyes. And he saw. And behold, the mountains were full of horses and chariots of fire, all around Elisha!

Scene 3
[18]Then the army[2] descended upon them. And Elisha prayed to the Lord, saying:

> *O strike these foreigners with a blinding light!*

And he struck them with a blinding light, according to the word of Elisha. [19]And Elisha said to them:

> *This is not the way. And this is not the city. Walk behind me, and I will lead you to the man whom you are seeking.*

And he led them to Samaria.

CLIMAX

Scene 4
[20]And when they entered Samaria, Elisha said:

> *O Lord, open the eyes of these men that they might see!*

And the Lord opened their eyes. And they saw. And behold, they were in Samaria! [21]And the king of Israel said to Elisha when he saw them:

> *Can I strike them? Can I strike them, my father?!*

[2.]The subject of this verb is ambiguous in the Hebrew. The options are either the Aramean army or the horses and chariots of fire. The horses and chariots of fire are the nearest antecedent, but the Aramean army is the more logical referent, given the context of their mission to capture Elisha and the ensuing action Elisha takes to pray that they would be blinded. The human army's descent upon Elisha and his servant lends an urgency to Elisha's prayer. See below for a fuller treatment of this translation decision.

²²And he said:

> *No, you will not strike them! Those whom you have taken captive*
> *with your sword or with your bow, do you strike them? Set bread*
> *and water before them, that they might eat and drink. And then*
> *let them go to their lord.*

²³And he set before them an elaborate feast. And they ate. And they drank. And he sent them on their way. And they went to their lord.

DÉNOUEMENT

And thereafter the bands of Aram no longer went into the land of Israel.

Setting / Conflict (vv. 8–10)

The narrator immediately establishes the initial equilibrium as a season of continual warfare between the king of Aram and Israel (הָיָה נִלְחָם, *hayah nilcham*, "he was warring").[3] This explanation introduces the conflict that is most evident at the surface layer of the script, which Tom Boogaart—writing from the perspective of performance—has described as a power struggle between the various kings in the passage: the king of Aram, the king of Israel, and the King of Kings—represented by his messenger Elisha, the אִישׁ הָאֱלֹהִים (*'ish ha'elohim*, "man of God").[4] The two earthly kings strategize and compete for dominance, seeking any chance to gain the upper hand, but the God of Israel—through the prophet Elisha—foils *both* of their plans (vv. 9, 22).

    According to Boogaart, the true conflict operates beneath the surface of the text, however, and is oriented not at the power struggle between the kings, but is about the nature of power itself.

---

[3] This is one of a number of elements that connect this story to that of 2 Kgs 5, in which the גְּדוּדֵי אֲרָם (*g'dudei 'aram*, "raiding parties of Aram," cf. 2 Kgs 6:23 and 2 Kgs 5:2) also infiltrate Israel, and while there take the little girl captive.

[4] Boogaart, "Drama and the Sacred," 43.

The scenes in the play show that the king of Aram as well as the king of Israel use power in a way that contrasts sharply with the way the King of the Universe uses it. The abiding question is whether people—both the characters in the drama and the audience—are capable of seeing the difference between these two uses of power. The issue of *seeing* is closely related to the issue of *power* in the narrative.[5]

Indeed, "seeing" is a central motif in the drama's approach to exploring the dimensions and dynamics of power as it functions in the kingdoms of the earth and in the kingdom of heaven.[6] Power is expressed through the capacity to see—and thus, to know.[7] Powerlessness is expressed through the inability to see (literal or metaphorical blindness), and is equated with ignorance.[8] This interconnected web of power, sight, and knowledge is worked out dramatically through the effective (and extensive) use of irony and humor,[9] largely (but not exclusively) through the "gentle mockery of Aram."[10] Indeed, this story seems to employ humor more than tension in the service of its formational objectives. Humor, like tension, functions to engage the audience, but unlike tension it lightens the mood. In this drama, humor is a strategy to open the hearts of the audience for the final turn toward the serious in which the heart of the drama's message lies (vv. 20–23).

---

[5] Boogaart, "Drama and the Sacred," 43; emphasis original.

[6] I use the phrase "kingdom of heaven" not in the technical sense as a term in Christian theology developed around New Testament writings, but as a general reference to the way God, as the "third king" in the drama—who has his own "army" of horses and chariots of fire—uses power in a way that contrasts sharply with the ways of the kings and kingdoms of earth.

[7] Cf. vv. 13, 17, 20. In the Naaman story, discussed in Chapter 5, the king of Israel explicitly pairs seeing and knowing when he is confronted by both his ignorance and impotence in the face of Naaman's illness and the king of Aram's demand for healing in 2 Kgs 5:7.

[8] Cf. vv. 11–13, 15b–17a, 18, 21–22.

[9] Cf. Hobbs, *2 Kings*, 73, 74.

[10] Wray Beal, *1 & 2 Kings*, 345.

A challenge that presents itself to any performance of this drama is how adequately to portray the multivalent character of power represented in the script. The very first group of students I worked with on this story came up with a solution that was as brilliant as it was unexpected: a table. Although it may seem an unlikely choice at first glance, the table is quite a fitting solution. And indeed, every group I have worked with after that initial group also chose to incorporate a table (generally the communion table) into the performance, with no prodding from me. Tables are, of course, commonly the place where families and friends gather to eat together, and as such they represent the familiarity, abundance, and joy of a shared meal.[11] But tables are not only for eating. Tables have also represented power in various forms from antiquity until today. In Israel, for example, the table in the Tabernacle and later the Temple held a sacred power by holding the bread of the Presence.[12] In Medieval Europe, a legendary table came to represent a masculine form of power (though non-hierarchical as it had no head), chivalry, and secrecy with the "Knights of the Round Table." In the present day the power held by governing boards is represented by the large tables that dominate board rooms. The solution of the table was also fitting for the liturgical context of this particular performance, which was to be a Communion chapel service at the seminary where I teach. The liturgical context added rich layers of meaning to the performance and allowed the themes in the script to "spill over" into the communal celebration of the Meal.[13]

---

[11] Of course, tables can also effectively be used to represent the opposite of all those things. If it is empty it can represent lack; if someone sits at it alone it can represent isolation and loneliness, etc.

[12] For the Tabernacle see, e.g., Exod 25–26, 30–31, 35, 37, 39–40. For the Temple see 1 Kgs 7:48; 1 Chron 28:16; 2 Chron 4:8, 19; 13:11; 29:18.

[13] During one performance of this drama the connection between the shared meal in v. 22 and Communion was made explicit as the celebration of Communion actually took place *between* the performance of v. 23a (concluding with "And he set before them an elaborate feast") and v. 23b (beginning with the narrator's comment "And they ate. And they drank.").

Most performances I have seen have used a table in some way, but the very first group's use of it was particularly effective.[14] I will briefly describe the role the table played in that performance as a whole, but will return at various points later on to fill in this initial sketch with insights from that and other performances. At the outset of the drama, the table sat downstage center, near the audience. A cluster of Israelites stood around it in a tableau discussing military strategy. A cluster of Arameans stood upstage center, furthest away from the audience. At the narrator's opening line—"The king of Aram was waging war with Israel" (v. 8a)—the king of Aram motioned toward Israel and his soldiers responded by moving downstage, throwing the Israelites to the ground, and stealing the table. The king directed them to set it before him (upstage), and he assumed position behind it, flanked by his counselors to instruct them where to set the ambush (v. 8b). But, as his plans repeatedly fail (v. 9) and his soldiers stagger home empty-handed and embarrassed, the table becomes the platform for his rage as he attempts to cling to a power that is clearly crumbling. He bangs both fists on its surface as he decries the suspected traitor in his midst: "Will you not tell me who among us is for the king of Israel?" (v. 11). As his soldiers leave to capture Elisha the king retreats again to the table, alone, places his hands on its surface and hangs his head, assuming a posture that suggests doubt, fear, and confusion.

The table is abandoned during the episode at Dothan (vv. 15–19), implying that another power is at work than that wielded by earthly kings. The stage then shifts to Samaria and as Elisha leads the blind army to the palace, the king of Israel assumes the same posture the king of Aram had previously taken (hands on table surface, head down)

[14.]Some performances of this drama are available for viewing on YouTube. The first performance I refer to, with the table, is accessible from this link (unfortunately the picture quality is low, and the final verse is cut off): https://www.youtube.com/watch?v=KIAsEPcNgdA. A performance that does not use a table but draws effective attention to the role of humor in the story, performed by the theatre touring company at Northwestern College in Orange City, IA under the direction of professor Jeff Barker is available here: https://www.youtube.com/watch?v=klrx0Jqtfcc.

drawing a subtle connection between them and their assumptions about power. When Elisha brings the Arameans to the king of Israel's doorstep, the king moves from his position behind the table to attack—gesturing to have a bow strung with an arrow pointed at the unarmed, defenseless Aramean soldiers (vv. 20–21). At Elisha's rebuke the table is transformed from a locus of royal and military power to the gathering place for a shared meal as the king transforms from archer to host, the soldiers from enemies to guests (vv. 22–23). The table then becomes the place from which the Aramean soldiers are sent home in peace (v. 23). The table aided the development and resolution of the conflict and helped us portray the various notions of power in the drama in an appropriately complex and nuanced way.

Now that we have identified the conflict and introduced an important theatrical strategy employed to flesh out the conflict in tangible ways (the table), we are ready to meet the principal characters. The king of Aram is the first character to be introduced, though by title only; no name is given.[15] The initial impression made by the narrator is that the king of Aram is in total control. He is the subject of two significant action verbs in verse 8: "waging war" (הָיָה נִלְחָם, *hayah nilcham*) and "took counsel" (וַיִּוָּעַץ, *vayyivva'ats*). The presentation of his character is complexified by his opening dialogue, however, which is shrouded in mystery—or perhaps secrecy.[16] The king takes every

---

[15.] Both kings are left unnamed in this drama. This is no doubt an intentional decision made by the composer. The lack of specificity actually broadens the scope of possible application, implying that the conflict was not necessarily between Elisha (representing God) and two particular earthly kings, but rather may be a conflict inherent to the office of the king, a perspective consistent with the so-called Deuteronomistic corpus (which includes the books from Deut–2 Kgs).

[16.] The adage "knowledge is power" is certainly applicable to this drama, as has already been mentioned. The role of secrets is related to this theme, namely, that those in power (or who imagine themselves to be powerful) love secrets because it makes them feel "in the know," and therefore gives them power over others who are ignorant. This theme is effectively worked out by another biblical drama: the story of Ehud's assassination of the Moabite king Eglon in Judg 3. Ehud gets Eglon alone on the rooftop by telling him he has a "secret message" (דְּבַר־סֵתֶר, *d'var-seter*, lit. "a word of secrecy") for him. So eager to hear this word is the king of Moab that he sends all of

precaution in relaying his military strategy, even resorting to using code to communicate his plan to his generals (פְּלֹנִי אַלְמֹנִי, *ploni 'almoni*, "such and such").[17] The composer's strategy is to caricature the king of Aram as power-hungry but paranoid, in charge but ignorant. He will ultimately be shown to be powerless in the face of the true power of the King of the Universe and his subjects.

The cracks in the king of Aram's power are revealed as soon as he sets his plan in motion. The one shining a light through these cracks is the drama's next principal character: Elisha, the "man of God." Despite all the king's efforts at secrecy, Elisha repeatedly sends word to the king of Israel (also unnamed, whom we come to know better at the end of the

---

his courtiers away, giving Ehud the perfect opportunity to assassinate him *and* get away before anyone notices.

[17.]Clearly this is not the actual speech the king of Aram gave to his generals and counselors. It is more of a summary, an abstraction, or a generalization. Given that there were numerous attacks, this scene is indicative of the king of Aram's strategy. Cf. Cogan and Tadmor, *II Kings*, 72. Adele Berlin discusses the use of פְּלֹנִי אַלְמֹנִי to refer to a place (as opposed to a person) here and in 1 Sam 21:3 and concludes: "The poetic explanation might be that the name itself had been forgotten, but it seems more likely that the narrator is intentionally abstracting, or generalizing, certain specific facts, as if he were saying, 'Reader, you don't need to know the name of the place/person. You just need to understand what I tell you about it/him.' . . . The story then becomes more story-like—less of an actual reality and more of a reflection of reality. It is not a videotape of a particular incident, but a recounting of that incident in someone's artful words. The presence of the narrator, subtle though it be, is one of the hallmarks of narrative." Berlin, *Poetics and Interpretation*, 110. I mostly agree with Berlin, but in light of my comments on the role of the narrator in Chapter 3, I would argue that the narrator is not at all a subtle presence in the story, but the central figure through whom the world of the story and the world of the present converge. Further, in light of the distinction I made in Chapter 3 between the composer and the narrator, I would argue that this is, in fact, not the result of the narrator inserting his/her influence on the story, but rather the expression of the composer's desire to keep the audience in the dark about the specific "place," while simultaneously beginning to reveal the power-hungry paranoia of the king of Aram. As Berlin suggested elsewhere, its use here may simply be for the purpose of "mysteriousness" (100). It is, rhetorically speaking, akin to the intentionally elusive summary of the little girl's speech that Naaman provides the king of Aram in 2 Kgs 5:4: "Thus and so (כָּזֹאת וְכָזֹאת) said the girl from the land of Israel" (see Chapter 5).

drama) to inform him of the Aramean ambushes (vv. 9–10). The drama leaves little doubt that the source of Elisha's knowledge is divine revelation.[18] Blocking the unsuccessful ambushes highlights the inherent comedic nature of the scene while introducing the theme of the powerlessness of earthly power. The theater's ability to present simultaneous action allows the king of Aram to send his forces at the same time Elisha informs the king of Israel of Aram's plans, creating the possibility of ironic humor. It could be done in a number of different ways. Perhaps an Aramean band moves toward a group of Israelite actors and makes a war-like attacking gesture, but the Israelites were ready, and they make a defensive gesture and easily repel the attack. A particularly effective possibility (which highlights the humorous element, and is closer to the sense of the Hebrew in v. 9) would have an Aramean band lie in wait next to a path they suspect Israel to take, but as they wait, their delicious over-confidence erodes to embarrassment as the Israelites never pass by that way[19] (perhaps the informed Israelite army creeps behind them and snickers at them as they wait in ignorance). After waiting for too long, the Aramean band returns home to their lord to report (another) unsuccessful ambush—"not once, not twice" (v. 10).[20]

[18.] Bergen is undoubtedly correct in judging Gray's elaborate attempt to find a natural explanation for Elisha's knowledge in his extensive network of relationships, and the possible infiltration of the Aramean court by the little girl of 2 Kings 5—who he postulates may have grown up to be one of the king's concubines—as "clearly outside the world of the narrative." Bergen, *Elisha and the End of Prophetism*, 129, n. 233. Gray's quote is as follows: "In view of the Israelite prisoners, such as the Hebrew maid of Naaman's wife, and others who, perhaps, became concubines of the king and his officers, there might well have been a leakage of secrets from the bedchamber, if not of the king, at least of the leaders of the raid." Gray, *I & II Kings*, 515.

[19.] The story of Ehud's assassination of Eglon also takes advantage of this kind of embarrassment. In particular, the scene in which the servants of Eglon wait for far too long for him to come out of the "bathroom," which buys Ehud—who has just assassinated Eglon in secret—sufficient time to escape back to Israel as the hero and rally the troops to return to Moab and finish what he started (cf. Judg 3:12–30, esp. 23–26).

[20.] Yet another option (developed by students at Northwestern College), which intentionally plays off the scene's humor, has the Israelite army (represented by a

The scene can be accentuated further by the king of Aram and the king of Israel being situated on opposite sides of the stage. The king of Aram becomes more and more animated, clearly frustrated by the situation, while the king of Israel sits comfortably on his throne laughing at his good fortune (this could be used to develop a sense of over-confidence that could be exploited later on when he misinterprets Elisha's act of delivering the bands of Aram to his doorstep in v. 21). The chess match has begun as the two kings with the prophet between them advance and retreat, move and counter-move.

Rising Action (vv. 11–19)

The conflict develops over the course of four scenes, with the climax arriving in the fourth, decisive scene. The four scenes follow the Aramean army as it (1) is sent by the king of Aram to capture Elisha (vv. 11–13), (2) remains ignorant of the heavenly host surrounding it even as the army surrounds Elisha (vv. 14–17), (3) encounters blindness in its failed attempt to capture Elisha (vv. 18–19), and (4) recovers from blindness at a point of profound vulnerability, namely, facing death at the hand of the king of Israel (vv. 20–23). Elisha's presence and influence dominates each scene and he is in control of every situation he finds himself in. He calms fears, opens and closes eyes, defies armies and kings, and ultimately teaches the king of Israel and the Aramean army how true power is wielded—through service and feasting as opposed to swords and fighting. Multiple perspectives converge in the telling of the story: "those of the characters, the audience, the narrator, and God" (represented by Elisha). "All these levels intersect each other in the presentation, and this interaction creates the rich matrix from which the portrayal of God emerges."[21]

---

single character, who holds a hand drum) "hide" behind a stool on the stage and, as each successive Aramean ambush approaches (three rounds of a single actor approaching, representing three waves of planned attacks), the Israelite actor stands up and bangs the drum several times, spooking the Aramean actor and sending them back to their camp defeated and embarrassed.

[21.]Boogaart, "Drama and the Sacred," 54.

Scene 1 - The Aramean Court (vv. 11–13)

The king of Aram is coming unravelled. The narrator's wonderfully imaginative description of "a storm erupting" in the king's heart (וַיִּסָּעֵר לֵב, *vayyissa'er lev*, v. 11) paints a picture of a state of confusion and helplessness expressed in uncontrollable rage. The certainty of his power is being de-threaded by a knowledge he knows nothing of— although he is apparently the only one ignorant of it.[22] The king rages: "Who among us is for the king of Israel?!" (v. 11).[23] In yet another case of humor and irony—made explicit through staging and the actor's tone of voice—the king's servant responds that the problem is not a traitor, but the improbable reach of Elisha's ears. Elisha—"the prophet in Israel"[24]—apparently hears everything, even the words the king speaks

---

[22.]"Not until he asks does an officer tell him about Elisha, as if it is common knowledge to everyone but the king. The king of Aram is represented as being 'out of the loop,' needing instruction from his servants as he did in the case of Naaman." Cohn, *2 Kings*, 45. Wray Beal also noted the presence of ironic humor in the scene: "Sarcastically, he asks to be 'told' (*ngd*) the traitor's identity, revealing that, while the prophet knows what Aram is doing, the king of Aram is clueless about what the prophet is doing—so clueless, in fact, that even his advisors know what he does not!" Wray Beal, *1 & 2 Kings*, 342.

[23.]One performance group capitalized on the humorous elements of the king's rage and expressed it through physical humor, playing up the "gentle mockery of the king of Aram" Wray Beal noted (345) through a childish expression of anger. In the space between the king realizing his ambushes have failed and his suspicion that there is a rat in his outfit, this group had the king begin stomping his foot on the ground, which grew into stomping both feet at the same time while jumping around in a circle. This interpretation moves the drama in the direction of parody.

[24.]The addition of this formal title on the lips of an Aramean counselor is significant. "The force of this statement is found not only in the quantity of information it contains, nor only in its 'confessional' quality, but also in its placement in the mouth of an Aramean." Bergen, *Elisha and the End of Prophetism*, 129. It also echoes the sentiments of the little girl in 2 Kgs 5:3, and Elisha's own claim to the king of Israel later in the same drama (v. 8). Perhaps Elisha's fame has spread throughout the Aramean court through Naaman's testimony; perhaps the composer is touching on a consistent theme throughout the Old Testament (which is picked up also in the New Testament), that of the "faithful foreigner" (cf. Ruth in The Book of Ruth; Rahab with the spies in Jericho in Josh 2:1–21; the sailors and the Ninevites in The Book of Jonah; Balaam's Ass in Num 22:22–35—yet another story in which sight plays a prominent

in his bedroom![25] How does the servant declare such a profound and provocative line? On the one hand, his statement is the clearest declaration of the power of Elisha in the entire narrative—a serious statement to be sure. On the other hand, his retort pulses with ribald humor, suggesting a degree of hubris. Does he speak with condescension in exasperation at the king's ignorance? Is he actually afraid of the king's anger and in his panic says more than he means to? Perhaps he responds with eyebrows raised in a subtle look of disbelief— with periodic glances to his colleagues—suggesting surprise at the king's ignorance. Perhaps he speaks in a measured cadence, pausing periodically for support and encouragement from his colleagues who urge him to continue down the path he started on, come what may. Perhaps the delivery is more nuanced, combining a number of these and other emotions. Each possibility would accentuate a different element of this dynamic and potentially funny exchange.

The portrayal of the king's density deepens as he struggles to comprehend the practical implications of this new-found knowledge. The composer has woven even more humor and irony into the king's speech, deepening also the parody of power he unwittingly embodies. One way to demonstrate this would be for the king to become very animated, quickly building intensity throughout the line ("Go! See!" v. 13) and perhaps pounding the table at the line "Where is he?!" (v. 13). Then, the force of the noise created by the table slap and his own shouts shocks him back to his newly discovered reality—Elisha can hear!— and so he gathers his counselors close and sinisterly whispers (perhaps Elisha cannot hear when he whispers!): "I will send, and I will capture

---

role. New Testament examples would include the Samaritan in the parable of the Good Samaritan in Lk 10:25–37 and Cornelius in Acts 10). The king of Aram's servant certainly does not end up worshiping Israel's God, but is nevertheless a conduit of revelation in the drama.

[25.]It does not take strong imaginative powers to see how an original audience composed of Hebrews would find such a revelation hilarious on the lips of Aramean soldiers. It also requires little imagination to see some in that same audience taking the next step to realize that divine ears likely *also* hear the words spoken—and divine eyes see the goings on—in bed chambers closer to home as well!

him!" Significantly—and ironically—the king blindly introduces the theme of seeing when he commands his counselors to "go and see" (לְכוּ וּרְאוּ, *lekhu ur'u*) where Elisha is. Apparently he is, yet again, the only one who does not know, for the immediate response is: "Behold, in Dothan."[26] Elisha's location at Dothan is significant from a geopolitical and strategic point of view because it was one gateway to the Jezreel Valley, which Marvin Sweeney describes as "the geographical key to northern Israel's military and economic power."[27]

Scene 2 - Dothan (vv. 14–17)

The king of Aram's worldview is, as yet, impenetrable. Perhaps he imagines his ambushes against Israel were unsuccessful because of the size of the forces he sent. He takes no such chance this time, sending "horses and chariots and a great army" (v. 14). The scene demonstrates the brilliance of Hebrew storytelling. As the king of Aram doubles down on his commitment to a militaristic worldview, he also (blindly) plays into Elisha's hands, ultimately setting up his own "defeat," creating the

---

[26.] הִנֵּה (*hinneh*, "behold") is repeated three more times in the drama (vv. 15, 17, 20), all by the narrator. Each instance expresses an element of surprise or indicates something unexpected. The narrator uses it to shift the audience's perspective, to see an event through the eyes of a particular character.

[27.] The full quote is as follows: "Dothan is a crucial location, both for narrative purposes and for understanding the strategic issues of Aram's invasion of Israel. . . . [I]f the Emeq Dothan provides access to the Jezreel from Samaria, it also provides access to Samaria from the Jezreel. Elisha's location at Dothan would therefore place him at the very site that determines Israel's ability to control the Jezreel. Given the Jezreel's importance, both as an agricultural breadbasket and as the site of the key east-west trade route between the Mediterranean coastal plain and the Transjordanian routes to Damascus and the Gulf of Aqaba, the Jezreel emerges as the geographical key to northern Israel's military and economic power." Sweeney, *I & II Kings*, 308. Sweeney's description of the geopolitical significance of Dothan suggests that Elisha's location there was not random but purposeful, both in the mind of Elisha and the composer. The strategic nature of Elisha's location further reinforces the drama's primary theme of power—where does it come from, who holds it, and how ought it be used?

opportunity for Elisha to "kill him with kindness."[28] Irony and humor combine, yet again, to reveal the king's folly. Lissa Wray Beal noted that "despite the evidence that Elisha knows Aram's troop movements, the king dispatches the force by night, thinking to mount a surprise attack. The king is truly blind."[29] The audience—although not as blind as the king—has nevertheless not yet learned how to see, and the twin themes of power and sight are only beginning to be developed. To facilitate the audience's training in seeing rightly, the composer introduces Elisha's servant as a proxy for the audience,[30] through whose eyes the audience is invited to probe more deeply the correspondence between perception and reality.[31] This effect is fundamentally experiential as the audience literally sees beyond the veil of visible reality along with Elisha's servant. A number of performative techniques could be employed to achieve this effect.

The challenge is to block the scene in a way that deepens the audience's empathetic connection with the servant, taking advantage of whatever theatrical techniques will allow the audience to see through his eyes, and therefore come to see anew along with him. One possibility would be to block the scene as follows. After the king of Aram sends his forces to Dothan, he exits the stage while his army fans out into the audience to get into position to surround Dothan. If possible, the lights

---

[28.]Cf. Selena Gomez, "Kill Em With Kindness," by Selena Gomez, Antonina Armato, Tim James, Benjamin Levin, and Dave Audé, released May 3, 2016, on *Revival*, Interscope Records and Polydor Records, digital download. The song celebrates nonviolent responses to violence in the world. Elisha, of course, does not kill the king of Aram or any of his soldiers, but through (strategic) kindness and hospitality calls their entire worldview into question. I will have much more to say about this later on.

[29.]Wray Beal, *Kings*, 343.

[30.]"The lad is a stand-in for the reader." Nelson, *First and Second Kings*, 186.

[31.]Indeed, Elisha's servant—and the entire scene in vv. 15–17—is central to the story, from a narrative, dramatic, and thematic perspective. This contra Jones, who claimed they (the character of the servant and the entire scene in vv. 15–17) were later revisions by the so-called "Yahwist" editor and played "no part in the development of the narrative." Jones, *1 and 2 Kings*, 422. Rofé makes a similar argument to Jones in Rofé, "Elisha at Dothan," 346–49.

could dim to indicate the darkness of night, and make it more challenging for the audience to see what is happening, which introduces a sense of uncertainty and confusion. Elisha and his servant enter the stage, transforming it from the palace in Aram to Elisha's location in Dothan. Elisha and his servant lay down to indicate they are asleep. The audience hears the soldiers moving, but because they are crouched down and the lights are dim, they cannot see them. The lights come up when Elisha's servant rises and proceeds to walk downstage center (toward the audience) to make the morning preparations while the narrator introduces him (v. 15a). When he lifts his sleepy eyes, the narrator, standing next to him, exclaims (speaking quickly, anticipating the servant's emotion), "And behold (הִנֵּה, *hinneh*), an army was surrounding the city! Plus horses and chariots!" (v. 15b). Simultaneous action increases the scene's effect: in the same moment the servant lifts his eyes, the Aramean soldiers rise from their crouched position among the audience and assume aggressive, war-like postures (arrow slung in a bow, sword held high, javelin prepared to throw). The servant stumbles backward, terrified: "Ah! My lord! What can we do?" (v. 15b).

The narrator's use of הִנֵּה (*hinneh*, "behold!") in verse 15 shifts the audience's perspective away from Elisha's calm confidence to the servant's anxiety and fear. Whatever confidence the servant has in Elisha is now complicated by fear of what is visible: The city is surrounded—"Plus horses and chariots!" (v. 15). How could Elisha *possibly* get out of this situation? Audiences may be tempted to laugh at the servant's exasperated plea (and laughter may be the intended response), which implies the level of felt tension is low at this moment. The level of felt tension notwithstanding, the audience is nevertheless *engaged*, curious to see how Elisha will respond.

His response introduces more humor. What he says is not humorous. In fact, it is extremely serious and an utterance of prophetic revelation. Its *effect* is humorous, however. "Do not be afraid, for many more are there with us than there are with them" (v. 16). In the blank space between Elisha's declaration of the true state of reality (v. 16) and that reality actually being revealed (v. 17) lies a moment of poignant humor, which functions to unite the audience's perception of reality with that of the servant. After Elisha declares the truth as he sees it, he pauses to let it sink in. The audience awaits the servant's response, which, as it turns out, is (very likely) the way everyone in the audience would respond if they were in the servant's place. He looks back and forth from Elisha to the army surrounding them, perhaps counting "1 – 2" on his fingers while looking from Elisha to himself, then looking out the window at the Aramean host. Brueggemann captures the moment well: "The statement must have bewildered the servant, because he can see and he can count. There is a large host outside and two inside. The prophet's arithmetic is clearly out of touch with reality."[32] Indeed, it is precisely this contradiction between sight and reality that the composer is intending to highlight in the audience's experience, preparing them to have their eyes opened, along with the servant's.

Elisha offers the first of three prayers related to sight and blindness. "Open his eyes that he may see" (v. 17). Elisha prays that the servant, whose eyes already see one plane of reality, would be opened to see a deeper dimension than normal sight can see. The servant's new capacity to see reveals his former seeing as a form of blindness. Again, Brueggemann articulates well the paradox in the revelation: "The servant is granted a vision of transhistorical reality or, as I choose to think, the servant can now see what conventional discernment misses in its self-assured blindness." He continues, "the prophet's count of allies and enemies is validated and his 'fear not' is grounded in reality"—it is just a reality of a different sort.[33]

But how is this actually accomplished? *How* does the audience come to see as the servant sees? And what, exactly, does the servant *see*? Spectacle of this sort is the currency of theater. A professional theater (with set designers, lighting, and creative professionals) would likely find no end to the possibilities for creative representation. A biblical scholar with minimal theatrical training preparing a minimalist performance for a community service requires a more modest approach to blocking the scene. Even when taking a more modest approach,

---

[32.] Brueggemann, *1 & 2 Kings*, 346.

[33.] Brueggemann, *1 & 2 Kings*, 347.

multiple opportunities present themselves. I will offer one suggestion that prioritized audience participation and infused an un-rehearsable element into the performance, which resulted in a genuinely authentic connection between actors and audience in which the result was greater than the sum of its individual parts. This particular performance took place during a community worship service. The bulletins for the day were printed on red, orange, and yellow paper. Right before the performance began, I explained to the audience we were going to invite their participation at a crucial moment in the story. Their cue would be Elisha raising his hands after praying over the servant, at which point they would each stand and wave their bulletin in the air, until the actor lowered her hands (Elisha was played by a woman), indicating they could sit back down. We did not rehearse it so as to preserve the spontaneity of the moment. During the performance, when Elisha prayed, the audience became the answer to the question they had silently asked with the servant: "How could there be more with us than there are with them?" The audience's privileged position, knowing they were going to fulfill this role, did not prevent them from engaging the servant's question, but created an anticipation in them for it. And their response resulted in a moment of spontaneous delight and surprise. The sound of the papers waving was significantly louder than anyone expected, and the look of shock on the servant's face (an untrained actor) was genuine and believable. The audience was invited to believe there was more to reality than meets the eye *because for a moment they became the reality revealed beyond the veil of human vision.*[34]

---

[34] Another, simpler option would be to have Elisha walk up to the servant and, as he prays over him, places his hand over the servant's eyes, indicating blindness. Then, at the conclusion of his prayer ("and let him see") Elisha raises his hand, and instantly the servant would behold the new reality as the narrator described what he saw. In this scenario the servant would simply pretend to see horses and chariots of fire surrounding them, and would turn around on stage with a look of awe as Elisha looked on, perhaps with a look of awe inspired by his servant's joy, perhaps with a knowing smile tinged with sadness that recalls his own (first?) experience with the horses and chariots of fire across the Jordan as Elijah was taken from him (cf. 2 Kgs 2:1–18), or perhaps with some other emotion.

Scene 3 - The (Intended) Captive Becomes the Captor (vv. 18–19)

The sanctity and security created by the revelation ends as suddenly
as it began. The servant, Elisha, and even the audience are thrown back
into "reality" as the Aramean army descends to capture Elisha.[35]
Although the Aramean host is oblivious to the presence of the fiery hosts
around them, for a moment we are led to wonder if it will even matter
in the end. Are the "invisible" hosts of heaven sufficient in the face of
the very visible hosts of earth? Whose power is greater? Elisha's second
prayer—the reversal of his first prayer—points to the answer: "Strike
these foreigners with a blinding light!" The narrator's response confirms
Elisha's power: "And he struck them with a blinding light, according to
the word of Elisha" (v. 18). Does Elisha speak his line with a sense of
urgency or concern? Does his heart beat faster as the army descends?
Does the volume and pitch of his voice rise? Or is he calm and collected
and still in control?

Two words in this verse require further comment. The first word is
הִכָּה (*hikkah*). In the hifil stem it is a violent word, meaning "strike,
smite." It often carries the connotation of a strike that results in death,
which is clearly the intended meaning later on in the drama (v. 21).[36]

[35.]Nelson argues that the most likely subject of the first verb in v. 18 (וַיֵּרְדוּ,
vayyerdu, "and they went down") is the horses and chariots of fire mentioned in v. 17.
Nelson, *First and Second Kings*, 186. This is unlikely (cf. Wray Beal, *1 & 2 Kings*,
344; Cogan and Tadmor, *II Kings*, 74). From a dramatic perspective, Elisha's prayer
is made more urgent and the tension increases if the Aramean army descends upon
him than if the horses and chariots descend. In the latter scenario the expected effect
would be the destruction of the Aramean army, but that clearly does not happen. The
most logical explanation is that the Aramean army "descended" upon the city and
Elisha but were struck "blind" before they could reach the door. This parallel's the
only other use of סַנְוֵרִים (*sanverim*) in the Hebrew Bible, when the men of Sodom were
struck with blindness and were unable to find the door of Lot's house (Gen 19:11).
This scenario would also locate Elisha's interaction with the army in the vicinity of
the city, after they descended upon it, and not out in the Aramean camp (where they
would still be if they did not "attack" the city). The "descent" of the Aramean army
would be figurative as opposed to literal/geographical, since Elisha is apparently in an
elevated location inside the city of Dothan.

[36.]Cf. Gen 4:15b; Exod 2:12; Josh 10:26.

Here on the lips of Elisha it has an altogether different meaning. Elisha asks the Lord not for a strike that leads to death, but a strike that *preserves life*, namely, his own (for now). The second word is סַנְוֵרִים (*sanverim*, "blindness" or "bedazzlement"). Its exact meaning is uncertain as it appears only here and in Gen 19:11, a similar context in which a divine agent "strikes" (הִכָּה) a hostile force with סַנְוֵרִים to protect Lot and his family from the Sodomite mob, leaving the mob "unable to find the door" (v. 11). Whether its intended meaning is "blindness" or "bedazzlement," the effect is clear: those "struck" by it lose their powers of perception.[37] A simple dramatic solution is to have the army descend from their positions in the audience and form a ready-to-strike[38] freeze frame (tableau) immediately surrounding Elisha and his servant while Elisha prays. When the narrator confirms Elisha's prayer is answered the Aramean actors momentarily break their tableau and create a new tableau using the arm not pretending to hold a weapon to cover their eyes. The invading army is now utterly helpless; Elisha has "by prayer, completely inverted the military realities of the situation."[39] All the power of Aram—symbolized by the sword and bow and spear—have been rendered powerless by the prayer of the prophet.

[37.]"Most interpreters understand the Hebrew term *sanwērîm* to refer to some temporary blindness (e.g., Hobbs, *2 Kings*, 78; Cogan and Tadmor, *II Kings*, 74). . . . *A clinical diagnosis of the blindness, however, misses its ironic narrative function.*" Sweeney, *I & II Kings*, 309; emphasis added. As I see it, "blinding light" (so JPS) seems a better fit than "blindness" (so NRSV, ESV, TNIV, KJV, ASV, NET) with respect to the context and the basic meaning of the word, which apparently has to do with "dazzling" light that results in blindness (e.g., "bedazzlement"). The precise meaning is uncertain as it appears only here and Gen 19:11. The root of the word is נור, which is also the root of the substantive נֵר, "light," as in an oil lamp. *HALOT*, s.v. "סַנְוֵרִים;" and *HALOT*, s.v. "נֵר." "Blinding light" clarifies both the result (blindness) and the means (light) through which YHVH "struck" (הִכָּה) the Arameans.

[38.]The king of Aram seemed to desire to capture Elisha, not to kill him ("I will send for him and capture him!" v. 13). The objective of this tableau is not to communicate Elisha's imminent death, but rather the imminent threat of the army's descent upon him and his servant. The gestures are symbolic and could be portrayed in various ways to achieve a similar effect.

[39.]Brueggemann, *1 & 2 Kings*, 347.

Elisha's dialogue in verse 19 is central to the drama's theological affirmation and political message—as relevant today as it was then. Movement and gesture accent the double meaning of the critical Hebrew word דֶּרֶךְ (*derekh*, "way, path"), and the context created by Elisha pairing his speech with action renders the composer's point explicit. Recall that the Aramean soldiers are in their "blinded" tableau in which one arm covers their eyes, and the other holds their weapon aloft. Elisha approaches each soldier and, as he says "this is not the way," he lowers their weapon-carrying arm. Indeed, the statement "this is not the way" has more to do with the purpose and methods of Aram's mission than the particular road on which they are standing.

Further, Elisha tells the army he will lead them to the one whom they are seeking (v. 19). This is a claim which, of course, stands in direct contrast to (visible) reality. Elisha and the audience know what the army does not: they are being led *by* the one whom they are seeking! Each dazed soldier "blindly" receives Elisha's guidance, but the audience is left to ponder Elisha's intentions, still unsure what this unpredictable prophet has in mind. How will Elisha wield the power *he* has, which is clearly superior to the power of Aram. As he leads the train of blinded soldiers to Samaria, the king of Israel assumes his position behind the table up stage center, flanked by his own soldiers—mirroring the king of Aram with his counselors in verses 8–13. As the scene unfolds, the audience perhaps begins to wonder if Elisha has set the Arameans up for a bloodbath in the streets of Samaria. Perhaps the composer wanted the audience to consider this—and perhaps even desire it. This would begin to establish an empathetic connection between the audience and the king of Israel, preparing them to be transformed along with him, just as they were invited to see anew with Elisha's servant in verse 17.

Climax / Resolution - Scene 4 - The Palace in Samaria (vv. 20–23)

Elisha leads the Arameans into the heart of Samaria, subtly showing how Elisha—not the king of Aram—is the true leader of the Aramean army on their mission.[40] As he guides the blinded train up the aisle and

---

[40.]Cf. Nelson, *First and Second Kings*, 187.

onto the stage, the king of Israel, from his position behind the table, responds with shock and awe, an expression of disbelief at his good fortune, and perhaps surprise that an entire host of Aramean soldiers could be in Israel without his knowledge—subtly connecting the two kings through their mutual ignorance. Elisha prays as soon as he enters Samaria, apparently in front of the king of Israel and his men. This third and final prayer repeats his first prayer (prayed over his servant, v. 17) and undoes the effects of his second (v. 18) by re-opening the Aramean soldiers' eyes (v. 20).

The blocking of the scene can serve to build the tension and set up the narrator's shift of perspective. For example, after they stop marching, the soldiers huddle together, blind, vulnerable, and unaware of where they are. As Elisha begins to pray over them the king of Israel abandons his position behind the table and purposefully approaches the group. As the narrator announces that their eyes are open (and as the soldiers lower their arms from their eyes) the king of Israel (and perhaps the actors representing his entourage as well) assumes a position holding a taught bow directed at the defenseless group.[41] At the same time, the narrator's repetition of הִנֵּה (*hinneh*, "behold") and the revelation that they are "in the heart of Samaria!" (v. 21) shifts the audience's perspective to see (וַיִּרְאוּ, *vayyir'u*, "and they saw") the scene unfold from the Aramean soldiers' point of view—and feel the shock of revelation with them. The soldiers' response to Elisha's final prayer is the mirror opposite of the servant's response. The servant's move from ignorance to knowledge extinguished his fear; the soldiers' move from ignorance to knowledge compounds their vulnerability and intensifies their fear!

This identification with the powerless and vulnerable soldiers increases the experience of tension and compels the audience (both ancient and modern) to choose sides. Perhaps the response is empathy

---

[41.]Of course a bow and arrow is not the only option, but it is an immediately recognizable gesture and the tension of the moment is symbolized in the tension he holds on the string. It is likewise released as he brings his hands back together, releasing the tension on the bow and indicating his acceptance of Elisha's command (v. 22).

for the Aramean soldiers—who were just following orders and got caught in the middle—which leads to a desire for them not to be harmed. Perhaps the response is similar to the king of Israel: This is your chance, kill them all! My read is the composer has employed humor throughout the drama to this point in order to establish a connection with the audience and the story, to soften their defenses, and to draw out their nationalistic and militaristic longings. Thus, the *intended* response is to cheer for the king of Israel who cries: "Can I strike them? Can I strike them, my father?" (v. 21). How will Elisha respond? Is this the next phase of Elisha's military partnership with the king of Israel (see vv. 9–10), or will the prophet call the legitimacy of (earthly) power and a kingdom built on the power of violence into question? Either way, the audience is poised to hear Elisha's response.

In this climactic scene, dialogue, point of view, blocking, and narration converge as the plot takes an altogether unexpected turn on its way to resolving the conflict. Elisha now articulates his point of view unequivocally: "No, you will not strike them!" (v. 22). He justifies this with reference to the prevailing practice regarding prisoners of war (they would not be killed, but would be taken as captives and used as slaves).[42] But Elisha does not stop there. He even calls the legitimacy of that practice into question by calling the king to a demonstration of radical grace: "Set bread and water before them, that they might eat and drink. And then let them go to their lord" (v. 22b).

The contrast between the worldviews of the king and Elisha are brought into sharp focus through their dialogue, but the blocking truly reveals this scene's profound message. Our performances have led to two significant discoveries. Both are examples of biblical performance criticism uncovering meaning in the script that is latent in the words, but undiscoverable until it moves from the page to the stage. *There is meaning in the movement*—in the bodies that take up space in various ways and communicate what words alone cannot. The first discovery has to do with Elisha's posture and position as he denies the king's request to strike. Recall that in one portrayal of the climactic scene, the

---

[42.]Hobbs, *2 Kings*, 78.

king of Israel shouts his death request to Elisha as he stands above the cowering Aramean soldiers with his bow drawn—perhaps with the Israelite army behind him following suit. The force of Elisha's response is reinforced through physical action. We discovered the most logical and compelling way for him to embody his message to the king was to put himself *between* the king and the Aramean army. Elisha stands in the gap between the powerful king and the powerless army, between the king's drawn bow and the Arameans' unprotected flesh. Thus, Elisha teaches the king what "the way" of power truly is as he stands in the way of the king's path of violence.[43] Word paired with action demonstrates the integrity of Elisha's character, and drastically increases the likelihood that the king of Israel will comply.

But it does more than that as well. This discovery reflects echoes of other stories throughout the canon, in both the Old and New Testaments, through what John Miles Foley called traditional referentiality.[44] Elisha standing in the gap between a weapon and its intended object recalls the climactic moments of at least two Old Testament dramas I have discussed in previous chapters—the Angel of the Lord stopping Abraham from slaughtering Isaac in Gen 22, and God standing in the gap between Moses' rod and the rock in the wilderness to save the people from dying of thirst in Exod 17.[45]

The second discovery has to do with how the king of Israel relates to the Aramean army and ultimately convinces them to join him at the table—one would imagine they might have suspected a trap, or at least needed some convincing to sit down and eat the food the king had

---

[43.]Our group discerned that it might take the king a bit of time to accept Elisha's paradigm-shifting command. To demonstrate this the king of Israel tried a couple of times to maneuver himself into a new position with a clear shot past Elisha, but each time the king repositioned himself Elisha followed suit and remained in the gap, protecting the army and preventing the breakout of violence and bloodshed.

[44.]See Chapter 1.

[45.]Both of these stories (Gen 22:1–19 and Exod 17:1–7) have been interpreted throughout Christian history as anticipating Jesus' death. Water From the Rock is placed within the season of Lent, and The Binding of Isaac is a Good Friday passage in versions of the Revised Common Lectionary.

provided. Again, a number of options are available. Most performances have included some variation on the following. After Elisha's compelling act, the king acquiesces and makes the preparations for the feast, enlisting his men to move the table out of the space that represents power and to set it in a more open and accessible space. The table is then set with food.[46] The king then approaches the army and shows them the table with a sweep of his arm, but they do not budge. Perhaps he brings a plate over to show them the delicious food, but they remain where they are. Then the king understands their hesitancy and responds with two actions to convince them of the trustworthiness of his intentions. First, he takes something from the plate and eats it himself to demonstrate that the food is not poisoned. Then—and this is the most significant gesture the king will make—he kneels before them and holds the plate out to them. His posture of kneeling is a demonstration of a transformation of power. He embodies before them what the feast itself represents: a profound act of service; an invitation to friendship—even if only temporarily.[47]

The shared meal around the king's table—which follows Elisha's selfless and symbolic act (vv. 22–23)—is the drama's climax.[48] It is the

---

[46.]Some performances have set the table with actual food that the king actually eats with the army; others have set the table with the Communion elements (this happened in a performance that took place during a Communion service), and others have not had an actual table and simply mimed the actions of setting the table and eating together.

[47.]This act of service echoes in the ministry of Jesus told in the New Testament. Perhaps the NT authors had this story from 2 Kgs 6 in mind as they reflected back on Jesus' life and told his stories. Consider, e.g., "The greatest among you will be your servant. All who exalt themselves will be humbled, and all who humble themselves will be exalted" (Matt 23:11–12); "A dispute also arose among them as to which one of them was to be regarded as the greatest. But he said to them, 'The kings of the Gentiles lord it over them; and those in authority over them are called benefactors. But not so with you; rather the greatest among you must become like the youngest, and the leader like one who serves'" (Lk 22:26). NRSV.

[48.]Much has been made of the potential chiastic structure of the drama, which locates Elisha's prayer and the subverting of the Aramean army's objective (vv. 18–19) as the center/climax (Cf. Wray Beal, *1 & 2 Kings*, 340–41; Cohn, *2 Kings*, 44; Long identifies vv.18–19 as the "climactic center" but does not identify a chiasmus.

experience through which the conflict is resolved, moving the drama from war to peace.[49] In this scene the transformation of the king of Israel and the Aramean army is seen. Through it the audience is likewise invited to be transformed along with these characters. One way to achieve this in performance is to return the focus to the table. The table is a symbol of power throughout the entire drama, although now it represents power of an entirely different sort. In the opening scene it was stolen from its original location down stage center and placed up stage center; now it is moved back to its original place, or perhaps a different location on stage altogether, to suggest it represents something altogether different. No longer will it be the location from which kings strategize their enemy's defeat through secret military tactics. No longer will it be the place where warriors and counselors huddle to strategize the downfall of their enemies. Now it is the platform for a shared meal, for breaking bread, perhaps even the sharing of stories. It becomes a humanizing table, and as such it works to undermine the friend-versus-foe way of viewing the world that is fundamental to the way the kings of Aram and Israel have seen the world to this point. The feast scene develops as described above. Slowly, as the Arameans eat and drink, they begin to relax and even enjoy themselves. The scene takes a few seconds to develop, but could easily end in a tableau that suggests the passage of time. As the actors freeze with food and cup in their hands—faces smiling, Israelite and Aramean looking each other in the eyes, acknowledging their shared humanity—the narrator walks through the

---

Long, *2 Kings*, 84). The interaction between Elisha and the bands of Aram in vv.18–19 may be the structural center of the drama, but the scene is not the climax (whether or not the claim of a chiasmus is justified). This final scene leading up to and at the table is the climax, for through it the drama's primary conflict is resolved and the characters (save Elisha) are transformed. The spectacle of the heavenly host (v. 17) and the specter of Elisha's subversion of the "great army" of Aram (vv. 18–19) are critical (and spectacular) elements, but they serve the larger purpose of propelling the plot and setting up the audience for the quotidian-yet-transformational encounter between Israel and Aram over the shared meal (v. 23).

[49]."At least provisionally, the feast produced a momentary pause in the hostilities, an occasion of friendship and peaceableness." Brueggemann, *1 & 2 Kings*, 348.

scene and says, "And they ate. And they drank. And he sent them on their way" (v. 23).

The foregoing interpretation of the feast scene, as well as Elisha's intentions for it, differ starkly that offered by Hobbs, who suggests "Elisha humiliates them by having them fed and sent on their way."[50] And again later he says, "Elisha, however, seems more intent upon embarrassing his foes with kindness than sparing them for purely humanitarian reasons."[51] It may be true that Elisha's decision was motivated by the power of embarrassment, but it is not the whole truth. Something more fundamental—and more theologically profound—is being indicated here than how to humiliate your enemies with kindness.

Elisha enlists the king of Israel to help him illustrate the character of power in what I earlier called the kingdom of heaven,[52] which contrasts sharply with the understanding of power at work in the kingdoms of earth. The shared meal is the means through which the drama's vision of power is ultimately expressed. In it Elisha helps the king of Israel and the Aramean army learn what "the way"[53] truly is, so that they—along with the audience—can see it and know it for themselves. The way of God, according to Elisha, is the way of service, of vulnerability, of love. The power of God enables people to rise above the forces that divide them and to see each other as humans, as neighbors. It achieves peace by ending hostility through service rather than attempting to secure peace through violence, which always begets more violence, as Martin Luther King Jr. famously said.[54]

---

[50] Hobbs, 2 Kings, 74.

[51] Hobbs, 2 Kings, 78.

[52] Again, I use this not as a technical term as it is used in the New Testament, but as a way of contrasting the character and conduct of earthly kings with the King of Kings, which is a focal point of this drama's message.

[53] 2 Kgs 6:19.

[54] King, A Testament of Hope, 17. The full quote is: "To meet hate with retaliatory hate would do nothing but intensify the existence of evil in the universe. Hate begets hate; violence begets violence; toughness begets a greater toughness." Martin Luther King's comments resonate with the message of Jesus when he rebuked a disciple for cutting off the ear of the high priest's slave in the Gospel of Matthew, saying "All who take the sword will perish by the sword." Matt 26:52, NRSV.

The image created by the king of Israel and the Aramean army gathered around a table breaking bread together, through the process of traditional referentiality,[55] can evoke in knowledgeable audiences memories of other significant shared meals throughout the Old and New Testaments. These stories would likely include the people of Israel discovering manna in the wilderness in which the gift of food forestalled the Israelites' hostility toward Moses and God;[56] the meal that YHVH shared with Moses, Aaron, Nadab, Abihu, and the seventy elders of Israel on Mt. Sinai as God was confirming the covenant with the people of Israel during which the people not only ate (apparently with YHVH) but also *saw* YHVH and were not killed;[57] and the miracle meal Elisha multiplied for the one hundred men gathered for the first fruits offering during a season of famine.[58]

[55.]See Chapter 1.

[56.]Exod 16.

[57.]Exod 24:9–11, cf. Exod 19:10–25, 33:20.

[58.]2 Kgs 4:42–44. The prophet Isaiah foretells of a great eschatological feast that God will serve on Mt. Sinai (with apparent reference to the meal described in Exod 24:11) that will be given "for all peoples" (Isa 25:6–9). The feast foretold in Isaiah and the feast shared by Israel and Aram may share some echoes, but there is dissonance between them as well. For example, it is unlikely that the feast Isaiah declares involves the coming together of enemies, since the Hebrew עַם ('*am*, "people") generally refers to members of a kinship group, and the verses immediately following the description of the feast speak of the destruction (rather than reconciliation) of one of Israel's neighbors to the southeast, Moab (Isa 25:10b–12). This vision contrasts with another eschatological vision in Isaiah, however, in which the prophet envisions both the people of Israel (עַמִּים, '*ammim*) *and* the surrounding nations (גּוֹיִם, *goyim*) coming together to the Lord's house, which will result in a permanent end of hostilities in which even the memory of war will cease (Isa 2:1–4). Although this vision does not involve a meal, it clearly imagines the ending of hostilities among Israel and her neighbors through a powerful shared experience in the Lord's house, the Temple. Perhaps Isaiah's vision of the ending of hostilities *in God's house*, when read together with Elisha's successful (though temporary) reconciliation of enemies through a shared meal *at a table*, provides a different interpretive context to understand the table-scene in God's house at the end of Ps 23, suggesting the meal the Lord sets for the psalmist "in the presence of my enemies" means the psalmist sits at the table across from—in other words, *with*—his (perceived) enemies, as opposed to the traditional reading in which the enemies remain hostile but the psalmist eats while they look on

The New Testament also includes stories in which meals feature prominently, and have a transformational effect. The last supper is one such meal. Interestingly, it contrasts with 2 Kgs 6 in that, instead of the meal making friends out of enemies, this supper anticipates the ultimate betrayal by one who had been a friend.[59] Bill Brown has connected 2 Kgs 6 with Luke's account of the disciples with Jesus on the road to Emmaus in Luke 24.[60] Both stories—Luke 24 and 2 Kgs 6—draw on the themes of blindness and sight, perception and misperception, which come together at a shared meal. The disciples do not recognize Jesus the entire time they are together until Jesus "took bread, blessed and broke it, and gave it to them. *Then their eyes were opened, and they recognized him.*"[61] Their recognition echoes that of Elisha's servant whose eyes were opened to see as Elisha saw, to see what normal sight blinded him to. But, just as the vision of the horses and chariots of fire came and went, as soon as the disciples recognize Jesus "he vanished from their sight."[62] In the Emmaus story in Luke, just as in 2 Kgs 6, "a simple act of sharing food becomes the vehicle of a dramatic revelation."[63] This revelation, this gift of prophetic vision—fleeting though it may be— empowers the recipient to live with courage, and to embody the vulnerable power of service, humility, and peace, despite appearances.

(either in shame or malice). For the traditional interpretation of Ps 23:5 see Dahood, *Psalms 1–50*, 147–48; Craigie, *Psalms: 1–50*, 208; Buttrick, ed., *Interpreter's Bible*, 128. For one scholar's take on connecting the table in 2 Kgs 6 with the table in Ps 23:5 see Boogaart, "Drama and the Sacred," 56.

[59.]Cf. Matt 26:17–25; Lk 22:14–23.

[60.]Brown, *Sacred Sense*, 142–43.

[61.]Lk 24:30–31, NRSV.

[62.]Lk 24:31, NRSV. The disciples' perception of Jesus as a stranger (v. 18) is, perhaps, another point of connection between these two stories, subtle though it may be. The meal in 2 Kgs 6 humanizes and particularizes the Arameans in their eyes, raising them from enemies to the level of (at least temporary) acquaintances (if not friends). The meal in Lk 24 humanizes and particularizes Jesus in their eyes, transitioning him from stranger to savior.

[63.]Brown, *Sacred Sense*, 143.

The Communion meal in the Christian tradition also resonates deeply with the meal shared in 2 Kgs 6.[64] Walter Brueggemann and Peter Liethart have both noticed the sacramental impulses of the meal the king of Israel hosted for his enemies. For Brueggemann, the great feast is "a most remarkable gesture, surely against the expectations of both the Syrians and the Israelite king.... The prophet seems to know that there is something elementally transformative (and therefore sacramental) about shared food."[65] Liethart drew more explicit connections between this shared feast and the Church's Eucharistic meal, seeing in the connection an invitation to action. "God calls his enemies and spreads a 'great feast' before us, and to the church he says: go and do likewise."[66]

After the Arameans finish eating, the drama ends with them leaving the table to return to Aram as the narrator concludes: "And thereafter the bands of Aram no longer went into the land of Israel" (v. 23). What began with war (v. 8) now ends in peace (v. 23).[67] As many have noted,

---

[64.]This is not only so from a theological perspective, but also from a performance perspective. John Miles Foley's description of traditional referentiality is, again, one way to see the connections between the two meals. The gestures the king of Israel would enact in order to set the table and preside over the meal with the Arameans are very likely going to be similar gestures to those enacted by a pastor or priest presiding over the Eucharist, regardless of denomination. And if the performance arena (another of Foley's categories in Chapter 1) of 2 Kings 6 was a place of worship, the references to Communion would be significantly strengthened. In each performance I have participated in these connections have been made by audience and actor alike, and not every performance has taken place in the context of worship or in a worship space.

[65.]Brueggemann, *1 & 2 Kings*, 352.

[66.]Leithart, *1 & 2 Kings*, 203.

[67.]Yet another interesting connection exists between the opening and closing scenes, but is lost in translation. The word for "waging war" in v. 8 (נִלְחָם, *nilcham*) and the word for "bread" in v. 22 (לֶחֶם, *lechem*) have similar roots, generally indicated by לחם I and לחם II. The precise relationship between the root(s) is unclear (e.g., are both words from the same root, or are the roots homonyms that imply a word play?), but what is clear is that there is some sort of connection between them, either at the etymological or poetic/figurative level. Regardless of the precise relationship, given the historical reality that the king was responsible to provide sustenance for his people (cf. Sweeney, *1 & II Kings*, 311; also Boogaart, "Drama and the Sacred," 46–47), the relationship suggests "that the people of Israel understood war fundamentally as a means of 'securing bread for oneself'" (Boogaart, "Drama and the Sacred," 47). In

however, the peace occasioned by this surprise feast does not last,[68] and
the two nations are again at war in the very next verse (v. 24). Bergen
interprets this as an indelible stain on the ministry and legacy of Elisha,
arguing that the first three words of 2 Kgs 6:24 "collapse" the prophet's
credibility.[69] I am more convinced by Wray Beal and Boogaart, for
example, who see this as a recognition of—and a testimony to—the
"vulnerable" and "unspectacular" nature of the sort of power that
brought about this momentary end of hostilities, embodied in the shared
meal made possible by the king's willingness to serve his enemies.[70]
Elisha called on the king of Israel to move into uncharted political
territory, calling him to live into an ideal beyond geopolitical
aspirations, anxieties about border security, and fruitless wars with
neighbors. Elisha called the king to serve instead of strike, to fellowship
instead of fight, to break bread instead of breaking bodies and breaking
up families, whether at home or abroad. Elisha called the king to a
radical expression of love: to spurn violence and choose hospitality[71]—
even in a time of war.

---

other words, the war Aram waged to secure (more) bread for themselves (at a high
cost to Israel) comes to an end when bread is freely given (by Israel). As Lissa Wray
Beal put it, the Arameans return home "empty-handed but full bellied, telling of the
surprising events and attesting to the power of the prophet in Israel." Wray Beal, *1 &
2 Kings*, 344.

[68.]See, for example, Bergen, *Elisha and the End of Prophetism*, 134–36; Boogaart,
"Drama and the Sacred," 56–58; Hobbs, *2 Kings*, 74–75; Cohn, *2 Kings*, 48.

[69.]Bergen, *Elisha and the End of Prophetism*, 135. They are: וַיְהִי אַחֲרֵי־כֵן (*vayehi
acharey chen*, "And it happened after this" or "Sometime later").

[70.]Wray Beal, *1 & 2 Kings*, 346–47; Boogaart, "Drama and the Sacred," 56–57.

[71.]Hospitality was an enormously important value in the ancient world (of both the
Old and New Testaments), demonstrated in numerous biblical dramas in which the
stakes for failing to offer hospitality are extremely high (Cf. Gen 18:1–15, 19:1–29
(this drama also includes the only other reference to blindness by סַנְוֵרִים in the Hebrew
Bible); Judg 19–21). Hospitality is given a central place in Mosaic Law with respect
to the treatment of vulnerable members of society (Lev 19:9–10; Deut 14:28–29,
24:19–22, to name a few). It is also a central issue in the New Testament. Jesus teaches
on its significance when he is a guest (Lk 7:38–50; see also Mk 2:15–17), and
demonstrates its significance as host (Mk. 6:30–44 (cf. 2 Kgs 4:42–44); Lk 24:13–35),
and Paul sees hospitable table fellowship as the foundation of a life empowered by the

The character of Elisha—the "man/God" (אִישׁ הָאֱלֹהִים, *'ish ha'elohim*), the representative of God's presence—is the one around whom the entire drama revolves. He is in control from beginning to end, and offers a glimpse into the generous and mysterious sovereignty of God. He is the recipient of divine knowledge, and uses it to prevent bloodshed. He sees reality *and* what is behind it. He prays and the Lord responds. He speaks and the king obeys. His word opens and closes eyes, revealing and obscuring reality. He speaks and he acts, and his words and deeds avert violence and initiate peace. He stands in the gap to prevent suffering. He ends a war through an act of hospitality. Elisha was certainly not perfect; the dramas collected in the cycle of stories about him[72] reveal a complicated, unpredictable man. But this story presents him as "a force for peace."[73] His power is unrivaled, but it is expressed not through a show of force or acts of violence,[74] but through acts that prevent violence, reveal the edifice of military conquest as a sham, and point to a reality beyond what "normal" sight can see. As audiences—both ancient and modern—see this story unfold, they are invited to see their own lives through the eyes of Elisha's servant, the king of Israel, or the Aramean soldiers, and are invited to consider how their own acts of hospitality and service may put an end to hostilities and bring about peace in their own lives, homes, communities, and world.

---

death and resurrection of Jesus and the faithful practice of Communion (1 Cor 11:17–34).

[72.] 1 Kgs 19:19–21; 2 Kgs 2:1–9:13; 13:14–21.

[73.] Brueggemann, *1 & 2 Kings*, 348.

[74.] One could say that the revelation of the horses and chariots of fire is a "show of force." However, it is significant that the only character who sees it is the servant, and that its function (here and elsewhere, cf. 2 Kgs 2) is neither militant nor violent. The heavenly army does not come to Elisha's aid; they are revealed to the servant (and the audience) to teach him (and us) that reality is not what it appears to be, that we are never alone, and that Elisha's word is trustworthy.

CONCLUSION

In the preceding pages I have attempted both to lay a foundation for
biblical performance criticism, and also construct a methodology upon
it—a stage, perhaps—that is sufficiently useful and powerful to gain the
interpreter access to meaning in (and between) the words preserved in
the scripts known as the Old Testament narratives. I began with the
premise that, although orality has been increasingly accepted and
researched by scholars of the Bible, it has not been incorporated
sufficiently at the methodological level, even by some of the scholars
that affirm its historical priority and its ongoing influence on the
received texts in the Hebrew Bible. This study joined that of a small but
growing number of others—particularly those published in the Biblical
Performance Criticism series by Cascade Books—that have attempted
to contribute to rectifying this widespread oversight.

We began in Chapter 1 by digging through the soil, unearthing a
long line of scholars that have engaged the topic of orality in and/or
behind the texts of the Hebrew Bible beginning with Gunkel, and tracing
the development of his seminal discovery as it morphed and received
nuance and further application for more than a century until today. We
discovered that the cultural realities of ancient Israel, at least up until
the Babylonian exile, suggest that oral performance was a primary
means of sustaining the community's memory, and textual version of
these performances—when they existed—served a secondary and
supportive function to the performance, which was primary.

The primacy of performance in the transmission of Israel's sacred
tradition calls for a reconsideration of the genre of the narratives, which
could be considered the core of Israel's sacred tradition as it constitutes
the collective memories celebrating their ancestors, and their ancestors'
profound encounters with Israel's God. In Chapter 2 this reconsideration
led to the conclusion that the narratives are neither historicized fiction
nor historiography nor another explicitly literary genre, but rather

dramas, the scripts of ancient plays. Their dramatic character calls for a paradigm shift in biblical studies away from text-oriented methodologies and toward medium-oriented ones. At the end of Chapter 2 I offered one such methodology that is appropriate for Old Testament narratives, which achieves the paradigm shift to a medium-oriented approach while by no means abandoning traditional text-oriented discoveries into the nature of the script, as well as the historical context in which its story is placed, and out of which the story arose (as those two are not always the same). This paradigm shift changes the scholar's relationship with the Bible in important ways by offering a way of holding the tension between objectivity and subjectivity in the interpretive process. Biblical performance criticism elevates the subjective, emotional engagement between the scholar and the story in ways that are both constructive and more honest to the realities of interpretation, since pure objectivity is unachievable, not to mention ultimately undesirable. Chapter 2 concluded with an explanation of the steps involved in applying biblical performance criticism to the narratives.

Chapter 3 identified five essential elements that are the constituent parts of Israel's dramatic tradition, and that a performance approach to interpreting the dramas must attend carefully to. These five elements are: dramatic structure, the role of the narrator (audience participation), the presence and function of dialogue, point of view, and finally movement and gesture. Some of these elements have been used by other scholars of the Bible (mostly literary scholars), such as Robert Alter, to demonstrate the distinctive character of Israel's *literary* achievements and contributions. However, when taken altogether and combined with the insights of cultural anthropology and orality from Chapter 1, these elements seem to point beyond the text's literary character to reveal a latent—but nevertheless pervasive—dramatic tradition.

Several of these dramatic elements, identified by performance criticism, contribute new insights to the field of Old Testament's understanding of various elements of the narratives, how they are told, and how they communicate meaning. For example, the role of the narrator as a character *within* the drama, who is distinct from the composer—and given a wholly unique role to fill within the telling of the story by the composer—opens the door to further explorations into this dynamic character and this unique storytelling technique. That the narrator both participates in the story as a character and stimulates the audience's involvement with the unfolding plot is a new insight, and could benefit from further reflection and comparison with narrative scholars such as Sternberg, Alter, and Amit who wrote about the narrator from a literary perspective and conflated the narrator and the author into a single individual.

The elevation of movement and gesture as essential exegetical elements that embody and demonstrate the conflict of each drama and help to build and release tension is another important contribution of biblical performance criticism. Not only do movement and gesture help the tension rise and fall, but they also are a critical part of how the audience becomes emotionally involved in the story. They help humanize the story and prompt audience participation. Facial expressions can evoke laughter or wonder; movements can highlight and build suspense; gestures can be humorous or profound, they can stand on their own and also reveal connecting threads within the tradition through metonymic referentiality; tone of voice can communicate the difference between a joke and a revelation, and so on.

Attention to these elements leads the scholar to give their full, embodied attention to the scripts contained in the Bible, which in turn often will reveal various types of gaps in the telling of the story. Some of these gaps are narrative gaps insofar as the narrator has chosen not to include some essential (or peripheral) detail—such as when/how the widow collects the empty vessels in 2 Kgs 4. Other gaps are physical or gestural—such as how Isaac gets off the altar in Gen 22. Still others are chronological—such as how Naaman comes to learn of the little girl's prophetic revelation before we find him relaying it to the king.[1] Biblical performance criticism not only provides the conditions necessary to

---

[1.]This also includes a narrative gap since the narrator elected to summarize the little girl's message and not allow Naaman to relay it word-for-word, perhaps suggesting Naaman didn't receive the message in full, and perhaps contributing to the mixup that almost derails Naaman's quest and starts a war!

identify these gaps, but also provides the requisite conditions that allow the gaps to be filled in ways that are logical, that resonate with the other details of the story, and ultimately embody powerful meaning, latent in the script.

Chapters 4–6 offered numerous examples, both large and small, of how biblical performance criticism achieves what I have described in the previous three paragraphs, along with providing practical examples of how biblical performance criticism handles the particular performative challenges raised by each unique drama. Each of the three dramas I discussed in depth contain different challenges for representation, such as how to show a large army moving across long distances, how battle scenes could play out, how an ambush is set up and avoided, how multiple locations across nations can be accessibly represented simultaneously on stage. Other challenges these stories presented were how to handle narrative silence about the passage of time between events, how miracles actually unfold, and how to represent the supernatural revealed within the natural world.

Another layer to the challenge of representation is how to represent the great theological themes these dramas bring to life. For example: life and death, fear and faith, God's sovereignty and human choice, the source and structure of power (both human and divine), God's presence in time, the nature of sickness and its causes and cures. One particularly challenging representational theme is the representation of God, either as an explicit character with agency within the drama, or as a representation of divine power and influence inherent in the composer's theological worldview as it is expressed in the story. I offered justification for God being represented as a character in performance (without dictating precisely how that representation should happen) that drew from the Bible itself and also history and anthropology, with respect to the meaning associated with the roles of the priests and prophets as representatives of God's presence and voice. Much more reflection could be done on this important representational challenge, which would benefit not only biblical performance criticism by sharpening its approach to this important matter, but to the field of Old Testament as a whole by deepening its understanding of how the people of Israel thought about God, about God's activity in their lives and in history, and where they may have drawn a line in their demonstration of the reality of God's presence in their midst.

The present study is in no way intended to be the final word on biblical performance criticism and the biblical narratives. I have attempted to offer historical, biblical, cultural, theological, and performative justification for the interpretive method I and others have been developing for over a decade at Western Theological Seminary. My hope is that the present study will continue a conversation that has been ongoing for several years among a few Old Testament scholars (and a number of New Testament scholars) about the nature of Israel's orality and the methodological implications it has for how we interpret the various portions of the Hebrew Bible. I have attempted to contribute to this conversation by reflecting deeply on the application of biblical performance criticism to a single genre in the Old Testament: the narratives, in the hopes that others will take up the banner with other genres (some have already done so), and also add further nuance and insight to what I have offered here about performing the narratives (dramas), by performing other biblical dramas themselves and offering what they discover therein. A world of meaning and insight awaits us, if we are willing to change the way we approach the Bible, get out of our offices, and walk across a stage.

BIBLIOGRAPHY

Alter, Robert. *The Art of Biblical Narrative*. New York: Basic Books, 1981.

Amit, Yaira. *Reading Biblical Narratives: Literary Criticism and the Hebrew Bible*, translated by Yael Lotan. Minneapolis: Fortress Press, 2001.

————. "Endings—Especially Reversal Endings." *Scriptura* 87 (2004), 213–26.

Arnold Bill T., and John H. Choi. *A Guide to Biblical Hebrew Syntax*. Cambridge: Cambridge University Press, 2003.

Auerbach, Erich. *Mimesis: The Representation of Reality in Western Literature*, translated by Willard R. Trask. Princeton: Princeton University Press, 1953.

Bakhtin, Mikhail. *Problems of Dostoyevsky's Poetics*, edited and translated by Caryl Emerson. Minneapolis: University of Minnesota Press, 1984.

Ball, David. *Backwards and Forwards: A Technical Manual for Reading Plays*. Carbondale: Southern Illinois University Press, 1983.

Balthasar, Hans Urs von. *Theo-Drama: Theological Dramatic Theory Vol. 1, Prolegomena*. San Francisco: Ignatius Press, 1983.

Bar-Efrat, Shimon. *Narrative Art in the Bible*. Sheffield: Sheffield Academic Press, 1989.

Bar-Ilan, Meir. "Illiteracy in the Land of Israel in the First Centuries C.E." In *Essays in the Social Scientific Study of Judaism and Jewish Society, II*, edited by S. Fishbane, S. Schoenfeld and A. Goldschlaeger, 46–61. New York: Ktav, 1992.

Barkay, Gabriel. "The Iron Age II-III." In *The Archeology of Ancient Israel*, edited by Amnon Ben-Tor, 302–73. New Haven: Yale University Press for the Open University of Israel, 1992.

Barton, John. *Reading the Old Testament: Method in Biblical Study*, 2nd ed. Louisville: Westminster John Knox Press, 1996.

Beardslee, William A. "Poststructuralist Criticism." In *To Each Its Own Meaning: An Introduction to Biblical Criticisms and Their*

Application, edited by Seven L. McKenzee and Stephen R. Haynes, 253–67. Louisville: Westminster John Knox Press, 1999.

Ben Zvi, Ehud, and Michael H. Floyd, eds. *Writings and Speech in Israelite and Ancient Near Eastern Prophecy*. Atlanta: Society of Biblical Literature, 2000.

Ben Zvi, Ehud, and Marvin Sweeney, eds. *The Changing Face of Form Criticism for the Twenty-First Century*. Grand Rapids: Eerdmans, 2003.

Bennett, Gordon C. *Acting Out Faith*. St. Louis: CBP Press, 1986.

Bennett, Harold V. *Injustice Made Legal: Deuteronomic Law and the Plight of Widows, Strangers, and Orphans in Ancient Israel*. Grand Rapids: Eerdmans, 2002.

Bergen, Wesley J. *Elisha and the End of Prophetism. Journal for the Study of the Old Testament Supplement Series*, vol. 286. Sheffield: Sheffield Academic Press, 1999.

Berlin, Adele. *Poetics and Interpretation of Biblical Narrative*. Winona Lake, IN: Eisenbrauns, 1994.

Berrigan, Daniel. *The Kings and Their Gods: The Pathology of Power*. Grand Rapids: Eerdmans, 2008.

Boer, Roland. "Introduction: Bakhtin, Genre and Biblical Studies." In *Bakhtin and Genre Theory in Biblical Studies*, edited by Roland Boer, 1–7. Atlanta: Society of Biblical Literature, 2007.

Boogaart, Thomas A. "Drama and the Sacred: Recovering the Dramatic Tradition in Scripture and Worship." In *Touching the Altar: The Old Testament for Christian Worship*, edited by Carol M. Bechtel. Grand Rapids: Eerdmans, 2008.

———. "Vessels Full of Grace and Truth." Keynote address, inauguration of the Dennis and Betty Voskuil Chair of Old Testament at Western Theological Seminary, Holland, MI, October 27, 2009.

———. "The Arduous Journey of Abraham: Genesis 22:1–19." In *Yes! Well . . . : Exploring the Past, Present, and Future of the Church: Essays in Honor of John W. Coakley*, edited by James Hart Brumm. Grand Rapids: Eerdmans, 2016.

Boomershine, Thomas E. *The Messiah of Peace: A Performance-Criticism Commentary on Mark's Passion-Resurrection*

Narrative. Biblical Performance Criticism. Eugene, OR: Cascade Books, 2015.

Botha, Pieter J. J. *Orality and Literacy in Ancient Israel*. Biblical Performance Criticism. Eugene, OR: Cascade Books, 2012.

Brook, Peter. *The Empty Space*. New York: Touchstone, 1968.

Brueggemann, Walter. *Finally Comes the Poet: Daring Speech for Proclamation*. Minneapolis: Fortress Press, 1989.

———. *1 & 2 Kings*. Smyth and Helwys Bible Commentary. Macon, GA: Smyth & Helwys Publishing, 2000.

———. *Testimony to Otherwise: The Witness of Elijah and Elisha*. St. Louis: Chalice Press, 2001.

———. "A Culture of Life and the Politics of Death." *Journal for Preachers* 29, no. 2 (Lent 2006), 16–21.

Buttrick, George Arthur, ed. *The Interpreter's Bible Commentary*. New York: Abingdon Press, 1954.

Campbell, Antony F., S.J. "Form Criticism's Future." In *The Changing Face of Form Criticism for the Twenty-First Century*, edited by Ehud Ben Zvi and Marvin Sweeney, 15–31. Grand Rapids: Eerdmans, 2003.

Carlson, Marvin. *The Haunted Stage: The Theatre as Memory Machine*. Ann Arbor: University of Michigan Press, 2003.

———. *Performance: A Critical Introduction*. 2nd ed. New York: Routledge, 2004.

Carr, David M. *Writing on the Tablet of the Heart: Origins of Scripture and Literature*. New York: Oxford University Press, 2005.

———. *The Formation of the Hebrew Bible: A New Reconstruction*. New York: Oxford University Press, 2011.

———. "Orality, Textuality, and Memory: The State of Biblical Studues." In *Contextualizing Israel's Sacred Writings: Ancient Literacy, Orality, and Literary Production*, edited by Brian B. Schmidt, 161–73. Atlanta: Society of Biblical Literature Press, 2015.

Center for the Constitution at James Madison's Montpelier. "2010 State of the Constitution: What Americans Know." Accessed 10 May,

2014. http://www.montpelier.org/sites/default/files/2010%20State%20of%20the%20Constitution.pdf.

Charry, Ellen. "Walking in the Truth: On Knowing God." In *But Is It All True?: The Bible and the Question of Truth*. Grand Rapids: Eerdmans, 2006.

Cheney, Marvin. "You Shall Not Covet Your Neighbor's House." *Pacific Theological Review* 15.2 (Winter 1982): 3–13.

Childs, Brevard. *The Book of Exodus: A Critical and Theological Commentary*. The Old Testament Library. Philadelphia: Westminster Press, 1974.

Chisholm, Robert B., Jr. *Interpreting the Historical Books: An Exegetical Handbook*. Grand Rapids: Kregel, 2006.

Clark Wire, Antionette. *The Case for Mark Composed in Perforamnce*. Biblical Performance Criticism. Eugene, OR: Cascade Books, 2011.

Cogan, Mordechai, and Hayim Tadmor. *II Kings*. Anchor Yale Bible Commentaries. Garden City: NY: Doubleday, 1988.

Cohn, Robert L. "Form and Perspective in 2 Kings V." *Vetus Testamentum* 33 (1983): 171–84.

———. *2 Kings*. Berit Olam: Studies in Hebrew Narrative & Poetry. Collegeville, MN: Liturgical Press, 2000.

Cole, David. *The Theatrical Event: A Mythos, A Vocabulary, A Perspective*. Middletown: Wesleyan University Press, 1975.

Conrad, Edgar. "Heard But Not Seen: The Representation of 'Books' in the Old Testament." *Journal for the Study of the Old Testament* 54 (1992): 45–59.

Conquergood, Dwight. "Performance Studies: Interventions and Radical Research." *The Drama Review* 46, vol. 2 (T174, Summer, 2002): 145–56.

Craigie, Peter C. *Psalms: 1–50*. Word Biblical Commentary. Waco, TX: Word, 1983.

Dahood, Michael, S.J. *Psalms 1–50*. Anchor Bible. Garden City, NY: Doubleday & Company, 1966.

David, Marcus. *From Balaam to Jonah: Anti-Prophetic Satire in the Hebrew Bible*. Atlanta: Scholars Press, 1995.

Dewey, Dennis. "The Mnemonics of the Heart: Marinating in the Stories of Scripture." Paper presentation, Orality and Literacy: Memory Conference, Rice University, Houston, October 11, 2003. Accessed October 12, 2016. https://sacredstoryjourneys.files.wordpress.com/2016/01/spiritual -mnemonics.pdf.

———. "Performing the Living Word: Learnings from a Storytelling Vocation." In *The Bible in Ancient and Modern Media: Story and Performance*, edited by Holly E. Hearon and Philip Ruge-Jones, 142–55. Biblical Performance Criticism. Eugene, OR: Cascade Books, 2009.

Dewey, Joanna. *The Oral Ethos of the Early Church: Speaking, Writing, and the Gospel of Mark*. Biblical Performance Criticism. Eugene, OR: Cascade Books, 2013.

Dever, William. *Did God Have a Wife? Archeology and Folk Religion in Ancient Israel*. Grand Rapids: Eerdmans, 2005.

Diamond, Elin. *Writing Performances*. London: Routledge, 1995.

Doan, William, and Terry Giles. *Prophets, Performance, and Power: Performance Criticism of the Hebrew Bible*. New York: T&T Clark International, 2005.

———. "Performance Criticism of the Hebrew Bible." *Religion Compass* 2, no. 3 (May 2008): 273–286.

———. *Twice Used Songs: Performance Criticism of the Songs of Ancient Israel*. Peabody, MA: Hendrickson Publishers, 2009.

Eichrodt, Walter. *Theology of the Old Testament*. Vol. 2. Philadelphia: The Westminster Press, 1967.

Eickmann, Paul E. "The Long Imperative in Biblical Hebrew." *Wisconsin Lutheran Quarterly* 100, no. 2 (Spring 2003): 125–32.

Eliade, Mircea. *The Sacred and the Profane: The Nature of Religion*, translated by Willard R. Trask. New York: Harcourt Brace Jovanovich, 1957.

Eng, Milton. *The Days of Our Years: A Lexical Semantic Study of the Life Cycle in Biblical Israel*. The Library of Hebrew Bible/Old Testament Studies 464. London: T&T Clark, 2013.

270

Esler, Philip Francis. *Sex, Wives, and Warriors: Reading Biblical Narrative With Its Ancient Audience.* Eugene, OR: Cascade Books, 2011.

Fassberg, Steven E. "The Lengthened Imperative קָטְלָה in Biblical Hebrew." *Hebrew Studies* 40 (1999): 7–13.

Fewell Danna, and David Gunn. "Abraham and Sarah: Genesis 11–22." In *Narrative in the Hebrew Bible*, 90–100. Oxford: Oxford University Press, 1993.

Fokkelman, J.P. *Reading Biblical Narrative: An Introductory Guide.* Louisville: Westminster John Knox Press, 1999.

Foley, John Miles. *Immanent Art: From Structure to Meaning in Traditional Oral Epic.* Indianapolis: Indiana University Press, 1991.

———. "Plenitude and Diversity: Interactions Between Orality and Writing." In *The Interface of Orality and Writing: Speaking, Seeing, Writing in the Shaping of New Genres*, edited by Annette Weissenrieder and Robert B. Coote, 103–118. Tübingen, Germany: Mohr Siebeck, 2010.

———. *The Singer of Tales in Performance.* Bloomington: Indiana University Press, 1995.

Fowler, Alastair. *Kinds of Literature: An Introduction to the Theory of Genres and Modes.* Cambridge, MA: Harvard University Press, 1982.

Fretheim, Terence. *First and Second Kings.* Westminster Bible Companion. Louisville: Westminster John Knox Press, 1999.

Fuchs, Esther. *Sexual Politics in the Biblical Narrative: Reading the Hebrew Bible as a Woman.* Sheffield: Sheffield Academic Press, 2000.

Giles, Terry, and William Doan. *Prophets, Performance, and Power: Performance Criticism of the Hebrew Bible.* New York: T&T Clark, 2005.

———. "Performance Criticism of the Hebrew Bible." *Religion Compass* 2/3, (2008): 273–286

———. *Twice Used Songs: Performance Criticism of the Songs of Ancient Israel.* Peabody, MA: Hendrickson Publishers, 2009.

————. *The Story of Naomi—The Book of Ruth: From Gender to Politics*. Biblical Performance Criticism. Eugene, OR: Cascade Books, 2016.

Goldman, Michael. *On Drama: Boundaries of Genre, Borders of Self.* Ann Arbor: University of Michigan Press, 2000.

Goody, Jack, and Ian Watt. "The Consequences of Literacy." *Comparative Studies in Society and History* 5, no. 3 (April 1963): 304–45.

Goody, Jack. *The Interface Between the Oral and the Written.* Cambridge: Cambridge University Press, 1987.

Gray, John. *I & II Kings*. The Old Testament Library. Philadelphia: Westminster Press, 1964.

Gunkel, Hermann. *The Legends of Genesis: The Biblical Saga and History*. Translated by W.H. Carruth. New York: Schocken Books, 1964.

————. *The Folktale in the Old Testament*. Sheffield: Almond Press, 1987.

Harris, Max. *Theater and Incarnation*. Grand Rapids: Eerdmans, 1990.

Havelock, Eric A. *Preface to Plato*. Cambridge: Harvard University Press, 1963.

————. *The Muse Learns to Write: Reflections on Orality and Literacy from Antiquity to the Present*. New Haven: Yale University Press, 1988.

Hearon, Holly E., and Philip Ruge-Jones. *The Bible in Ancient and Modern Media: Story and Performance*. Biblical Performance Criticism. Eugene, OR: Cascade Books, 2009.

Hens-Piazza, Gina. *1–2 Kings*. Abingdon Old Testament Commentaries. Nashville: Abingdom Press, 2006.

Heschel, Abraham Joshua. *The Prophets: An Introduction*. Vol. 1. New York: Harper Torchbooks, 1962.

Hobbs, T. R. *2 Kings*. Word Biblical Commentary. Nashville: Thomas Nelson, 1985.

Holman, C. Hugh. *A Handbook to Literature*. Indianapolis: The Bobbs-Merrill Company, 1980.

272

Horsley, Richard A. "The Origins of the Hebrew Scriptures in Imperial Relations." In *Orality, Literacy, and Colonialism in Antiquity*, edited by Jonathan A. Draper, 107–34. Atlanta: Society of Biblical Literature, 2004.

———. *Text and Tradition in Performance and Writing*. Biblical Performance Criticism. Eugene, OR: Cascade Books, 2013.

Iverson, Kelly R. *From Text to Performance: Narrative and Performance Criticisms in Dialogue and Debate*. Biblical Performance Criticism. Eugene, OR: Cascade Books, 2014.

Jaeger, C. Stephen. *The Envy of Angels: Cathedral Schools and Social Ideals in Medieval Europe, 950–1200*. Philadelphia: University of Pennsylvania Press, 1994.

Jones, Gwilyn H. *1 and 2 Kings*. New Century Bible Commentary. Grand Rapids: Eerdmans, 1984.

Joüon, Paul. *A Grammar of Biblical Hebrew*, translated by T. Muraoka. Rome: Editrice Pontificio Istituto Biblico 1923.

Kaminsky, Joel S. *Corporate Responsibility in the Hebrew Bible*. Sheffield: Sheffield Academic Press, 1995.

King, Martin Luther, Jr. *A Testament of Hope: The Essential Writings and Speeches of Martin Luther King Jr.*, edited by James M. Washington. San Fransisco: HarperCollins Publishers, 1986.

King, Philip J., and Lawrence E. Stager. *Life in Biblical Israel*. Louisville: Westminster John Knox Press, 2001.

Kirova, Milena. "Eyes Wide Open: A Case of Symbolic Reversal in Biblical Narrative." *Scandinavian Journal of the Old Testament* 24, no. 1 (2004): 85–98.

Knapp, Mark L.. Judith A. Hall, and Terrence G. Horgan. *Nonverbal Communication in Human Interaction*. 8th ed. Boston: Wadsworth, 2014.

Knierim, Rolf. "Old Testament Form Criticism Reconsidered." *Interpretation* 27, no. 4 (October, 1973): 435–468.

Kuhn, Karl Allen. *The Heart of Biblical Narrative: Rediscovering Biblical Appeal to the Emotions*. Minneapolis: Fortress Press, 2009.

LaBarbera, Robert. "The Man of War and the Man of God: Social Satire in 2 Kings 6:8–7:20." *The Catholic Biblical Quarterly* 46, no. 4 (October 1984): 637—51.

Lambdin, Thomas O. *Introduction to Biblical Hebrew*. New York: Scribner, 1971.

Lanfranchi, Pierluigi. *agoagoge d'Ezéchiel le Tragique: Introduction, texte, traduction et commentaire*. Studia in Veteris Testamenti Pseudepigrapha 21. Leiden: Brill, 2005.

Lash, Nicholas. *Theology on the Way to Emmaus*. London: SCM Press Ltd., 1986.

Lasine, Stuart. "'Go in Peace' or 'Go to hell'? Elisha, Naaman and the Meaning of Monotheism in 2 Kings 5." *Scandinavian Journal of the Old Testament* 25, no. 1 (2011): 3–28. Accessed September 18, 2014. http://dx.doi.org/10.1080/09018328.2011.568207.

Leeb, Carolyn S. *Away From the Father's House: The Social Location of na'ar and na'arah in Ancient Israel*. Sheffield: Sheffield Academic Press, 2000.

Lessing, Reed. "Orality in the Prophets." *Concordia Journal* 29, no. 2 (April 2003): 152–165.

Levenson, Jon. "The Bible: Unexamined Commitments of Criticism." *First Things* 30 (February 1993): 24–33.

Levtow, Nathaniel B. "Text Production and Destruction in Ancient Israel: Ritual and Political Dimensions." In *Social Theory and the Study of Israelite Religion: Essays in Retrospect and Prospect*, edited by Saul M. Olyan, 111–39. Atlanta: Society of Biblical Literature, 2012.

Levy, Shimon. *The Bible As Theatre*. Portland: Sussex Academic Press, 2000.

Liethart, Peter. *1 & 2 Kings*. Brazos Theological Commentary on the Bible. Grand Rapids: Brazos Press, 2006.

Long, Burke O. *2 Kings*. Forms of the Old Testament Literature. Grand Rapids: Eerdmans, 1991.

Lord, Albert Bates. *The Singer of Tales*. Cambridge, MA: Harvard University Press, 1960.

274

————. *Epic Singers and Oral Tradition*. Ithaca: Cornell University Press, 1991.

Loubser, J. A. *Oral and Manuscript Culture in the Bible: Studies on the Media Texture of the New Testament—Explorative Hermeneutics*. Biblical Performance Criticism. Eugene, OR: Cascade Books, 2013.

Mathews, Jeanette. *Performing Habakkuk: Faithful Re-enactment in the Midst of Crisis*. Eugene, OR: Pickwick Publications, 2012.

Maxey, James A. *From Orality to Orality: A New Paradigm for Contextual Translation of the Bible*. Biblical Performance Criticism. Eugene, OR: Cascade Books, 2009.

————. "Biblical Performance Criticism and Bible Translation: An Expanding Dialogue." In *Translating Scripture for Sound and Performance: New Directions in Biblical Studies*, edited by James A. Maxey and Ernst R. Wendland, 1–21. Biblical Performance Criticism. Eugene, OR: Cascade Books, 2012.

Maxey, James A., and Ernst Wendland. *Translating Scripture for Sound and Performance: New Directions in Biblical Studies*. Biblical Performance Criticism. Eugene, OR: Cascade Books, 2012.

Mazar, Amihai. *Archeology of the Land of Israel*. New York: Doubleday, 1992.

Mead, James Kirk. "'Elisha Will Kill?': The Deuteronomistic Rhetoric of Life and Death in the Theology of the Elisha Narratives." PhD diss., Princeton Theological Seminary, 1999.

Menn, Esther M. "A Little Child Shall Lead Them: The Role of the Little Israelite Servant Girl (2 Kings 5.1–19)." *Currents in Theology and Mission* 35:5 (October, 2008): 340–348.

Miller, Robert D., II. *Oral Tradition in Ancient Israel*. Biblical Performance Criticism. Eugene, OR: Cascade Books, 2011.

————. "The Performance of Oral Tradition in Ancient Israel." In *Contextualizing Israel's Sacred Writings: Ancient Literacy, Orality, and Literary Production*, edited by Brian B. Schmidt, 175–96. Atlanta: Society of Biblical Literature Press, 2015.

Muilenburg, James. "Form Criticism and Beyond." *Journal of Biblical Literature* 88, no. 1 (March 1969): 1–18.

Nagy, Gregory. *Greek Mythology and Poetics*. Ithaca, NY: Cornell University Press, 1990.

———. *Poetry as performance: Homer and beyond*. Cambridge: Cambridge University Press, 1996.

Nelson, Richard D. *First and Second Kings*. Interpretation: A Bible Commentary for Teaching and Preaching. Louisville: John Knox Press, 1987.

Newbigin, Lesslie. *The Gospel in a Pluralist Society*. Grand Rapids: Eerdmans, 1989.

Newsom, Carol A. "Spying Out the Land: A Report From Genology." In *Bakhtin and Genre Theory in Biblical Studies*, edited by Roland Boer. Atlanta: Society of Biblical Literature, 2007.

Niditch, Susan. *Underdogs and Tricksters: A Prelude to Biblical Folklore*. San Francisco: Harper & Row, 1987.

———. *Oral World and Written Word: Ancient Israelite Literature*. Louisville: Westminster John Knox Press, 1996.

———. "Hebrew Bible and Oral Literature: Misconceptions and New Directions." In *The Interface of Orality and Writing: Speaking, Seeing, Writing in the Shaping of New Genres*, edited by Annette Weissenrieder and Robert B. Coote. Tübingen, Germany: Mohr Siebeck, 2010.

Nielsen, Eduard. *Oral Tradition: A Modern Problem in Old Testament Introduction*. London: SCM Press, 1954.

O'Mathúna, D. P. "Sickness and Disease." In *Dictionary of the Old Testament: Historical Books*, edited by Bill T. Arnold and H. G. M. Williamson. Downers Grove, IL: InterVarsity Press, 2005.

Oden, Thomas C. ed. *Ancient Christian Commentary on Scripture: 1–2 Kings, 1–2 Chronicles, Ezra, Nehemiah, Esther*. Downers Grove: InterVarsity Press, 2008.

Ong, Walter J. *The Presence of the Word: Some Prolegomena for Cultural and Religious History*. New Haven: Yale University Press, 1967.

———. *Orality and Literacy: The Technologizing of the Word*. New York: Routledge, 1988.

Pederson, Johannes. *Israel: Its Life and Culture*. London: Oxford University Press, 1940.

Perry, Peter. *Insights From Performance Criticism*. Minneapolis: Fortress Press, 2016.

Person, Raymond F. "Ancient Israelite Scribe as Performer." *Journal of Biblical Literature* 117, no. 4 (1998): 601–609.

—————. "Orality Studies and Oral Tradition: Hebrew Bible." *The Oxford Encyclopedia of Biblical Interpretation*, edited by Steven L. McKenzie, 55–63. Oxford: Oxford University Press, 2013.

—————. "Foley and the Study of the Hebrew Bible." Paper presentation, annual meeting of the Society of Biblical Literature, Baltimore, November 23–26, 2013.

Peursen, Wido van. "Participant Reference in Genesis 37." *Journal of Northwest Semitic Languages* 39, no. 1 (2013): 85–102.

Polak, Frank H. "Book, Scribe, and Bard: Oral Discourse and Written Text in Recent Biblical Scholarship." *Prooftexts* 31 (2011): 118–140.

—————. "Language Variation, Discourse Typology, and the Sociocultural Background of Biblical Narrative." In *Diachrony in Biblical Hebrew*, edited by Cynthia L. Miller-Naudé and Ziony Zevit, 301–38. Winona Lake, IN: Eisenbrauns, 2012.

Powery, Emerson B. "The Origins of Whiteness and Black (Biblical) Imagination: The Bible in the 'Slave Narrative' Tradition." In *The Bible in American Life*, edited by Philip Goff, Arthur E. Farnsley II, and Peter J. Thuesen, 81–88. Oxford: Oxford University Press, 2017.

Pratico, Gary D., and Miles V. Van Pelt. *Basics of Biblical Hebrew*, 2nd ed. Grand Rapids: Zondervan, 2001.

Rad, Gerhard von. *The Problem of the Hexateuch and Other Essays*, translated by E. W. Trueman Dicken, D.D. New York: McGraw-Hill Book Company, 1966.

Regt, L.J. de. *Participants in Old Testament Texts and the Translator: Reference Devices and their Rhetorical Impact*. Assen, The Netherlands: Van Gorcum, 1999.

Redford, Donald B. *A Study of the Biblical Story of Joseph (Genesis 37–50)*. Leiden: E. J. Brill, 1970.

Rentería, Tamis Hoover. "The Elijah/Elisha Stories: A Socio-cultural Analysis of Prophets and People in Ninth-Century B.C.E. Israel." In *Elijah and Elisha in Socioliterary Perspective*, edited by Robert B. Coote. Atlanta: Scholars Press, 1992.

Revell, E. J. *The Designation of the Individual: Expressive Usage in Biblical Narrative*. Kampen: Kok Pharos, 1996.

Rhoads, David. "Performance Criticism: An Emerging Methodology in Second Testament Studies – Part I." *Biblical Theology Bulletin* 36, no. 3 (2006): 118–133.

———. "Performance Criticism: An Emerging Methodology in Second Testament Studies—Part II." *Biblical Theology Bulletin* 36, no. 4 (2006): 164–84.

———. "What Is Performance Criticism?" In *The Bible in Ancient and Modern Media*, edited by Holly E. Hearon and Philip Ruge-Jones. Biblical Performance Criticism. Eugene: Cascade Books, 2009.

———. "Biblical Performance Criticism: Performance as Research." *Oral Tradition* 25, no. 1 (2010): 157–98.

———. "The Art of Translating for Oral Performance." In *Translating Scripture for Sound and Performance: New Directions in Biblical Studies*, edited by James A. Maxey and Ernst R. Wendland, 22–48. Biblical Performance Criticism. Eugene, OR: Cascade Books, 2012.

Robb, Kevin. "Preliterate Ages and the Linguistic Art of Heraclitus." In *Language and Thought in Early Greek Philosophy*, edited by Kevin Robb, 153–206. La Salle, IL: The Hegeler Institute, 1983.

Rodríguez, Rafael. *Oral Tradition and the New Testament: A Guide for the Perplexed*. London: Bloomsbury T&T Clark, 2014.

Rofé, Alexander. "The Classification of the Prophetical Stories." *Journal of Biblical Literature* 89, no. 4 D (1970): 427–440.

———. "Elisha at Dothan (2 Kings 6:8–23): Historico-Literary Criticism Sustained by the Midrash." In *Ki Baruch Hu: Ancient Near Eastern, Biblical and Judaic Studies in Honor of Baruch A.*

Levine, edited by Robert Chazan, W. W. Hallo, and L. H. Schiffman, 346–49. Winona Lake, IN: Eisenbrauns, 1999.

Rokem, Freddie. *Performing History: Theatrical Representations of the Past in Contemporary Theatre.* Iowa City: University of Iowa Press, 2000.

Rollston, Christopher A. *Writing and Literacy in the World of Ancient Israel: Epigraphic Evidence from the Iron Age.* Atlanta: Society of Biblical Literature, 2010.

———. "Scribal Curriculum During the First Temple Period: Epigraphic Hebrew and Biblical Evidence." In *Contextualizing Israel's Sacred Writings: Ancient Literacy, Orality, and Literary Production*, edited by Brian B. Schmidt, 71–101. Atlanta: Society of Biblical Literature Press, 2015.

Sarna, Nahum M. *Exodus.* The JPS Torah Commentary. Philadelphia: Jewish Publication Society, 1991.

Schechner, Richard. *Performance Studies: An Introduction.* 3rd ed. New York: Routledge, 2013.

Schmidt, Brian B., ed. *Contextualizing Israel's Sacred Writings: Ancient Literacy, Orality, and Literary Production.* Atlanta: Society of Biblical Literature Press, 2015.

Schniedewind, William, and Daniel Sivan. "The Elijah-Elisha Narratives: A Test Case for the Northern Dialect of Hebrew." *Jewish Quarterly Review* 87, no. 3/4 (Jan–Apr 1997): 303–37.

Schniedewind, William M. "Orality and Literacy in Ancient Israel." *Religious Studies Review* 26, no. 4 (October 2000): 327–332.

———. *How the Bible Became a Book: The Textualization of Ancient Israel.* Cambridge: Cambridge University Press, 2004.

Schulte, Hannelis. "The End of the Omride Dynasty: Social-Ethical Observations on the Subject of Power and Violence," translated by Carl S. Ehrlich. *Semeia* 66 (1994): 133–48.

Seow, Choon-Leong. "The First and Second Books of Kings: Introduction, Commentary, and Reflections." In *The New Interpreter's Bible, Vol. 3*, 1–295. Nashville: Abingdon Press, 1999.

Shulman, Ahouva. "The Use of Modal Verb Forms in Biblical Hebrew Prose." PhD diss., University of Toronto, 1996.

Spencer-Miller, Althea. "Rethinking Orality for Biblical Studies." In *Postcolonialism in the Hebrew Bible: The Next Step*, edited by Roland Boer, 35–68. Atlanta: Society of Biblical Literature, 2013.

Sternberg, Meir. *The Poetics of Biblical Narrative: Ideological Literature and the Drama of Reading.* Bloomington: Indiana University Press, 1987.

Strine, Mary, Beverly Long, and Mary Hopkins. "Research in Interpretation and Performance Studies: Trends, Issues, Priorities." In *Speech Communication: Essays to Commemorate the Seventy-Fifth Anniversary of the Speech Communication Association*, edited by Gerald Phillips and Julia Wood, 181–93. Carbondale: Southern Illinois University Press, 1990.

Stuhlmueller, Carroll. "The Influence of Oral Tradition Upon Exegesis and the Senses of Scripture." *Catholic Biblical Quarterly* 20, no. 3 (July 1958): 299–326.

Sweeney, Marvin. *I & II Kings.* The Old Testament Library. Louisville: Westminster John Knox Press, 2007.

Sweet, Jeffrey. *Solving Your Script: Tools and Techniques for the Playwright.* Portsmouth, NH: Heinemann, 2001.

Taylor, Diana. *The Archive and the Repertoire: Performing Cultural Memory in the Americas.* Durham, NC: Duke University Press, 2003.

Turner, Victor. *From Ritual to Theatre: The Human Seriousness of Play.* New York: Performing Arts Journal Publications, 1982.

Tyson, Craig W. "Who's In? Who's Out?: II Sam 5,8b and Narrative Reversal." *Zeitschrift für die alttestamentliche Wissenschaft* 122, no. 4 (2010), 546–557.

VanHoozer, Kevin. *The Drama of Doctrine: A Canonical Linguistic Approach to Christian Doctrine.* Louisville: Westminster John Knox Press, 2005.

Veldhuis, Niek. "Levels of Literacy." In *The Oxford Handbook of Cuneiform Culture*, edited by Karen Radner and Eleanor Robson, 69–89. Oxford: Oxford University Press, 2011.

Vries, Lourens de. "Views of orality and the translation of the Bible." *Translation Studies* 8, no. 2 (2015), 141–55.

Walton, John H., Victor H. Matthews, and Mark W. Chavalas. *The IVP Bible Background Commentary: Old Testament*. Downers, Grove, IL: IVP Academic, 2000.

Walton, John H., and D. Brent Sandy. *The Lost World of Scripture: Ancient Literary Culture and Biblical Authority*. Downers Grove, IL: InterVarsity Press Academic, 2013.

Ward, Richard, and David Trobisch. *Bringing the Word to Life: Engaging the New Testament Through Performing It*. Grand Rapids: Eerdmans, 2013.

Weissenrieder, Annette, and Robert B. Coote, eds. *The Interface of Orality and Writing: Speaking, Seeing, Writing in the Shaping of New Genres*. Biblical Performance Criticism. Eugene, OR: Cascade Books, 2015.

Wells, Samuel. *Improvisation: The Drama of Christian Ethics*. Grand Rapids: Brazos Press, 2004.

West, Travis. "Unseen Grace: Lent in the Book of Exodus." *Perspectives* 26, no. 3 (March, 2011): 5–8.

———. *Biblical Hebrew: an interactive approach*. Wilmore, KY: GlossaHouse, 2016.

Wolff, Hans Walter. *Anthropology of the Old Testament*. Philadelphia: Fortress Press, 1974, 88.

Worthen, W. B. *Shakespeare and the Authority of Performance*. Cambridge: Cambridge University Press, 1997.

Wray Beal, Lissa M. *1 & 2 Kings*. Apollos Old Testament Commentary. Downers Grove, IL: InterVarsity Press, 2014.

Townsend Gilkes, Cheryl. "Jesus Must Needs Go Through Samaria: Disestablishing the mountains of race and the hegemony of whiteness." In *Christology and Whiteness: What Would Jesus Do?*, edited by George Yancy, 59–74. New York: Routledge, 2012.

Young, Ian M. "Israelite Literacy: Interpreting the Evidence, Part I." *Vetus Testamentum* 48, no. 2 (April 1998): 239–53.

———. "Israelite Literacy: Interpreting the Evidence, Part II." *Vetus Testamentum* 48, no. 3 (July 1998): 408–22.

Zanella, Francesco. *The Lexical Field of the Substantives of "Gift" in Ancient Hebrew*. Leiden: Brill, 2010.
Zink, James K. "Scandinavian Oral Tradition School." *Restoration Quarterly* 9, no. 4 (1966), 249–256.

Made in United States
North Haven, CT
17 November 2024

60353013R00163